William De Loss Love

Sabbath and Sunday

William De Loss Love

Sabbath and Sunday

ISBN/EAN: 9783743325029

Manufactured in Europe, USA, Canada, Australia, Japa

Cover: Foto ©ninafisch / pixelio.de

Manufactured and distributed by brebook publishing software (www.brebook.com)

William De Loss Love

Sabbath and Sunday

SABBATH AND SUNDAY

BY REV. WM. DeLoss LOVE, D. D.
Author of "St. Paul and Woman," Etc.

FLEMING H. REVELL COMPANY

CHICAGO   NEW YORK   TORONTO

Publishers of Evangelical Literature

COPYRIGHTED 1896, BY FLEMING H. REVELL CO.

DEDICATION

This book, entitled

SABBATH AND SUNDAY

Is hereby respectfully and affectionately dedicated to the memory of

GEORGE EDWARD DEXTER

My college class mate of more than fifty years ago, who lived past our semi-centennial, which occurred in June, 1893, and died at his home, Charles City, Iowa, August 20, 1894. It was contemplated to have Mr. Dexter prepare a legal department to this volume, giving an outline of the Sabbatic laws in the several half hundred States of the Union, and a statement of the principles which justify the enforcement of the civil law to sustain the Sabbath in a free government. But his death came too soon for the completion of my plan. One ever with him after their union speaks of his strong love for the Sabbath, and says that he read only the best of books and papers on that day, and always thanked God in family worship for the Lord's Day, at its close. Mr. Dexter was an Elder in the Presbyterian Church. He became a practitioner at law in three different states, New York, Wisconsin and Minnesota. He acquired a large property, and, in his will, remembered his Alma Mater, Hamilton College. With a Christian character and useful living and prosperity in business and length of days—life was with him a noble success. Ever green and fruitful of good be his memory.

PREFACE.

Every book, by its inherent value, should prove its right to have an existence. It is often well to preface a book with a statement or testimonies bearing on its value. These should be of the nature of proofs, not merely of opinions. The first ten chapters of the following work were first published in seven articles in the Bibliotheca Sacra between Oct. 1879 and July 1881. But all of that part has been revised, abridged and simplified in some respects and brought to date. The remaining seven chapters have not before been published.

Rev Prof. Edwards A. Park, D. D., LL. D. then chief editor of the Bibliotheca Sacra, beside admitting the seven articles—199 pages in all—to the columns of that portly quarterly, about ten years afterward wrote as follows, "I thought very highly of your articles on the Sabbath and I now think it would be well to republish them. . . . I thought that the value of your articles consisted largely in their extensive quotations from men eminent in the church." The greater portion of those quotations were from the early Fathers and pertain to these several points:

1. That the *civil* and *ceremonial* laws of the Jews were temporary. 2. That all *moral* laws are permanent. 3. That the early Christians under direction of the Apostles sacredly observed the

Lord's Day, and chiefly refused to regard the observance of the seventh day as binding. 4. That the Apostles and early Fathers did not consider the fourth commandment abolished but held to the contrary. 5. That some of them taught that the Lord's Day takes, in substance, the place of the seventh day Sabbath. 6. That the early Fathers did not appoint the Lord's Day as sacred, but the Apostles did so appoint it and the early Fathers so observed it.

Since the early Christian Fathers held and taught these things, they can hardly fail to be true, and it is highly important for the Sabbath cause that they be widely known to be true. Oehler's Old Testament Theology, translated from German into English by Rev. Geo. E. Day, of Yale Theological Seminary, at the close of its chapter on the Sabbath, cites the aforementioned articles in the Bibliotheca Sacra as on the "Conservative" side in respect to Sabbatic views.

Prof. A. E. Waffle, author of the "Green Prize essay on the Lord's Day," in his appendix says, "Among the review articles I would call especial attention to a series of able articles in the Bibliotheca Sacra (1879-81) by Rev. Wm. DeLoss Love, D. D." He speaks with like approval of an article by Prof. Schaff in the Princeton Review Vol. xxxv.

Rev. W. F. Crafts, D. D. in his volume "The Sabbath for Man," gives like credit to the same articles, and in his appendix, makes a very long quotation from the present writer's article on "St. Paul and the Sabbath" in "Sabbath Essays," which in meaning is the same, in respect to that portion of Scripture, as that of the Series of Articles. The "essays" were given at Sabbath Conventions in Springfield and Boston in the Autumn of 1879.

It is thought that the above and other similar testimony, which might be given, will seem to justify the publication of the following work.

CONTENTS

CHAPTER I. - - - - - - - - 7
    Introduction.

CHAPTER II. - - - - - - - - 10
    Origin and History of the Sabbath.
        1 Its basis for appointment that "God rested."
        2 The early seventh day.
        3 The week a seven of days.
        4 The Sabbath at the giving of manna.
        5 Septenary time among Gentile nations.
        6 The early appointment of public worship.
        7 The Sabbath in cuneiform inscriptions.
        8 The Fourth Commandment itself shows a previous sacred seventh day.

CHAPTER III. - - - - - - - - 33
    Christ did not abolish or modify the Sabbath of the Fourth Commandment.

CHAPTER IV. - - - - - - - - 48
    Christ's apostles did not teach or hold that either the Law or the Fourth Commandment is abolished.

CHAPTER V. - - - - - - - - 75
    The change of observance from the seventh to the Lord's Day possible and probable.

CHAPTER VI. - - - - - - - - 83
    "The First Day" becomes the sacred weekly day among the early Christians.

CHAPTER VII. - - - - - - - - 120
    The "Lord's Day" comes to be the Christian Sabbath.

CHAPTER VIII. - - - - - - - - 148
   The Early Fathers confirm the teaching of the Apostles.

CHAPTER IX. - - - - - - - - 182
   The Early Fathers on the ceremonial and moral laws

CHAPTER X - - - - - - - - - 224
   The Christian Sabbath in the New Dispensation.

CHAPTER XI - - - - - - - - 264
   The advantages of the Sabbath for man's physical being.

CHAPTER XII. - - - - - - - - 273
   The advantages of the Sabbath for mental rest, capacity and culture.

CHAPTER XIII. - - - - - - - - 280
   The advantages of the Sabbath for Society and Social Regeneration.

CHAPTER XIV. - - - - - - - - 285
   The advantages of the Sabbath for the welfare and preservation of the State.

CHAPTER XV. - - - - - - - - 293
   The advantages of the Sabbath in its reward for observance.

CHAPTER XVI. - - - - - - - - 301
   The advantages and necessity of the Sabbath in morals and religion.

CHAPTER XVII - - - - - - - - 309
   How to keep the Sabbath.

CHAPTER I.

INTRODUCTORY.

No great and beneficent reform was ever accomlished, no institution of value and power ever existed, without a firm basis of truth, of doctrine. Whenever the doctrine has become uncertain in the minds of the people, then the institution has languished, the revolution has faltered. This has been illustrated in the history of the Sabbath, and is now illustrated in its wide desecration. The lax continental Sabbath, now so much imported to America, comes from erroneous doctrine. First, it proceeds from deficient faith as well as evil practice long existing in the Romish church. Secondly, from the untrue position taken by the Reformers of the sixteenth century, in holding that the "external observance" of the fourth commandment was merely Jewish and ceremonial, and therefore is now void;[1] and, thirdly, from a widespread misrepresentation of the Reformers' actual views, which misrepresentation has been caused by ignoring their belief that the Sabbath was given to man at the beginning, and is moral and perpetual.[2]

Without a divine command for the Sabbath, men will but illy keep it. They require more basis of

---

[1] Calvin's Institutes, Book ii. c. 8, Fourth Com.; Luther on Gal. ii. 19.

[2] Calvin's Com., Gen. ii. 3; Ex. xx. 11; Luther on Larger Catechism; Augsburg Confession.

doctrine than doubt or example or expediency can afford. Nicholas Bownd's new doctrine of the Sabbath, whether strictly correct or not, resulted, in his day, in a revival of religion as well as of Sabbath observance. The Puritan revival of Sabbath doctrine, whether excessive or not, was both the fruit and the source of religious revival. But, on the other hand, every successful effort in the past to undermine or weaken the doctrine of the Sabbath has been attended or followed by bad morals and irreligion.

Probably the Sabbath, or Lord's day, was never more observed than now as a holiday, but is less observed than sometimes in the past as a holy day. The present increasing loss in respect to its sacred character has its chief cause in the wide-spread uncertainty in respect to its basis. Besides the imported defect in doctrine and practice, there exist serious errors among ourselves. The disciples of the seventh-day Sabbath have been increasing; and this has brought disesteem of the Christian Sabbath, or Lord's day, even among some who do not embrace their sabbatarian views. Much has been said against the Puritan Sabbath to the detriment of the real Sabbath. A growing number of scholars, and even ministers, have been teaching that we cannot found the observance of the Lord's day upon the fourth commandment; that that part of the decalogue, though not ceremonial, was positive, and not moral in its nature; and is annulled in the new dispensation. Some have said that the whole decalogue, as it stands in Exodus, has been abolished, because given to the Jews; and many have said that there was no Sabbath at all until the time of Moses, and after the exodus from Egypt.

Two opinions divide Christendom respecting the basis of the Lord's day; some holding that its authority is simply ecclesiastical, derived from the example and teaching of the church since the apostles, and others that its authority is from the apostles, or directly from Christ himself. The Roman Catholic church teaches that "Sundays and holy days all stand upon the same foundation. viz: the ordinance of the church"; and that Protestants inconsistently have to acknowledge the infallibility of the church, by depending on her authority to establish the observance of Sunday.[1] Thus, instead of standing on a firm foundation of doctrine, we are somewhat floating on a sea of uncertainty. Such diverse opinions tend to distraction of the public mind, to neglect and desecration of the weekly day of rest, and even to disbelief and unbelief in religion itself. Without salutary change we shall not have better but worse Sabbath observance. It will be the object of this book to awaken more interest in both the doctrine and sacredness of the Christian Sabbath, or Lord's day.

[1] Catholic Christian Instructed, p. 211. The Shortest Way to end Disputes in Religion. by Rev. Robert Manning. approved by Rev. Bishop Fitzpatrick, p. 19.

CHAPTER II.

THE ORIGIN AND HISTORY OF THE SABBATH.

1. Its basis for appointment was the fact that 'God rested.' The record of the appointment is conspicuously given in the first three verses of the second chapter of the Bible, really belonging to the first chapter. Drs. Paley, Hessey, R. W. Dale, and others tell us that the early reference to the Sabbath in Genesis is no proof of its early institution.² We reply, it belongs to them to prove their objection. The record of the appointment being given along with that of the creation, the *prima facie* evidence is that the Sabbath was very early instituted and given to man. It does violence to the record to suppose that the appointment was delayed twenty-five centuries—until the Israelites were approaching Sinai.

But was the seventh day given to man that of twenty-four hours, or that of God's rest from the close of the six days' creation to the beginning of some other? In the chief sense *man's* day; for its characteristics are those of the natural day in the fourth commandment. Both are blessed and sanctified. God blessed the day by making it a blessing—a blessing chiefly to man, not to himself: hence it

---

[1] Paley's Works, Bk. v. c. 7; Hessey on Sunday, p. 102; Dale on the Ten commandments, p. 88.

was man's day. Yet God's rest was, in some sense, the prototype for that of man.

Though in the early record the seventh day is not called the Sabbath, the characteristics of the two days being the same, there can be no reasonable doubt of their identity. In the commandment not only the first seventh day, but each succeding seventh, was consecrated; and probably at the close of creation each seventh day, as well as the first seventh, was devoted to religion and rest. The reason that induced the appointment of the day—"because that in it he had rested"—appeals to intelligence, and suggests that man was to know and regard the sacred time. And since he could know it in the beginning, it is presumable that it was then given him. He early could enjoy it, and by it commemorate his own origin as the last of God's earthly creation. God's delight in the day must have been much in having his creatures enjoy it; hence it is improbable that he withheld it all the way from Eden to Sinai. The day not being an ordinance of nature, and not causing any break or mark in physical events, man could not learn the specific hebdomadal time from nature. He needed its positive appointment, and it having in itself a blessing for him, evidence of its early appointment may be expected.

2. It appears probable that the primitive pair, with their immediate descendants, early began to observe the seventh day. Cain made an offering to the Lord "in process of time"--at the end of days— end of some number of days. That number, in this instance, was probably *seven;* for that was evidently

the more common multitude of days employed by Jehovah in his appointments with men, and by man in his reckoning of periods. The *first* length of time which, according to the record, we are *certain*, God used in his communications with men, was the seven days' notice he gave Noah before causing it to rain upon the earth (Gen. vii. 4. 10); and in the first account we have of *man's* first reckoning of time, Noah stayed seven days before sending forth the dove from the ark the second time, and other seven before sending it the third time (Gen. viii. 10, 12). If he had waited seven days only once, it would have been less noticeable; doing it twice indicates that he often or constantly observed the specific weekly time. It is improbable that he kept weekly time without a knowledge of the Sabbath that marked off for him the weeks. We know of no day or event that ever designated weekly time as the Sabbath or Lord's day has done. We cannot suppose that God gave primitive man the week without a sacred day; he would sooner give it for the sake of that day than for any other reason.

"God remembered Noah" (Gen. viii. 1). He did not let the flood continue too long; he stopped the fountains of the deep and the windows of heaven; he sent a wind to assuage the waters. And Noah remembered God; he doubtless consulted him about opening the ark, about sending forth the raven and the dove, about waiting other *seven days twice over;* naturally connecting the waiting with religious services appropriate to the seventh day; and when upon dry ground again he built an altar and sacrificed. "There is certainly indicated here a sevenfold division of days, whatever may be its reasons. Of these, no one seems more easy and natural than that which refers it to the traditionary remembrance of the creation and its seventh day of rest."[1]

3. Coming to the age of the early patriarchs, we find Jacob and Laban speaking so familiarly of the "week" (Gen. xxix. 27, 28)—a *seven of days*—that we infer the common acquaintance of their own families, and of their fathers, with that method of reckoning time. When Jacob died, Joseph "made a mourning for his father seven days" (Gen. l. 10), many Egyptians being with him. Here, in all, we find people of Haran,—a part of ancient Syria,—and of Canaan, and of Egypt, observing weeks. Measuring *some* time in that way, probably most of them so measured *all*, as we know was subsequently the case with the Jews. Seven days elapsed in Egypt between the smiting of the river and the Lord's next appeal to Pharaoh through his servant Moses (Ex. vii. 25).

That the number seven became representative and symbolical after the giving of the fourth commandment is not surprising; but what gave it such significance before the Mosaic period, except that God in the beginning made the seventh day conspicuous and sacred to man? The Lord protected Cain by a threatening of sevenfold vengeance upon any that should slay him (Gen. iv. 15); and Lamech boasted that he would be protected by a threatening of seventy and sevenfold vengeance (Gen. iv. 24). Jacob would serve seven years for Rachel (Gen. xxix. 18, 20), and he bowed before Esau seven times (Gen. xxxiii. 3).

[1] Tayler Lewis,—Lange on Genesis. p. 311.

In Pharoah's dream seven kine appeared, and seven other kine ate them up; seven ears of corn came up, and seven thin ears devoured them (Gen. xli. 2-7). Then Joseph showed Pharoah that seven years of plenty were to be followed by seven years of famine; and the two series of seven years came (Gen. xli. 25-30 xlvii. 53, 54). It is highly probable that this early symbolic use of the number seven had some connection with a sacred seventh day. Keil and Delitzsch affirm that the week was established at the creation.[1] But since nature did not mark off the weeks as it does the days, what did divide them from each other, save ceremonies or services, and those of a religious character? Times and seasons, or their limits,—their first and last days,—were customarily attended with religious services. What more natural than that their weeks were marked off to them by sacred or religious days? How did they know weekly time? By the mere approximate of the fourth of a lunar month? Or, by the seven notes of the diatonic scale? Or through the astronomical seven planets, then so awkwardly numbered as to embrace the sun and moon? Or was there the clear and dignified reason that God in the beginning, after the six days of creation, set apart, blessed, and sanctified the seventh day? Did the prominence of the number seven make the week, or did the sacred day make both? History ascribes the earliest knowledge of astronomical science to the Babylonians and Egyptians.[2] But Noah observed septenary time four hundred years before Egypt is even heard of, and near a thousand years

---

[1] Com. on Pent., Vol. i. p. 149.
[2] Lewis's Astronomy of Ancients, p. 256.

before Babylon appears. The celestial bodies, once named the seven planets, and numbered in the following order,—Saturn, Jupiter, Mars, Sun, Venus, Mercury, Moon,[1]—how much tendency have they to cause the observance of weekly time? But weekly time first observed, then how much tendency in men to name the seven days after the seven planets. Besides, no evidence appears that these seven heavenly bodies were early selected and named. Plato and authors contemporary with him discourse of the seven planets; but Homer and Hesiod were apparently ignorant of them, though speaking often of the stars.[2] Tayler Lewis says truly of those who claim to be "the higher school of criticism," had they found in some Hindoo or Persian book a reference to some sevenfold division of time, and in a similar writing closely connected with it an account of a hexameral creation with its succeeding day of rest, they would have discovered a connection between the two ideas. But they violate their own canon, "that the Bible is to be interpreted like any other ancient writings,"[3] and are unreasonably sceptical as to the connection between the week made up of God's creative work and his rest, and the week subsequently observed by man.

The hebdomadal division of time seems as well known to the Hebrews before the giving of the law, and previous to their leaving Egypt, as afterward: the passover, given before the exodus, being prolonged seven days, as well as the feast of tabernacles, given in the wilderness. God's rest began at man's origin; and apparently man's knowledge of that rest

[1] Ibid., p. 246. [2] Ibid., pp. 62, 144, 290.
[3] Lange on Genesis, p. 311.

and his observance of weekly time, also then commenced. Men, knowing the week and the reason, would even naturally have a special regard for the limit day, the seventh of the week.

4. When the Israelites journeyed in the wilderness, they were directed of God to gather twice as much manna on the sixth as on any other day, that the seventh might not be desecrated by gathering during its hours (Ex. xvi. 22, 23, 29). As this occurred before the decalogue was given on Sinai, it shows that the Sabbath existed previous to the latter event, and favors the view that the weekly day of rest was made known to man at the beginning. Dr. Heylin,[1] and Dr. Paley[2] a century and a half afterwards, with others following them, gave their opinion that this transaction in the wilderness was the first institution of the Sabbath.[3] But the first mention of the day in this passage, which is the first by the name "Sabbath" in the scriptures, refers to what God had said of it: "The Lord hath said" (Ex. xvi. 23). If that was just previous, and the Sabbath was originated on this occasion, then it was appointed in a private way, and first announced to Moses alone, which does not comport with its importance. We naturally should expect a fuller record, and more said

---

[1] Works, fol. p. 348, Part. i. c. 4. [2] Moral and Political Philosophy, Bk. v. c. 7.

[3] Dr. Paley's, or the Paley-Heylin views, evidently bore fruit after their kind. Rev. J. Willison of Dundee, Scotland, in a work on the "Santification of the Sabbath," published in 1819, refers to the same sentiments as advocated by Philip Limborch. Then, as now, they seem to have been inimical to the most sacred observance of the Sabbath.

of it, like that in the second of Genesis or the twentieth of Exodus.

The Lord, in his rebuke of some for going out on the Sabbath to gather manna, says: "How long refuse ye to keep my commandments and my laws" (verse 28)? This, with the strong language of the next verse, seems to imply a more familiar acquaintance with the command than the offenders had, if they heard it first only the day previous. They were evidently familiar with the *sixth* day, and, therefore, doubtless, with the *seventh*, and the *week*. The Sabbath, in this instance, seems to have come on the sixteenth of the month, and—it not being on the fourteenth—this fact is against the theory of the quarterly division of the month to constitute the week, and favors the independent and divinely appointed date of the Sabbath. The original—"Let to-morrow be rest, a holy Sabbath to the Lord" (ver. 23)—defines and emphasizes the *rest* by a phrase used here first, and only six times in the Bible; and this earliest use may have been to produce a new and strong impression on the multitude that had just issued from idolatrous Egypt, and needed more instruction and a more vigorous memory concerning that day.

Objection: The surprise of the Hebrews in finding a double quantity of manna on the sixth day shows that the Sabbath was not before known to them.[1]

Reply: It was the miracle of a double supply on one day that astonished them; a miraculous provision for the observance of the seventh day they had not before seen.

[1] Hengstenberg, Hessey, Sunday, p. 111; Garden, Smith's Bible Dict., p. 2764.

Objection second: The original is "*a*" and not "*the* holy Sabbath," and therefore the people were not familiar with the day, and it had just been appointed. *Reply:* The repetition of the word "rest," in the phrase "rest the holy Sabbath,"—Sabbath meaning rest,—to define and emphasize the nature of the day to those who in Egypt may have partially forgotten it, because as bondmen not permitted to observe it, or to those who may have been only proselytes from the Egyptians, might naturally cause the expression "rest," instead of "the rest." *Reply second:* The sabbatical year, each seventh year, and day of atonement, are also designated by the word "Sabbath," and therefore the definite article may have been omitted in reference to the seventh-day Sabbath. Some claim—probably with insufficient reason—that the passover, appointed previous to this occasion in the wilderness, was also sometimes called a Sabbath.[1] *Reply third:* Preceding this time the seventh day, though sacredly observed, may not have been known as the Sabbath,—rest,— and therefore now, when first called such, the definite article would naturally be omitted. We too readily suppose the day must have been called Sabbath, or nothing. One measuring rule of time then was seven days; and the seventh, being the concluding one, was a marked day, and independent of the divine appointment, might easily have become a sacred day. Previous to this, the seventh day of the passover feast had been made religious and devoted to "a holy convocation" (Ex. xii. 16). The early generations, especially, needed the appointment of

---
[1] Caspari, Bib. Sac., Vol. xxviii. p. 471.   [2] Paley.   [3] Paley.

convocation and worship. After the bondage of Egypt *rest* was more required and prized, and the usual name of the sacred day may then have been changed from seventh to Sabbath.

Objection third: In Ezekiel (Ezek. xx. 10—12) God is represented as *giving* his Sabbaths to Israel in the wilderness, as though they were then first instituted.[2] *Reply:* He did not merely give them; he gave them "to be a sign"; he *appointed* them then to be a sign of his covenant with Israel. That does not denote recent origin, any more than God's appointment of the bow in the cloud as a "token of a covenant" (Gen. ix. 13) denotes that it then first existed. All the commandments were to be the sign of a covenant (Deut. v. 3; vi. 8), but some, at least, were given long before their engrossment at Sinai.

Objection fourth: In Nehemiah (ix. 14) God is represented as *making known* his Sabbath upon Mount Sinai, as though then he first made it known.[3] *Reply:* He did there *emphatically* make it known to those who had in Egypt partially forgotten it, and not been allowed to observe it; but not then *first*, because he at least made it known in the wilderness before Israel arrived at Sinai. *Reply second:* God is elsewhere represented as making known his "mighty acts" and "glorious majesty (Ps. cxlv. 12; 1 Chron. xvi. 8); yet that does not imply the *first* proclamation of them, but a more *full* one. Though this record concerning the manna does not prove the previous knowledge of the seventh day as sacred, it does not prove the lack of such knowledge. It adds to other strong probabilities that the seventh was at **the beginning made known to man as religious.**

Objection: "If the Sabbath had been instituted at the time of the creation . . . and if it had been observed all along from that time to the departure of the Jews out of Egypt . . . it appears unaccountable that no mention of it, no occasion of even the obscurest allusion to it, should occur."[1] *Reply:* "To object that the Bible, in its few brief memoranda of their (the patriarchs') lives, says nothing about their Sabbath-keeping, any more than it tells us of their forms of prayer and modes of worship, is a worthless argument."[2] The sacred seventh day may have been given in Eden, and yet not "observed all along." We have shown that there is probably repeated allusion to it in the septenary division of time. Notwithstanding the impressive promulgation of the fourth command through Moses on Sinai, the Scriptures do not mention the Sabbath between the death of Moses and near that of David—about four hundred and thirty-six years,—and yet it was generally observed. We go through the histories of Joshua, of the Judges, of Samuel, and of Saul without its mention. It is the general belief that the institution of sacrifice was observed from the time of the fall; but no mention is made of it between Abel's offering and Noah's building an altar after he left the ark,— by the usual chronology, about sixteen hundred and fifty years. There is no record respecting circumcision—boasted rite of the Jews—between Israel's renewal of it by Joshua on entering Canaan and the circumcision of John the Baptist,—about

---

[1] Paley's Principles of Moral and Political Philosophy, Bk. 5, c. 7.

[2] Tayler Lewis,—Lange on Genesis, p. 197.

fourteen hundred and fifty years,—save Jeremiah's allusion once to the literal, and once to the figurative, observance (ix. 25, 26; iv. 4). Scripture history is given so much in outline and isolated sections, that the lack of any distinct mention of the seventh day as sacred between the creation and Moses is no approach to proof that it was not observed. The words "seven," "seventh," and "sevenfold" occur three hundred and eighty-three times in the Old and New Testaments, and not without some special cause. The cause and origin of so frequent use certainly preceded the giving of the fourth commandment; though that event amplified the cause and increased the use. What cause so probable as that God rested the seventh day, and blessed and hallowed it?

5. The Jewish weekly measurement of time had a striking similarity in a like reckoning among other nations—the Romans, Greeks, Egyptians, Assyrians, Chaldees, Persians, Hindoos, Chinese, Peruvians. The claim that the Greeks and Romans obtained their weekly divisions of time from the Egyptians,[1] and not until about the beginning of the Christian era, is not warranted. Some noted ancient Greek and Roman authors speak of the seventh day as sacred. Clement of Alexandria, writing in the second century, says: "The seventh day is recognized as sacred, not by the Hebrews only, but also by the Greeks."[2] He then quotes from ancient authors— Hesiod: "The first, fourth, and seventh day is holy"; Homer: "And on the seventh there came the sacred day"; "The seventh was sacred"; Callimachus.

[1] Smith's Bible Dict., p. 2764.
[2] Ant. Nic. Lib., Vol. xii. pp. 284, 285.

"Among good days is the seventh day"; "The seventh is among the prime, and the seventh is perfect." Further, Clement says: "The elegies of Solon, too, intensely deify the seventh day." "Among the Greeks says a modern writer, "seven was sacred to Apollo and to Dionysos, . . . particularly sacred in Eudoea, where the number was found to pervade, as it were, almost every sacred, private, or domestic relation."[1] Professor James Hadley enumerates nearly a score of instances where the number seven is significantly used in Homer, and four cases in Odyssey of noted action continuing six days, and terminating on the seventh in some critical event—"a curious circumstance," he says, "in which we might almost be tempted to trace either a dawning or a vanishing of the week."[2] He states, as other authors do, that the Pythagoreans had a special regard for the number seven, and that Philolaus, in an exposition of Pythagorean doctrine, says concerning God, the author and governor of all things, that "he is without variation, even like himself, and like no other, even as the number seven." Among the Persians, in the religion of Zoroaster, who was nearly or quite contemporary with Moses, the number seven was sacred; and Persian modern literature "abounds in sevens."[3] Far back in Brahminism the number seven was especially noted and frequent, and that without being traceable to Egypt or any other nation. Porphyry says: "The Phoenicians consecrated one day in seven as holy."[4]

---

[1] Chambers' Encyclopaedia, Vol. viii. pp. 364, 365.
[2] Essays p. 326.
[3] Hadley's Essays, p. 329.
[4] Cited by President Dwight, Works, Vol. iii. p. 255.

The Sclavonians, while yet in their ancient paganism, held a weekly festival.[1] Lucian speaks of boys as having the seventh day for play.[2] Theophilus of Antioch has this phrase: "Concerning the seventh day, which all men acknowledge."[3] Former inhabitants of the coast of Guinea observed a weekly day in social and religious services.[4] An ancient Chinese writer says: "Every seven days comes the revolution" —of the heavenly bodies, as Chinese scholars explain,—indicating some former septenary division of time; and Gillespie[5] says that by the Chinese calendar now there are four names in each lunar month, answering to our four Sundays of the month. Of Grecian wise men seven were singled out six centuries before Christ, and Plato gives the first list.[6]

There were also the seven wonders of the world, and the seven ages of human life. The book of Job shows the observance of Septenary time in some land other than that of Israel, and in an age probably before the time of Moses (Job ii. 13).

Philo, contemporary of Christ, wrote a dissertation on the number seven, and said: "That day is the festival not of one city or one country, but of all the earth"[7]; meaning, doubtless, that it was designed for all, though not observed by all. The Saracens had a weekly sacred day before the time of Mohammed[8]; and he made the number seven conspicuous in the

[1] Helmaldus, cited by Ussher, Works, Vol. xii. p. 578.
[2] Ibid., p. 580.   [3] Ant. Nic. Lib., Vol iii. p. 79.
[4] Hurd's Rites and Ceremonies (1799), p. 456.
[5] Land of Sinim, p. 161; cited by Gilfillan, p. 360.
[6] Hadley's Essays, p. 826.
[7] Yonge's Translation, Bohn's Ecclesiastical Library, Vol. i. p. 26.   [8] Purchas' Pilgrimage, cited by Gilfillan, p. 359.

Koran, though unable to read the Bible, by which he may, however, have been indirectly influenced.[1] The importance and dignity of the number seven is shown by Shakespeare's use of it. La Place said: "The week is perhaps the most ancient and incontestable monument of human knowledge."

Even if in some cases in the far past, as that of Hesiod, the reference be to the day of the month, and not of the week, still, the question is, How came the seventh to be a noted and sacred day in so many nations, and generally without known copying from each other? The weekly division might be forgotten during the long ages, and yet the number seven remain sacred. That other days than the seventh have been sacred or noted among gentile nations does not weaken the argument. There were other sacred days and numbers in the Jewish economy; though scarcely any number in any nation has been so conspicuous as "seven."

Notwithstanding the Egyptians and others named the seven days after the seven planets, that does not prove that there was an astronomical cause for the septenary division; for there are no phenomena of the heavens sufficient to suggest it. After that division was made and observed, and its cause and authority forgotten, the astronomical reason may have been originated in human fancy.[2] The fact that the seventh is so generally a marked or sacred day, with no satisfactory reason for it external to the Scriptures, favors the view that it was appointed as a religious day in the beginning. If so, it was indeed

---

[1] Hadleys Essays, p. 337.
[2] Tayler Lewis, —Lange on Gen. p. 311.

for man, and it may be expected to continue while the race endures.

Objection: "It is no safe foundation for our thinking ourselves bound to keep it [the Sabbath], that the patriarchs kept it before the law was given, and that the commandment had existed before the time of Moses, and was only confirmed by him and repeated. . . . For if the law itself be done away in Christ, much more the things before the law."[1] "And if Moses has vanished in the diviner glory of Christ, all that preceded Moses must have vanished, too."[2] *Reply:* Ceremonial and some other laws given expressly to the Jews were in force only while Judaism lasted. But moral commands—as, to worship God, and not to kill or steal—given to Adam, or Noah, or any other representative not of a nation, but of mankind, most certainly hold their binding force upon all men. Therefore, the Sabbath or any sacred day, having moral elements, if given to the race once, must, in respect to those elements, hold still, wherever known. Besides, moral elements, principles, laws, are not done away in Christ, even if their application and use be changed. The things done away, or vanished, in Christ are only such as have their fulfillment, completion or enlargement in him.

6. The fact of a septenary division of time in the early ages being established, the associated fact that public worship was in early time appointed and observed, gives a high degree of probability that the seventh day was sacred. "Then began men to call

---

[1] Dr. Thomas Arnold, Sermons, Vol. iii. No. xxii. pp. 256, 257.
[2] Dr. R. W. Dale, Ten Commandments, p. 94.

upon the name of the Lord" (Gen. iv. 26). Professor Stuart regarded this as teaching that social and public worship then commenced.[1] It cannot mean that there was previously no private worship; that Seth did not pray before his son Enos was born, nor any others prior to that date. Lange, and Keil and Delitzsch also hold that this passage announces the inauguration of public religious services. We know, further, that in that primitive era there were consecrated places of worship. Noah built an altar unto the Lord (Gen. viii. 20). So did Abraham at both his first and second stopping-place in Canaan (Gen. xii. 7, 8); and to the latter he came again for worship after returning from Egypt (Gen. xiii. 3, 4). He built another altar after separating from Lot (Gen. xiii. 18), and still another at Beersheba (Gen. xxi. 33). Isaac built an altar when he dwelt in Gerar (Gen. xxvi. 6, 25). Jacob built one at Shalem (Gen. xxxiii. 18, 20), and one at Bethel (Gen. xxxv. 7), and offered sacrifices at Beersheba. It must have been the custom to prepare and consecrate places of worship. Here are three positive factors, existing long before the time of Moses: septenary division of time, public worship, and places for public worship. When did they worship? On some particular day, at a stated time, doubtless, as we know their posterity soon did. When was that time, unless on the seventh day, the weekly limit in the hebdomadal period, which, at least, was the time a few centuries afterwards? Daily worship of equal length would have been unnatural. Daily sacrifices would have required too much time of each small community, and too much expenditure

---

[1] Phelps' Perpetuity of the Sabbath, p. 34.

of the life of animals. The later Jews were required to offer at Jerusalem, on the Sabbath, double the number of sacrifices they offered on other days; the earlier Jews were, therefore, more likely to offer weekly sacrifice on the seventh day than on any other.

7. But we have other important ancient evidence, in the Chaldean account of the creation, as given by the cuneiform inscriptions found in the ruins of ancient Babylon. The lamented George Smith, noted in Assyrian researches, says: "In the year 1869 I discovered, among other things, a curious religious calendar of the Assyrians, in which every month is divided into four weeks, and the seventh days, or 'sabbaths,' are marked out as days on which no work should be undertaken."[1] H. Fox Talbot, F.R.S., in his translation of these Creation Tablets, renders two lines thus:

"On the seventh day he appointed a holy day,
And to cease from all business he commanded."

He also says: "This fifth tablet is very important, because it affirms, clearly in my opinion, that the origin of the Sabbath was coeval with creation.... It has been known for some time that the Babylonians observed the Sabbath with considerable strictness. On that day the king was not allowed to take a drive in his chariot; various meats were forbidden to be eaten, and there were a number of other minute restrictions. . . . But it was not known that they believed the Sabbath to have been ordained at the creation. I have found, however, since this translation of the

[1] Assyrian Discoveries, p. 12.

fifth tablet was completed, that Mr. Sayce has recently published a similiar opinion."[1]

Rev. A. H. Sayce, M. A., so far as appears, has translated more of this "Babylonian Saints' Calendar" than any other person. Both he and Mr. Smith have translated a Babylonian list of the thirteen months of the year and their patron deities. Mr. Sayce has translated in full the memorandum of each of the thirty days of the month in this calendar. That for the seventh day reads thus:

"The seventh day. A feast of *Merodach* (and) *Zir=Panitu*. A festival.

A sabbath. The prince of many nations the flesh of *birds* (and) cooked fruit eats not.

The garments of his body he changes not. White robes he puts not on. Sacrifice he offers not. The king (in) his chariot rides not.

In royal fashion he legislates not. A place of garrison the general (by word of) mouth appoints not. Medicine for his sickness of body he applies not.

To make a *sacred spot* it is suitable. In the night in the presence of *Merodach* and *Istar*, the king his offering makes. Sacrifice he offers.

Raising his hand, the high place of the god he worships."[2]

That this is not merely for the seventh day of the month, without any weekly significance, is manifest from the fact that nearly the same language is used in these memoranda for the fourteenth, the twenty=first, and the twenty=eighth days. And nothing like

---

[1] Transactions of the Society of Biblical Archæology, Vol. v. Part ii. pp. 427, 428.

[2] Records of the Past, Vol. vii. pp. 160, 161.

it is used for any other of the thirty days except the nineteenth which seems to have been another sacred day, like the day of atonement in the Hebrew Calendar. Mr. Sayce says the month was divided into two lunations, each of "three periods of five days, the nineteenth ending the first period of the second lunation."[1] Being thus a limit day, it was sacred. Mr. Sayce further says of this calendar: "But the chief interest attaching to it is due to the fact that it bears evidence to the existence of a *seventh-day Sabbath*, on which certain works were forbidden to be done, among the Babylonians and Assyrians. It will be observed that several of the regulations laid down are closely analagous to the sabbatical injunctions of the Levitical law and the practice of the Rabbinical Jews. What I have rendered "sabbath" is expressed by two Accadian words, which literally signify "dies nefastus," and a bilingual syllabary makes them equivalent to the Assyrian *yum sulumi* or "day of completion (of labors), or a day unlawful (to work upon)." The word Sabbath itself was not unknown to the Assyrians, and occurs under the form *sabattu* in W. A. I., II. 32, 16, where it is explained as a day of rest for the heart." *Sabattu* is also explained to mean "complete" in W. A. I., II. 25, 14. The calendar is written in Assyrian. The occurrence, however, of numerous Accadian expressions and technical terms shows that it was of Accadian, and therefore non-Semitic origin, though borrowed by the Semites, along with the rest of the old Turanian theology and science. The original text must accordingly have been inscribed at some period anterior to the seven-

[1] Ibid., Vol. i. pp. 164, 165.

teenth century, B. C., when the "Accadian language seems to have become extinct."[1] An American Assyrian scholar, Rev. Selah Merrill, D.D., also affirms that the Accadian language became extinct at least seventeen centuries before Christ, except as some of its words were brought into the Assyrian. These cuneiform inscriptions, therefore, seem to give positive evidence, that the "Sabbath" existed at least two centuries prior to the giving of the decalogue on Sinai, and that, as Talbot says, "the origin of the Sabbath was coeval with creation." Therefore, having the whole evidence in view, the modern, frequent statement, that it 'is unwarrantable to infer that the Sabbath was instituted at the beginning,'[2] we claim is unfounded.

8. The fourth commandment in itself indicates the probability that God had made the seventh day sacred, and given it to man as such, long before he gave the decalogue. The injunction to "remember" the day naturally implies that it was previously known. Remembrance ordinarily signifies retrospection as well as prospection. It here implies retrospection; for the Sabbath was known at the giving of manna, even if not at creation. The command to remember is based on three reasons: God rested from his work, he blessed the seventh day, and he hallowed it. The past tense of the verb is used; each reason was an act of the past. The first one, God rested, we know dates at the close of creation. Were there two thousand and five hundred years between

[1] Records of the Past, Vol. vii. pp. 157, 158, and 2d. note p. 160.
[2] The Social Law of God, Sermons on the Ten Commandments, by E. A. Washburn, D.D., p. 73.

that and the date of the other two reasons? Improbable. If they all dated at the beginning of God's rest, then the seventh day was made sacred at that time; whether or not then made known to man. Yet was it not made known when made sacred?

If God's act of blessing and hallowing the seventh day occurred on the Mount while he wrote the decalogue, we should not have had the Hebrew perfect tense, but the imperfect, or participle, which in this case would be nearly equivalent to the English present: remember the Sabbath-day, for God rested on it, and *blesses* and *hallows* it.

The three reasons in the commandment for observing the Sabbath-day being the same as the three for the appointment of the seventh day, as stated in the narrative of the creation, is another fact that apparently dates the sacred day at the beginning of God's rest. The language in Malachi, "Remember the law of Moses" (Mal. iv. 4), naturally means not merely bear that law in mind in the future, but remember the law given through Moses heretofore; and, in like manner, the fourth command rationally means, remember the Sabbath-day given heretofore.

The command to remember has especial significance, because at that age so much of history and of knowledge of God's works and commands depended upon human memory. The book of Genesis did not exist to preserve the sacred narratives until Moses' hand could write it; though he doubtless embraced in it some accounts previously written by inspired men. By the usual chronology Adam could tell Methuselah of the sacred seventh day; Methuselah, Shem; Shem, Abraham; Abraham, Isaac; Isaac, Joseph; Joseph, Amram; Amram, his sons, Aaron and Moses. Memory had a high office.

It being a legal axiom that a law continues while its reason continues, it follows that under a wise ruler the law is in force as soon as the reasons for it exist. One of the three reasons, and doubtless all, for the appointment of the Sabbath, began at the close of the creation. Should not this increase the probabilities nearly into assurance, that the seventh was given to man as a sacred day at his origin?

CHAPTER III.

CHRIST DID NOT ABOLISH OR MODIFY THE SABBATH.

The decalogue had an ascendency over the other enactments of the Mosaic law, and was confirmed without repeal by Christ, in his own person and through his apostles. Its original superiority is evident from its having been written by Jehovah himself on the two tables of the covenant, made especially for them, and kept in the holy of holies. No part of that law can be abolished, except by the enacting authority.

But some claim that this decalogue was abolished by Christ, through himself and his disciples. Dr. Thomas Arnold speaks cautiously: "If the law itself be done away in Christ."[1] Dr. R. W. Dale says: "The Jewish revelation has become obsolete."[2] Dr. George B. Bacon says: "When I say that Christianity superseded the Jewish law, I mean, just as Paul meant, that it superseded the whole of the Jewish law."[3] And many suppose that Christ himself began to disregard and violate the Sabbath. Dr. Heylin, in the seventeenth century, said that Christ abated the estimation which the people had of the Sabbath, preparatory for the abrogation of the day.[4] Theodore

---

[1] Works, Vol. iii. p. 257, Sermon xxii. The Lord's Day.
[2] Ten Commandments (Fourth), p. 93.
[3] Sabbath Question, p. 101.
[4] Hist. Sab., fol. p. 401, Part ii. c. l. § 2.

Parker said, on this question, "Paul rejects the authority of the Old Testament."[1] *Reply:* When Christ was requested to tell the greatest commandment of the law, he gave a summary of the first four as our duty to God, and of the last six as our duty to man. He added: "On these two commandments hang all the law and the prophets" (Matt. xxii. 35-40). He made no exception of the fourth commandment; he therefore sustained that and the whole ten. In that day no question had been raised about the abrogation of the fourth commandment or the Sabbath. He said to another: "Keep the commandments." When asked, "Which?" he specified the last six; the direction to the inquirer to sell his possessions having pertained to the tenth (Matt. xix. 16-22). By not naming the first three he did not reject them, nor the fourth by not naming it. He convicted the young man by the second table of the law; much more was he a sinner by the first. Christ testified that he came not to destroy the law; therefore the Sabbatic part of it he did not abolish. He said: "Till heaven and earth pass, one jot or one tittle shall in no wise pass from the law, till all be fulfilled" (Matt. v. 18). The sacrificial and otherwise ceremonial law was fulfilled when Christ's propitiatory work was complete; but the chief elements of the sacred day did not pertain to that law, and no proof exists that their office has been fulfilled.

Dr. Washington Gladden says this: "One of the ten commandments was, as it seems to me, distinctly repealed by our Lord."[2] He is understood to refer

---

[1] Christian Use of Sunday, p. 18.

[2] Church and Kingdom, p. 51.

to the fourth commandment, but he does not prove or profess to prove the statement, yet such claims of repeal are hazardous for souls and sociology. Their effect with some is to undermine the authority of the Scriptures.

Jesus, instead of annulling the Sabbath, explained and enforced its observance, and purified it from rabbinical abuses. His justification of his disciples in plucking ears of corn on the Sabbath for their present need was on the ground of special necessity. like that of saving life or relieving suffering (Matt. xii. 1-13; Mark ii. 23-28; iii. 2-6; Luke vi. 1-10; xiii 11-17; xiv. 1-6). Thus was David justified in relieving his hunger by means not otherwise allowable (1 Sam. xxi. 1-6). But F. W. Robertson repeatedly implies that the fourth commandment—"In it thou shalt not do any work" (Ex. xx. 10) forbids doing even religious or necessary work.[1] *Reply:* Such cannot have been the meaning; for God required Joshua, with priests and armed men, to march around Jericho on the Sabbath (Josh. vi.); and the double sacrifices (Num. xxviii, 9, 10) and new baked shew-bread (Lev. xxiv. 5-8; 1 Chron. ix. 32), which the Lord appointed for the Sabbath, required a large amount of labor, yet it was not profanation of the day. The Sabbatic law forbade the ordinary secular work in order to promote rest and worship. Pharisaic dogmas added the prohibition of works of necessity and mercy; but Christ allowed them, and, by the case of David eating shew-bread, and that of the priests performing labor in the Temple on the Sabbath (Matt. xii. 5, 6), he showed

[1] Sermons (First Series), Shad. and Sub. Sab. Law, pp. 116, 118, 120.

that his course was not inconsonant with the law of the Sabbath. And it is not shown that Christ ever allowed anything which the law denied.

Jesus taught the application and adaptation of the Sabbath to the race, by saying that it "was made for man, and not man for the Sabbath" (Mark ii. 27). Dr. R. W. Dale and others object that he did not mean that the Sabbath was made for *man*, in distinction from the Jews, but for the *Jewish* man.[1] We reply: The first truth in this language of Christ is, man was not made for institutions and ordinances, but these—including the Sabbath—for man. An implied truth is, the Sabbath was made for mankind. "The Son of Man is Lord also of the Sabbath" (Mark ii. 28). As Son of *Man*, he belonged to the *race*, though he came first to the house of Israel. So the Sabbath made for man was designed for the race of men, though for the Jews it was especially the seal of the covenant. The elements of the Sabbath are chiefly of a moral nature, such as rest, physical and spiritual, worship, and time to be kept holy. It cannot be found that God has ever laid moral duties upon one nation or portion of mankind, without making the same binding upon all others where they were known and could be practiced. Moral duties are universal and permanent. Therefore, when Christ said the Sabbath was "made for man," he did not mean it was for *Jews* merely, but for *all* men. He gave no indication that he was defining the manner in which Jews only should keep the Sabbath, nor that he intended to have it abolished under the new dispensation.[2]

---

[1] Ten Commandments, by Dale, p. 92.
[2] Dr. J. S. Stone, in The Eclectic, Vol. iv. p. 554.

Dr. Dale gives no definite reason for his opinion that Christ referred merely to the Jews, as having the Sabbath made for them. But Dr. S. M. Hopkins says specifically: "What Jesus said was not that the Sabbath was made for man or humanity at large, but for the man (*ton anthropon*); the Jewish Sabbath for Jewish man; just as we should say that the constitution was made for the people (the American people), and not the people for the constitution. The failure of our translators to appreciate the force of the Greek article in this passage has largely contributed to mistaken views as to the universal and permanent obligations of the fourth commandment—an error which will undoubtedly be rectified in the new revision."[1] The revision shows no change. Alford, one of the revision committee until his death, translates it, "For the sake of man," without the article, meaning the *generic* man. Winer says: "To be particularly noticed, further, is the use of a singular with the article to express in the person of a definite individual a whole class; as when we say, The soldier must be trained to arms." He gives as an example Matt. xii. 35: ὁ ἀγαθὸς ἄνθρωπος . . . ἐκβάλλει ἀγαθά, "A good man out of the good treasure of the heart bringeth forth good things."[2] As we understand Professor Hopkins' rule, this must be a *Jewish* good man; according to Winer, and to reason, we think, it is *any* good man; the "definite individual" is taken for a "whole class." In this instance, and in the case of the Sabbath made for man (Mark. ii, 27), the Saviour is addressing unbelieving Pharisees;

[1] Address at Pittsburgh, before the Evangelical Alliance.
[2] New Testament Grammar (Am. ed.), p. 106.

yet in neither case does he say anything limiting his application to the Jews, nor anything more appropriate or needful to them than to other men. Dr. Robinson says the article is also used "in the singular when the noun expresses a generic idea, or stands as the representative of a class, where in English, also, we commonly put *the*."[1] He cites, as one example, the passage Winer does (Matt. xii, 35), where he would translate, as Alford does, "*the* good man," representing a class, the *generic* good man. Dr. Robinson speaks again of the Greek usage, "where the singular, ὁ ἄνθρωπος, *the man*, is used in a collective or generic sense, either for all mankind or for a particular class of men,"[2] and cites Matt. iv. 4: "Man shall not live by bread alone," ὁ ἄνθρωπος, *the* man, *man* used generically, though preceded by the definite singular. But as we understand the rule of Dr. Hopkins and others, it must be merely the Jewish man. Pray, then, what is there in Scripture that is applicable to us Gentiles? Professor Hadley gives a class where the noun, though preceded by the definite article, is used generically, and gives as his example, ὁ ἄνθρωπος θνητὸς ἐστι, *man is mortal; the* man; yet he says: "Man as such, comprehending every one of the species,"[3] not merely all of one nationality, or a definite individual. Professor A. C. Kendrick, on the particular passage in question (Mark ii. 27), says, "Had it been ἀνθρώπῳ, it must have been for *a* man, spoken of indefinitely, whoever he might be, where ἀνθρώπῳ was used loosely for τῳ ἀνθρώπῳ. The

---

[1] Lexicon of the New Testament, p. 490, col. 2.

[2] Ibid., p. 56, col. 2.

[3] Greek Grammar, § 526 b.

latter, τῷ ἀνθρώπῳ, may mean equally well 'the man,' *i. e.*, the man referred to in the particular case, or 'for man' collectively and generically, the *genus homo*, which the Greek language has no other way of properly designating. That the latter is meant here, I should not think there is a moment's ground for doubting. Otherwise, it can here (Mark ii. 27) have no proper reference whatever."[1] Professor Hopkins illustrates: "The Jewish Sabbath for the Jewish man, just as we should say that the constitution was made for the people (the American people)." *Reply:* 1. If Christ had said "the Jewish man," as Dr. Hopkins says, "the American people," it would have been a parallel case; but as the fact is. it is not. The simple phrase, "The constitution was made for the people," unexplained by word, allusion, or implication, would mean for all people; as God's "constitution" of natural rights, life, liberty, and the pursuit of happiness is for all people. 2. If Christ intended the truths of his gospel to be only for the Jews, then it might be that the Sabbath was made merely for them. But he says: "Preach the gospel to every creature." And under the old dispensation he desired to have the whole world made proselytes to the Jewish faith, as the Rechabites were—to that of the Sabbath with the rest. He made special promises to the strangers that should come and keep his "Sabbaths" (Isa. lvi. 3-8). 3. If Gentiles were not *men*, then the Sabbaths were not for them.

Finally, a class of writers have for a long time been saying that Christ did not teach that the Sabbath was for mankind in general, but that in saying

---

[1] Private correspondence.

that it "was made for man," he said only that it was made for the Jews. The only reason we have found for such doctrine is that so clearly stated by Dr. Hopkins, which we have now considered, and which we conclude has no real foundation.

Returning to Christ's instructions, when he inquired of the Pharisees: "Is it *lawful* to do good on the Sabbath days, or to do evil" (Mark iii. 4) ? "Is it *lawful* to heal on the Sabbath day" (Luke xiv. 3) ? and when he affirmed, "It is *lawful* to do well on the Sabbath days" (Matt. xii. 12), he each time implied, and intended to be understood, that he fully regarded the Scripture laws pertaining to the Sabbath, though he disregarded the rabbinical perversions of them. The Great Teacher corrected the abuses of both the Sabbath and marriage, but never those concerning circumcision, or any other institution not designed for all men and all time.

Objection: Christ attended a feast on the Sabbath, thus putting dishonor upon it, which apparently set it aside (Luke xiv. (1-25). *Reply:* This is not in Scripture called "a feast," but "eating bread" (ver. 1). Probably it was only the cold lunch, or meal at noon; for it is not called "supper." That it was the mid-day meal is apparent from the fact that great multitudes (ver. 25) attended Christ as he seems to have been going from the Pharisee's house; this occurrence, *after* the evening meal, it being so late, would be improbable. The synagogue services closed about noon, the sixth hour. Josephus speaks of an assembly being dissolved then, "at which hour," he says, "our laws require us to go to dinner on Sabbath days."[1] Then, probably, one of Christ's hearers, living near by, invited him and his company and some of his own Pharisee friends, to his house for refreshment. Jesus and his apostles numbered thirteen, and at such a time the number at the meal was naturally doubled or quadrupled. They must all eat somewhere, and eating together did not make it a secular occasion, which is what is generally meant by our term "feast." The Pharisees were 'watching him,' especially to see if he would heal on the Sabbath the man present who had the "dropsy" (ver. 1, 2). All this gives a religious, rather than a secular aspect to the scene. Bengel says: "There was no wedding on this occasion." What Christ says of a wedding was in a parable uttered then, and out of courtesy he would make the occasion in the parable different from that at the house of his host. So far as appears, the Saviour's conversation there was wholly religious, and nothing of hilarity is witnessed among the guests. It was probably not an expensive meal; for no fire was allowed for the cooking of food on the Sabbath (Ex. xxxv. 3).[2] The chief rooms

[1] Life, § 54.
[2] Professor Fairbairn argues that the prohibition of fires was only temporary, designed for wilderness experience, and quotes Josephus as implying that in his day only the Essenes refused to build fires on the Sabbath (Typology, Vol. ii. p. 143). The quotation is: "They are stricter than any other of the Jews in resting from their labors on the seventh day; for they not only get their food ready the day before, that they may not be obliged to kindle a fire on that day, but they will not remove any vessel out of its place," etc. (Wars, Bk. ii. c. 8). Contrary to Fairbairn's inference, the passage implies, we think, that other Jews *did* refuse to build fires on the Sabbath; otherwise, the

that some selected were simply the more conspicuous places for reclining at the table. No evidence appears that Christ disregarded the sacred day on this occasion, even though many were assembled together. In a day without printing, and with few manuscript books, there was more need of social religious communion, even on the Sabbath, than now.

The "supper" made for Jesus at Bethany (John xii. 2) was evidently not on the Jewish Sabbath. He seems to have come from Jericho on Friday, to have rested during the Jewish legal Sabbath, and at evening, after its close, to have had a meal with his usual company, and the few friends at the house of their host. Even if it were the Sabbath, nothing appears which was improper for that day, nothing like a secular feast.

The great feast given the Saviour by his disciple Levi—his apostle Matthew—(Luke v. 29), cannot be claimed to have been on the Sabbath. It was probably on Friday, as the next day seems to have been the seventh.

Many say that when Jesus ate bread with the Pharisee on the Sabbath (Luke xiv. 1) "the meal must have been a costly and ceremonious one," "a splendid entertainment."[2] Much against it is the

phrase "not only" would not have been inserted. In respect to removing vessels, etc., the Essenes went beyond other Jews. Philo says: "Moses, in many places, forbids any one to handle a fire on the Sabbath day" (Yonge's Translation, Vol. iii. p. 120), which shows that he understood the prohibition to be of universal application.

[2] See Alford and Trench, *in loc.*

fact that no cooking could be done, or fire built, on the Sabbath. Against it is one reason for no cooking, "that thy man-servant and thy maid-servant may rest as well as thou." (Deut. v. 14). Yet, closing their day at six o'clock in the evening, they could have one warm meal before daylight passed by, which, on other days at least, was their chief meal; though we, with the same rule against fires on Sunday, could not have a warm meal between midnight and midnight—commencing and closing the day, as we do, at that hour.

Objection Second: It was a feast that Christ attended on this occasion, because "the Jews used to give entertainments on the Sabbath. See Nehemiah viii. 9-12; Tobit ii. 1."[1] *Reply:* The day in this passage in Nehemiah is not called the Sabbath, but "holy unto the Lord" (ver. 9). It was on the first day of the seventh month (ver. 2). That was the time of the feast of trumpets. And though in Lev. xxiii. 24, 25 the day is called a Sabbath—in the Revised Version, a *solemn rest*—it was not the weekly one; it was not *shabbath*, but *shabbathon*, merely a day for sabbatizing, a sabbatical day—one on which "no servile work should be done," but not one on which "no work" should be performed, as was the case with the weekly Sabbath and the day of atonement. It were useless to hold that the feast of trumpets always came on the Sabbath. The varying nature of the Jewish month forbids it. The Mischna implies that the Sabbath and that feast were not identical; stating, as it does, that when the feast of trumpets came on the Sabbath the

[1] Alford on Luke xiv. 1.

trumpets were to be blowed only in the Temple, and not outside of it.¹

The passage in Tobit (ii. 1) to which Alford refers does contain the phrase, "There was a good dinner prepared for me"; but the same verse shows that the occasion was not on the Sabbath, but "day of Pentecost." Alford cites also Augustine; but the passages,² though indicating luxurious ease and idleness, do not prove expensive feasts, and, besides, they pertain to customs in Augustine's time, and not in that of Christ. In another passage, not referred to by Alford, Augustine³ speaks of reveling and drunkenness as practised by the Jews "of old"; but he doubtless refers to the prophets' day, when the desecrated Sabbaths were an abomination to God (Isa. i. 13). Alford's citations utterly fail to show that Christ attended a feast on the Sabbath.

Other writers, perhaps by following Alford, have fallen into his error. "Christ attended a feast made on that day in his honor. . . . Jewish usage, in that age, justified social gatherings on the Sabbath, and Christ by his practice sanctioned this usage, while by his words he never rebuked it;"⁴ "It was usual for the rich to give a feast on that day; and our Lord's attendance at such a feast," etc.⁵

"It was customary to give feasts on that day, and our Savior is expressly said to have been a guest at

¹ Surenhusius's Mischna, Parz ii. p. 344, Roch Hash. Caput iv. (§ 1). Amsterdam, 1699.

² On Ps. xxxii. 2; Ps. xci. 2, Latin numbering.

³ Commentary on Matt. xxiv. 20.

⁴ Dic. Religious Knowledge, by Lyman Abbott and Prof. T. J. Conant, p. 824. Art. "Sabbath."

⁵ Smith's Dictionary of the Bible, p. 2759.

one."[1] "Nehemiah, a Jewish reformer of the strictest principle, gave directions for eating the fat, and drinking the sweet, and sending portions unto them for whom nothing is prepared, on the Sabbath, after the sermon" (see Neh. viii. 8, 10).[2] *Reply*: This passage in Nehemiah has nothing to do with the observance of the Sabbath; but the writer here citing it, and writing the sentence which he hopes is proved by it, does cite this good sentence from Paulus on Luke xiv. 1-24: "We are not here to understand a public banquet." To sustain the charge against the Jews of holding social gatherings and giving feasts, —by which is meant those of a secular character,—we find adduced such passages as these: 2 Chron. xxix., which does not speak of the Sabbath at all, but of special services consequent on the revival of religion in the beginning of Hezekiah's reign, and subsequent to the cleansing of the Temple; and Neh. viii. 9-13, which refers to the feast of the trumpets (Lev. xxiii. 24, 25), and to memorial services at the completion of the rebuilding of the wall around Jerusalem, and Hosea ii. 11, which threatens divine judgments by taking away the Sabbath. But all these fail to sustain the foregoing charge.

The error is frequent of ascribing the celebrations of mere feast-days to the sacred Sabbath, probably because they are sometimes called "Holy unto the Lord" (Neh. viii: 9). And even the mirth (Neh. viii. 12) of feast-days was religious, rather than secu-

---

[1] Kitto's Bib. Cyc. (Alexander's ed., third and enlarged), p. 713.
[2] Questions of the Day, by John Hall, D. D., p. 201. See also Cox on "Sabbath Laws and Sabbath Duties," pp. 137, 436, 439; and George B. Bacon, D. D., on "The Sabbath Question," p. 74.

lar. Josephus approvingly quotes Nicholaus' plea for the Jews before Agrippa, in which he says of their observance of the seventh day: "It is dedicated to the learning of our customs and laws; we thinking it proper to reflect on them, as well as on any [good] thing else, in order to our avoiding of sin. If any one, therefore, examine into our observances, he will find that they are good in themselves."[1] Whiston, learned in such things, corroborates Josephus; and both give a historic impression utterly inconsistent with secular feasts, or even secular visiting on the Sabbath among the Jews in our Savior's time. The fact that the Pharisees and Essenes, and perhaps the Sadducees, of that age, were very scrupulous and superstitious in observing the Sabbath, and put much merit in the outward acts of life, is irreconcilable with the theory that they attended secular feasts or even social gatherings on that sacred day. Philo, contemporary of Josephus, treating of Jewish laws and customs, says: "But the seventh day had an especial honor; for it is not permitted to do anything whatever on that day"; and, "It was invariably the custom, . . . especially on the seventh day, . . . to discuss matters of Philosophy, . . . in accordance with which custom, even to this day, the Jews hold philosophical discussions on the seventh day, disputing about their national philosophy."[2] The learned Selden, after quoting various Jewish authorities, says: "The Jews, therefore, by no means

---

[1] Antiq., Bk. xvi. c. 2. § 4; see also ibid., c. vi. § 12; against Apion, Bk. i. § 22; Wars, Bk. iv. c. 9, § 12.

[2] Life of Moses, i. c. 36, Yonge's Translation, Vol. iii. pp. 46, 119.

count the Sabbath a burden, but a great blessing; they have it in high veneration, and affect to call it their spouse."[1] Buxtorf gives similar testimony.[2] Philo describes the "feasts" of "Barbarians and Grecians," with the apparent implication that Jewish feasts were free from all excesses and perversions.[3] We therefore conclude, though the Jews had their chief meal on the Sabbath near mid-day, instead of at evening, as on other days, and though they endeavored to make the occasion cheerful, and set their best food cold upon the table, and gave time to conversation, and frequently to short discourses, yet that they did not in our Saviour's time indulge in mere social visiting, carnal festivities, or secular amusements during the Sabbath hours. We also conclude that the frequent statement in modern times that Christ was on the Sabbath a guest at a feast made in his honor, has done much to secularize the Lord's day. Professor Barrows, D, D., of Oberlin, whose studies had led him to some special examination of this subject, states that he knows of no evidence that Christ attended a feast, in the ordinary sense of the term, on the Sabbath, or that the Jews of that age were accustomed to hold sumptuous entertainments on that day.

[1] Selden de Jure nat. et gent. lib. iii. c. 10; Oper. Vol. i. pp. 326, 327.
[2] Buxtorf, Synag, Judaic. c. xv. pp. 299, 300; Edit. Basil, 1661.
[3] Vol. i. p. 198, Cain and his birth.

CHAPTER IV.

CHRIST'S APOSTLES DID NOT TEACH OR HOLD THAT EITHER THE LAW OR THE FOURTH COMMANDMENT IS ABOLISHED.

The last chapter we closed by replying to some objections. They were, that Christ did much toward abolishing the Sabbath of the decalogue by his teaching and by his sanction of Jewish secular festivities on that sacred day. Several incorrect statements, having the weight of objections, have been made by Jahn,[1] Horne,[2] Lightfoot,[3] and Wetstein.[4] The last three of these writers depend on Luke xiv. 1 to maintain their claim. They all have misapprehended such passages as Ex. xv. 20, 21; 2 Sam. vi. 14; Neh. viii. 9, 10. We have already sufficiently replied to these objections. We may add a few words. Jahn's editor, Professor Upham, says that the practices which that author names were all religious. He should have added that none of his Scripture passages necessarily refer to the Sabbath at all. Horne quotes the standard text, Luke xiv. 1, and then refers to Lightfoot and Wetstein. They chiefly rely on the

[1] Archaeology (2d ed.), p. 443.
[2] Introduction, Vol. iii. p. 292.
[3] Horae Heb. et Talmud (London, 1823, p. 142, Lev. xiv. 1.
[4] On Luke xiv. 1.

Mischna. But that is composed much of traditions relative to Jewish customs, was very meagre as late as the close of the second century, was not completed (the Babylonian one) until about the close of the fifth century, and that of Jerusalem, the inferior one, not much sooner, if as soon.[1] It is poor authority on which to convict Jesus Christ of attending secular feasts on the Sabbath among the Jews, when its date is not at our Saviour's time, and the Jews had so much degenerated in national customs at the time of its date. Some of the practices attributed by these and other writers to the Jews of Christ's day, Philo, contemporary with him, denies, at least, with reference to the better class of Jews. Speaking of the joy the great lawgiver had provided in the Sabbath for the Hebrew people, and of their abstaining from secular labor and business on that day, he adds: "But not, as many do, running mad after the theater, the mimes, and dances, but philosophizing in the highest sense."[2]

2. But did the *apostles* teach that the fourth commandment was abrogated? They taught the binding nature of the whole moral law, without excepting that of a sacred day of rest. Paul, in one instance, names half the decalogue, and adds: "If there be any other commandment, it is summed up in this word, namely, Thou shalt love thy neighbor as thyself. . . . Love is the fufilling of the law" (Rom. xiii. 10). He says expressly: "The law is holy, and the commandment holy and righteous and good" (Rom. vii. 12);

---
[1] Prof. Samuel Adler, Johnson's Encyclopaedia, "Talmud"; Rees' and Chambers' Encyclopaedias on "Talmud and Mischna."

[2] De Mose, iii. p. 167, quoted by Milman, Hist. Jews, Vol. i. p. 203, note.

"Do we then make of none effect the law through faith? God forbid; yea, we establish the law" (Rom iii. 31). The apostle never could have written thus, if one-tenth of the decalogue—more than that in language and thought—were repealed, annulled, as F. W. Robertson and others say.[1] Paul could not have meant that the sacred seventh of time was, like circumcision and sacrifice, no longer needed, nor that all days should be equally devoted to the secular and religious. He himself still observed the seventh, and had added to it another religious day. Near the time he wrote the few sentences (Rom. xiv. 5; Gal. iv. 10; Col. ii. 16, 17) which some think imply the abolition of the Sabbatic principle, "he reasoned in the synagogue every Sabbath, as his custom was" (Acts xviii. 4; xvii. 2; xvi. 13; xiii. 14, 44); and on each Lord's day where he tarried he met with the disciples for worship (Acts xx. 7); and he, or some other sacred writer, expressly enjoined on others to do likewise (Heb. x. 25). No evidence appears that he kept all days alike, or that he grew lax, and threw off the restraints of holy time. If the Saviour intended to repeal the real Sabbath, why do we not find him or his apostles instructing the disciples to disregard the fourth commandment? Why not find him or them engaged on that day in secular labor, or diverting themselves by fishing? Why no case of conflict between them and the Pharisees where the former set aside the sabbatic ordinances?

3. Do the following apostolic statements imply that the law is abolished? "Ye are not under law,

[1] Robertson's Sermons, Sydenham Palace and Sabbath (Second Series); Shad. and Sub. of Sab. (First Series.)

but under grace" (Rom. vi. 15); "If ye are led by the Spirit ye are not under the law" (Gal. v. 18); "That he might redeem them which were under the law" (Gal. iv. 5); "Ye also were made dead to the law" (Rom. vii. 4); "We have been discharged from the law" (Rom. vii. 6); "The letter killeth, but the Spirit giveth life" (2 Cor. iii. 6). If in Christ we are not condemned by the law, nor in danger from its penalty, nor bound to seek justification by our own righteousness, nor longer burdened by ceremonial observances of the old dispensation; still love constrains to obedience, the rule of the moral law is sweet to us, wherein we fail of obedience we obtain forgiveness, and, as Augustine says, "The law itself, by being fullfilled, becomes grace and truth";[1] and hence it is not abolished.

Objection: "The law written and engraven in stones, with all its glory, is done away."[2] *Reply:* Though the preceding sentence is from the pen of a respected and representative author, who believed it founded on Scripture, yet it is not Scripture. He refers to 2 Cor. iii. 7, 11. Why, and of what, does the apostle speak? Unquestionably, he had been charged with boasting (ver. 1) on account of some statements in his former epistle (1 Cor. v. 9; xiv. 18; xv. 10). Replying, he declares his joy at being a minister of the New Testament (ver. 6); and then, conceding much to the glory of the "ministration of death,"—of the letter of the law,—he exalts far above it the glory of the "ministration of the Spirit." The comparison is between the two ministrations, not, as some authors

[1] Manichæan Heresy, p. 321.
[2] Dr. Geo. B. Bacon, Sabbath Question, p. 133.

suppose, between the law and the Spirit. The former ministration was characterized by a law "written and engraven on stones" (ver. 7), and given through Moses in great glory (ver. 13); but that ministration and the dispensation lying back of it are passed away to give place to the ministration of the Spirit. This is not teaching that the law is abolished, but that it and its dispensation need no longer be relied upon as a way and means of salvation. Although the laws given by Jehovah to the Jews were not formally divided into kinds, they evidently had different offices. First, in general, they offered a way of righteousness and salvation for sinners. With such meaning the term "law" is often employed in the New Testament. As such it embraced the typical and ceremonial part; and more, the law of rectitude, the expression of God's will relative to right and wrong in his rational creatures. While the whole system of types, and the ceremonies pertaining thereto, was temporary, the laws, principles and rules pertaining to the moral state and conduct are permanent. The chief duties required in the decalogue are, in general, ever required. They must be, since God is ever holy, and moral right and wrong will never change their nature. A ministration and its glory passing away is one thing; the abolition of that which ministers in some particular form is quite another thing. The law and its dispensation, as a dependence for redemption is void; the law, so far as it is the divine expression concerning the moral state and conduct of men, is in force, and is imperishable. Certain writers tell us that the "law written and engraven in stone, with all its glory, is done away";[1] but all that the Scriptures tell us is that the glory of Moses' countenance "was to be done away," and that the glory of the "ministration of condemnation .... is done away." Meyer, Stanley, DeWette and Neander say that the two ministrations in this passage are compared, not the two religions of the two dispensations. De Wette (*in loc.*) suggests that the old dispensation lying back of the ministration shares in the removal; but that is not the law as a guide of life, but the dispensation as a reliance for life eternal. That is abolished, because a better takes its place. But there are no better principles and rules of duty to supersede the moral precepts of the decalogue; hence they are not abolished.

Objection second: The following three passages indicate the abolition of the entire Sabbath, with other Jewish festive days, at the close of the old dispensation: "One man esteemeth one day above another; another esteemeth every day alike. Let each man be fully assured in his own mind" (Rom. xiv. 5); "Ye observe days and months and seasons and years" (Gal. iv 10); "Let no man therefore, judge you . . . in respect of a feast day or new moon, or Sabbath day" (Col. ii. 16). *Reply:* The first two of these passages would hardly be thought to refer to the weekly Sabbath, were it not for the third. Does that refer to it? The word *Shabbath*—Sabbath=rest, and its derivative *Shabbathon*—a keeping of the Sabbath, a resting, a Sabbatism—are applied to five different days and the seventh year. The days are, the weekly Sabbath, the day of the atonement (Lev. xxiii. 32), the feast of trumpets (Lev. xxiii. 24), and the

[1] Bacon, Sabbath Question, p. 133.

first and eighth of the feast of tabernacles (Lev. xxiii. 39). One Seventh=Day Adventist author says there were "seven annual Sabbaths,"[1] besides the weekly one, as named in Lev. xxiii. His error is in reckoning the first and seventh days of unleavened bread and the day of pentecost as Sabbaths, which the sacred writer does not term such. Yet they were days of holy convocation, and this twenty=third chapter of Leviticus is a catalogue of such days.

With us the word "Sabbath" is a technical name, not always suggesting its literal meaning—a solemn rest. With the Jews, accustomed to hear the Scriptures in the Hebrew, the literal idea was more prominent; and *Shabbath* and *Shabbathon* alike brought to their minds the thought of rest. Yet the weekly Sabbath and that of the atonement had a designation peculiar to themselves. In the fourth commandment it is, "day of the Sabbath" and "Sabbath of the Lord." In Lev. xxiii. 3 it is, *Shabbath Shabbathon,—rest of resting, a sabbath of rest;* and the same phrase occures with reference to the day of atonement (Lev. xxiii. 32.) But in the case of the feasts of trumpets (Lev. xxiii. 24.), and in that of the feast of tabernacles (Lev. xxiii. 39) only the word *Shabbathon— a resting, a sabbatism*—is used. The Septuagint notes this distinction. Another difference is this: In respect to the weekly Sabbath and the day of atonement the manner of command is, "Ye shall do no work" (Lev. xxiii. 3, 28); but in the case of the feast of trumpets and of the feast of tabernacles it is, "Ye shall do no *servile* work" (Lev. xxiii. 25, 26). By the former phrase all kinds of labor were forbidden—

[1] W. J. Littlejohn, The Constitutional Amendment: p. 114.

toil with the hands and business, trade; by the latter, labor with the hands was forbidden, while mere business and trade were allowed. But on each of the whole five days a holy convocation was enjoined, and also on the first and seventh days of the feast of unleavened bread, and at the feast of pentecost or the harvest (Lev. xxiii. 21). On these last three days, also, servile work was forbidden, but not all work. It seems certain that amid all these days of rest and convocation the apostle, by the word "Sabbaths,"— Sabbath, R. V.—rests, at least embraced the weekly Sabbath. It came so much more frequently than the yearly Sabbath or Sabbatisms, and seventh year Sabbath, that it were unreasonable to suppose the apostle by the term "Sabbaths" excluded it, and included them, without the least intimation of the omission. He would be more likely to exclude the Sabbatisms than the full Sabbaths, which were the one weekly day, and the one yearly day, the atonement. The seventh day was the only one of all usually called the Sabbath; the others had other names. The reasons are much stronger for supposing the apostle meant, by the word "Sabbath," the weekly days, rather than the yearly ones. The feast days are never called "Sabbaths." The day of atonement was a *fast* day, not feast day.

This word "Sabbaths,"—C. 2.—in Col. ii. 16, some suppose to be singular in meaning,—therefore referring to the weekly Sabbath only,—though plural in form, in Greek owing to one peculiar ending of the singular, which finally assumed the termination of the plural without its meaning. Possibly adverse to that view is the fact that in a similar list of public occasions (Gal. iv. 10) the word "days" occurs in plural form, referring to sacred festivals, and perhaps including the Sabbath. In the list in Colossians there is a descending scale—yearly festivals, monthly ones, weekly ones. This scale is the more noticeable, because in Gal. iv. 10, pertaining to the same subject, there is an ascending scale from days to years—the same scale reversed.

Assuming, now, that the apostle, in Col. ii. 16, embraced the weekly day in the word "Sabbaths," or Sabbath, does it show that the fourth commandment is obsolete? The apostles had to contend with Jews and the Judaizing Christians. Though the latter accepted Christ, and kept the first day of the week, they tenaciously held that Christians should continue the observance of some Jewish institutions, especially the seventh day. This Judaism was a stumbling to the Gentile Christians, and the cause of much discussion. The apostle's direction was: "Let every man be fully persuaded in his own mind" (Rom. xiv. 5) in respect to the observance of these Jewish days. His practice was indicated by the fact that he circumcised Timothy (Acts xvi. 3) to facilitate his acceptance with the Jews, since it was the young disciple's privilege by being of Jewish descent on his mother's side; and refused to circumcise Titus (Gal. ii. 3-5), because he was a Gentile, and Christianity did not require it, and those who deemed it obligatory needed correction. The apostle was inspired to allow non=essentials to the Jewish, and to disallow their being made essentials to the Gentile, Christians. Among these non=essentials was the observance of the annual and monthly religious feasts, and probably of the seventh day. Paul was taught by inspiration that circumcision was no longer necessary, and probably that the seventh day was no longer obligatory. But while the former was purely ceremonial and national, the latter was not wholly ceremonial or national or judicial. So far as it was Jewish, positive, it was set aside; as moral, it remained. In the moral were rest, hallowed time, worship, probably a day for worship[1] and holy convocations (Lev. xxiii. 3). In the positive were the septenary division, the seventh-day obligation, memorial of deliverance from Egypt (Gen. xxxi. 16), and the Jewish civil, ceremonial, and judicial relations; the last involving penalties for violation of sabbatic law. One evidence that the decalogue is moral, and was designed for man, is, that penalties are not annexed, and may therefore vary; as may also some specific duties not named in the decalogue itself. Doubtless the apostle was ignorant of these analytical distinctions; enough that he observed them, even if blindly, and as an inspired man could say, Christians need not keep the seventh, but should keep the first day, and on it observe their most sacred religious services. But if Paul rejected the Sabbath in any sense, it was merely the specific Jewish day, without embracing the moral elements of the

[1] Holy convocation requires a particular time or day for the assembling; and, the evils of making only half of Sunday religious, and the remainder secular, as by the Continental method, seem to indicate that *natural* as well as revealed religion calls for a *whole*, and not a mere *half* stated day for holy rest and worship. And the tendencies of *true worship* in holy convocation are towards the sacred observance of the whole day.

real Sabbath: for he was contending with Jews and Judaizing Christians, who were busy with the superficial positive, not with the deep-laid moral and spiritual, which the apostle was especially observing in the Lord's day.

Objection third: Still, according to the apostle Paul, "We are delivered from the law, that being dead wherein we were held" (Rom. vii. 6); and therefore it is not binding upon us. For, as Archbishop Whately says, "There are very many passages relative to the Mosaic law occurring in the writings of the apostle Paul, whose most obvious and simple interpretation, at least, would seem to imply the entire abolition of that law by the establishment of the gospel."[1] *Reply:* Bengel, Alford, Lange, and Meyer affirm, and Whately admits, that the phrase "that being dead wherein we were held" should read, "we being dead to that law wherein we were held." The law is not dead, or abolished, but believers are dead to it. Meyer even says: "Paul is not discussing the abrogation of the law, but the fact that the Christian as such is no longer under it."[2] The apostle has just used the figure of the marriage relation. Believers are married to another, even Christ, and not to the law. In the law, with all its types, ceremonies, deeds, is not their hope; but it is in Christ Jesus. The extent of the apostle's meaning in saying, "We have been discharged from the law," (Rom. 7:6) "Ye are not under law" (Rom. vi. 14) is indicated by another of his statements: "For I testify again to every man that receiveth circumcision that he is a debtor to do the whole law" (Gal.

---

[1] Difficulties, etc., p. 142.   [2] Com., Rom. vii, 1.

v. 3). He must conform to all its ceremonial observances, and obey all its moral requirements. No other course is left him, if he insists on salvation by law. But believers, accepting grace, enjoy the Antitype,—types and ceremonies having passed away,—and delight in forgiveness for all violations of the moral law. Yet the law in its moral character and requirements, pointing out the way of duty, demanding holiness, and forbidding sin, is unabolished and unabolishable. As Dr. Bushnell says, "Plainly enough, the law of God can never be taken away from any world or creature; for with it, in close company, goes abroad all the conserving principle, moral and physical, in which God's kingdom stands."[1]

However, admit that it is all abolished. What then? Surely the apostles ought not to use it; we shall not find them using it. Alas for the theory! After Paul wrote his Epistle to the Romans, in which the foregoing passage occurs (Rom. vi. 14), he writes that to the Ephesians, in which he actually appeals to this abrogated law: "Children, obey your parents in the Lord; for this is right. Honor thy father and mother, which is the first commandment with promise; that it may be well with thee, and thou mayest live long on the earth" (Eph. vi. 1-3). He does not even stumble at using the Jewish promise of long life in Canaan; the *priciple* in it makes it serviceable, applicable. Nor does he hesitate to employ this commandment in addressing Gentile, as well as Jewish Christians. The fifth commandment and the fourth and all the others are for *man* not for Jews only. He does not tell us that the law is abolished,

[1] Forgiveness and Law, p. 119.

that he refers to this command as only a law of nature; he summons it as embracing the authority of Jehovah descended on Mount Sinai. More, in the same Epistle where we are told that "we have been discharged from the law" (Rom. vii. 6), we find the apostle subsequently bringing forward the law itself, as still a law and obligatory: "He that loveth his neighbor hath fulfilled the law"; hence he is delivered from its condemnation. "For This, thou shalt not commit adultery; Thou shalt not kill; Thou shalt not steal; Thou shalt not covet; and if there be any other commandment, it is briefly summed up in this word, namely, Thou shalt love thy neighbor as thyself" (Rom. xiii, 8, 9). He speaks of the second table. Is love abolished? Nay. Then all that which is condensed into love is not annulled. The apostle is consistent with himself, and must mean: If we love, we are delivered from the condemnation of the law, because now obedient, and forgiven for past disobedience; delivered from the ceremonies and deeds of the law as our hope, because salvation is offered on the easier condition of repentance and faith; not delivered from obligation to obey any of the law's moral precepts, yet privileged to obey them all by the one comprehensive principle of love. Nor is all this merely a Pauline peculiarity. The inspired James, at least twelve or fifteen years after the death of Christ, when the new dispensation had been more than fully inaugurated and established, appeals expressly to the decalogue as a rule of duty, in an address to believers, who are dead to the law as a means of hope and merit: "If ye have respect of persons, ye commit sin, and are convinced by the law as transgressors. For whosoever shall keep the whole law, and yet stumble in one point, he is become guilty of all. For he that said, Do not commit adultery, said also, Do not kill. Now, if thou dost not commit adultery, but killest, thou art become a transgressor of the law" (ii. 9-11). Definite commands are referred to, not as abolished, but as though in force as much as ever. What the sovereign God hath *said* is appealed to—what he said on the mount, amid thunderings and lightnings, and the noise of the trumpet, and the mountain smoking. It is in our dispensation, as it were in our time, that the apostles summon the law of Sinai to their aid in proclaiming the gospel; and it becomes uninspired men not to say any more that the law is abolished. If apostles of Jesus Christ may remind their hearers and readers of the commandments as still expressive of God's will, we need not recall our appeals to them, nor be troubled by the many assertions in our time that the decalogue and all the Old Testament laws are abrogated.

Moreover, twenty-seven years after Christ's death, and after the law was abolished by his death—as some say—the apostle Paul pronounces the law holy, and "the commandment holy and righteous and good" (Rom vii. 12), and points out the good services of the law in making him know his sins (vii. 7-11) and in making others know their sins (vii. 5). He refers to the ten commandments; for, by way of illustration, he names one of them—that of covetousness (vii. 7). Have we outgrown the good services of the law? Yet all this the apostle says just after declaring that believers "are not under the law" (vi. 14), "are discharged from the law" (vii. 6). Only one conclusion is rationally deducible: They who are risen with Christ are not under the law as their ground of salvation; yet are not delivered from the law as an instructor in the evils of sin and the fruits of righteousness. Further, if Christ abolished the law, how did he deliver from its curse? If abolished, it had no curse; that, too, was abolished.[1]

Objection fourth: Dr. Hopkins says: " Neither our divine Lord nor his apostles ever recognized the fourth commandment as containing a law for Christians."[2]

Reply: The fourth commandment stood by previous enactment. It did not need recognition in order to its continuance. The question is, did Christ or his apostles ever reject it? 1. The apostles, so far as we learn, did not reject it. Both James and Paul directly appeal to the commandments; not naming all of them at any time, not rejecting any, not intimating that the fourth or any other was annulled. Had it been annulled, a fact so striking would have received attention. Paul's indication that no one might impose upon Christians the obligation to observe the seventh day, after the first had become the Lord's day (Col. ii. 16), is no evidence that the commandment had become void. That command, analyzed, had the following parts: (1) A division or part

---

[1] After we had given the manuscript of this Article to the press, we found that the honored Rev. Amos A. Phelps, in a discussion held in the year 1840, made the clear distinction that the *law* is "done away as a means of justification," but is not done away " as a rule of duty;" and he is original in the manner in which he has applied that fundamental analysis to this subject.—See Phelps on the Perpetuity of the Sabbath, p. 11.

[2] Sabbath Question, p. 11.

of six days; (2) A division of one day immediately following the division of six; (3) An appointment for all secular work during the first division; (4) An appointment for rest and holy keeping of time during the second division; (5) A commemoration of God's creation of the world by the first division, and of his rest by the second division; (6) A reckoning of time that made the first division the first six days, and the second division the seventh day. The apostles never said aught to set aside any one of these first five parts. Their teaching and example simply affected the element of time, and gave an additional object of commemoration—that of Christ's resurrection. They did not revoke the commemoration of God's act of creation, nor of his rest; for still six days are devoted to labor, and one to rest. They put the original commemoration in the background by placing another before it. By changing the reckoning of time they did not make void the original commemoration; because, with such variation of time as the daily revolution of the earth gives, what is the seventh day to some is the first to others, and exact identity of observance would be impossible, and is not required. Though Paul taught that observance of the seventh day was optional (Col. ii. 16), he and the other apostles taught, by word and example, the duty and privilege of keeping the first day, and of laboring six days; and therefore in respect to its chief (the first four) elements, they "recognized the fourth commandment as containing a law for Christians," and did not teach or allow the doctrine that it is annulled. Even failure to enforce the fourth commandment would not be its abolition.

2. If they were Christians who followed Christ

during his earthly ministry, then he did repeatedly "recognize the fourth commandment as containing a law for Christians." Even his corrections of the abuses of the Sabbath were indirect recognitions of the validity of the fourth commandment. Not one word did he ever say against it.

A consideration of the decalogue has led us into the New Testament with the question: Has the decalogue or fourth commandment been abolished? Returning to the Old Testament, we should note the fact that the primal reasons given in both Genesis (ii. 1-3) and Exodus (xx. 11) for observing the Sabbath pertain to man, and not specifically to Jews, and that they agree well with Christ's declaration, that the Sabbath was made for man, and not man for the Sabbath (Mark ii. 27). The reasons, God rested, and he blessed and hallowed the Sabbath, are too broad and benevolent to be confined to one nation.

Objection: "The Sabbath is described as a sign between God and the people of Israel"; therefore, it seems, "the observance of it was peculiar to that people, and designed to be so"[1] (Ex. xxxi. 16, 17; Ezek. xx. 12). "That rest . . . being only commemorative of their deliverance from Egyptian servitude, was not moral nor perpetual."[2] *Reply:* Previous to the above from Dr. Paley and Bishop Jeremy Taylor, Dr. Heylin had said the same;[3] and they all seem to have written without due consideration. The Sabbath may have been, and was, an especial sign of one thing to the Jews, and a sign of other things for all

---
[1] Dr. Paley, Moral and Political Philosophy, chap. vii.
[2] Jeremy Taylor, Law and Conscience, sec. 58.
[3] History of the Sabbath. Part i. chap. iv. sec. 6.

men. The former does not exclude the latter. The sign described in Ex. xxxi. 16, 17 is consonant with that in Ex. xx. 11; and the reasons in the latter instance show that it was for man, and not Jews only.

The Jewish nation existed as such long before the recognition of the Sabbath at the giving of manna in the wilderness. Who can say that the Sabbath was not a weekly sign long before, against all nations that serve not the true God? No doubt the Egyptians robbed the Jews much of this badge of their consecration to Jehovah. Israel desired to go three days' journey into the wilderness to "hold a feast unto the Lord" (Ex. x. 9). May not the feast have embraced a Sabbath, which was one of "the set feasts of the Lord" (Lev. xxiii. 2, 3), and afterwards, at least, was a high feast day? The passover was an emphatic sign of Jewish nationality, and a marked memorial of Israel's departure from Egypt (Ex. xii. 11, 27). But the law of the passover, being Jewish and temporary, was not put into the decalogue; while the law of the Sabbath was. The former was a memorial of deliverance from Egyptian bondage; the latter of the creation. The reason of the former was limited; that of the latter was world-wide. The Sabbatic institution, in its whole range, seems to be commemorative of three events: First, of God's rest, and the close of creation; secondly, of God's special choice and appointment of the Jews; thirdly, of Christ's resurrection, and the completion of redemption. The Sabbath of the Jews in the wilderness, and to the end of the old dispensation, may not have been the exact successor of the sacred day instituted in the beginning, and observed by the patriarchs; though the latter, as

4

well as the former, may have been the seventh by the current reckoning in its period. The weeks and days may have been disarranged during the Egyptian bondage, and a correction or redating may have been commenced at the giving of manna or at the institution of the passover, when a holy convocation was appointed.

Objection Second: Archbishop Whatley says: "The very law itself indicates, on the face of it, that the whole of its precepts were intended for the Israelites exclusively."[1] Dr. Thomas Arnold speaks doubtfully about it;[2] Dr. R. W. Dale implies that "the fourth commandment was given to the Jews" only;[3] Dr. Geo. B. Bacon says the Sabbath commandment was "addressed not to the Christian church, but to the Jewish church;"[4] Bishop Robert Sanderson (born A. D. 1587) said "that no part of the law delivered by Moses to the Jews doth bind Christians under the gospel by virtue of that delivery—no, not the ten commandments themselves, but least of all the fourth, which all confess to be, at least in some part, ceremonial";[5] and Jeremy Taylor speaks of "laws which were to separate the Jews from the Gentiles."[6]

Reply: It was not the design of the Jewish laws, or of the Sabbath in particular, to separate the Gentiles from the Jews, if the former would forsake their idolatry, and embrace the true religion. The Sabbath being made for *man*, as most of these writers admit, it inevitably follows that the fourth commandment,

---
[1] Difficulties in the Writings of St. Paul, p. 147.
[2] Sermons, Vol. iii. No. 22, pp. 255-258.
[3] Ten Commandments, p. 93.
[4] Sabbath Question, p. 97.
[5] Dr. Hessey on Sunday, p. 327.
[6] Christian Law and Conscience, sec. 44.

which gave or confirmed the Sabbath, had in its moral part a binding force upon man. We prefer what Tertullian says: "For why should God, the Founder of the Universe, the Governor of the whole world, the Fashioner of humanity, the Sower of universal nations, be believed to have given a law through Moses to one people, and not be said to have assigned it to all nations? For, unless he had given it to all, by no means would he have habitually permitted even proselytes out of the nations to have access to it. But—as is congruous with the goodness of God and with his equity as the Fashioner of mankind—he gave to all nations the self-same law."[1] Whether the Sabbath be for us or not, being made for man, at the time it was made it was not exclusively for Jews. Though the Decalogue was *addressed* to the Israelites, that does not prove Whately's claim that it was "*intended* for the Israelites exclusively." The teaching of Christ and his apostles especially indicates that the Jews were as much bound to give the moral law to the world as Moses was to Israel from the mount. It has ever been God's way to speak unto one, or a few, that they might communicate to the many. Bishop Sanderson may say that "no part of the law delivered by Moses to the Jews doth bind Christians under the gospel by virtue of that delivery"; but the inspired Paul and James reiterate that law as though binding alike on Jews and Gentiles as far as known to them, as though obtaining its divine force not from their lips, but from the voice of Jehovah, sounding in sublime peals from Sinai across the centuries.

[1] Ans. to the Jews, Ant. Nic. Lib., Vol. xviii. p. 203.

The Sabbath, besides having its place in the decalogue, is throughout the old dispensation ranked with things moral, permanent, and highly important. It is placed above feasts, ceremonies, and sacrifices. Sacrifices and other solemnities are commanded to be observed upon it; but while it is admitted to the decalogue, they are not. In all parts of the Pentateuch it is treated as though worthy of its place in the first table of the moral law. Its essential and great importance is indicated by the fact that a wilful violation of it by the Jews was made punishable with death (Ex. xxxi. 14). Its observance is ranked as an essential aid to the highest virtues, and as equally binding. Is Israel pointed to the first commandment as of especial significance? the fourth is placed by its side: "Six days thou shalt do thy work, and on the seventh day thou shalt rest; . . . And in all things that I have said unto you take ye heed; and make no mention of the name of other gods, neither let it be heard out of thy mouth" (Ex. xxiii. 12, 13). In another passage the first, second, and fifth commandments are ranged with the fourth," and the observance of them all is made requisite to holiness! "Ye shall be holy; for I the Lord your God am holy. Ye shall fear every one his father and his mother, and keep my Sabbaths; I am the Lord your God. Turn ye not unto idols, nor make to yourselves molten gods: I am the Lord your God" (Lev. xix. 1–3). One passage declares that the Sabbath is a sign, and implies that it is a direct means for the sanctification of the people: "Verily, ye shall keep my Sabbath; for it is a sign between me and you throughout your generations; that ye may know that I am the Lord which doth sanctify you. Ye shall keep the Sabbath therefore; for it is holy unto you" (Ex. xxxi. 13, 14). These Scripture facts unmistakably indicate that the Sabbath has in it very essential moral elements. It is not simply typical of a future rest; it is an absolute means to the rest and peace of holiness, here and hereafter.

Farther on in Jewish history the true prophets are ever endeavoring to maintain the strict observance of the Sabbath in Israel. False and formal observances, ceremonies without the heart, the Lord through his prophets contemns (Isa. i. 11-14). But the highest divine favor is upon him that truly keeps the Sabbath. Its observance is ranked with keeping judgment and doing justice and keeping from evil: "Keep ye judgment, and do righteousness . . . Blessed is the man that doeth this, and the son of man that holdeth fast by it; that keepeth the Sabbath from polluting it, and keepeth his hand from doing any evil" (Isa. lvi. 1, 2). And all strangers that observe the Sabbath have equal blessings with Israel: "For thus saith the Lord of the eunuchs that keep my Sabbaths, and choose the things that please me, and hold fast by my covenant; unto them will I give in mine house and within my walls a memorial and a name better than of sons and of daughters; I will give them an everlasting name that shall not be cut off. Also, the strangers that join themselves to the Lord, to minister unto him, and to love the name of the Lord, to be his servants, every one that keepeth the Sabbath from profaning it, and holdeth fast by my covenant; even them will I bring to my holy mountain, and make them joyful in my house of prayer" (Isa. lvi. 4-7). Keeping the Sabbath is ranked with making and keeping a covenant with God, and with loving the name of the Lord. Sabbath-keeping, when fully right, involves moral character, embraces the intent of the heart, and in itself must have moral elements. As Bishop Daniel Wilson says, the sanctification of the Sabbath is described as a main proof of essential piety.[1] It involved principles and services demanded by our relations to God, and taught us even in the nature of things.

7. A *moral law* pertains to the duties of rational beings, and has its reasons in the nature and relations of things. A *positive law* pertains also to the conduct of rational beings; but has not its reasons in the nature and relations of things, but in the will of a governmental authority. Moral and positive laws are often combined. There is a moral law against murder; the state makes it also a positive law. The decalogue is composed of laws having each a moral nature; but in respect to their enactment merely for the Jewish nation they were positive laws. The Jewish civil and ceremonial laws were positive, because enacted for that nation, and in part for that age of the world. Yet they had some moral elements. All moral laws and elements are binding, wherever applicable; but positive laws, so far as they are positive, are binding only on those for whom they were enacted. "Moral duties," says Bishop Butler, "arise out of the nature of the case itself, prior to external command. Positive duties do not arise out of the nature of the case, but from external command; nor

[1] Divine Authority and Perpetual Obligation of the Lord's Day, p. 75.

would they be duties at all, were it not for such command, received from him whose creatures and subjects we are."[1] The decalogue—given when God met the great Hebrew host, and spake to them from Mount Sinai, written twice by his finger on tables of stone, preserved in the ark of the covenant—received this amazing enactment as positive law to the Jews, because it was, in general, supreme moral law to mankind. "Moral precepts are precepts," says Butler, "the reasons for which we see." The reasons for labor, for rest, for keeping holy time, for worship, we can see; and thus far the fourth commandment is *moral* in its nature. The reasons for the proportions of time devoted to labor and to rest, and for the number of the day that shall be sacred, we cannot see until expressly told; and in these respects this command is of the nature of *positive* law. The decalogue as a whole is moral; as a merely national law for the Jews, positive, like their civil and ceremonial law. The penalties of the decalogue, not being in the commands themselves, but in positive enactments for the Jews, were binding only on them, and in the Jewish dispensation, except as they involved moral principles. Some duties pertaining to the several commands, not being stated in them, but growing out of positive laws, were binding only upon that people, except as they had a moral, and therefore permanent nature.

All of the ten commandments, with penalties, were undoubtedly more or less in force before their engrossment at Sinai. The offerings to God by Abel, Noah, and others, implied a knowledge of the duty

[1] Complete Works, p. 176.

to love and serve him. Idolatry and the use of images were known to be evil; for Jacob required his household and all with him to put away the "strange gods" (Gen. xxxv. 2). The early frequent administration of oaths doubtless implies a knowledge of the third commandment. The honor due to parents is indicated by the conduct of Noah's sons, and their father's blessing and the curse pronounced; and parental authority was honored in the fact that Abraham was blessed for commanding his children after him (Gen. xviii. 19). Cain was cursed for murder, and the world was destroyed by flood because of corruption and violence (Gen. vi. 11). Shechem suffered judgment for breaking what was afterwards the seventh commandment (Gen. xxxiv. 1-31). Four kings were smitten by Abram and his servants for breaking the eighth of the decalogue (Gen. xiv. 1-24); and Joseph's brethren protested against the charge of theft (Gen. xliv. 8). Abimelech remonstrated with Abraham for falsely testifying that his wife was his sister (Gen. xx.); and covetousness was a violation of law, and, especially with kings, a common sin. Enoch was translated, and Noah preserved from destruction, because they walked with God (Gen. v. 24; vi. 9); while Sodom and Gomorrah were destroyed by fire, because the men were sinners before the Lord exceedingly (xiii. 13). Previous to the giving of the law at Sinai nine commandments of the decalogue had been given, and had been broken times without number; the fourth commandment was probably no exception. Even Archbishop Whately, in arguing that the whole Mosaic code, including the decalogue, had been abrogated,[1] claims "that some

[1] Difficulties of the writings of St. Paul, pp. 148, 150, 152.

Sabbatical institution, in memory of the creation, existed in the patriarchal times, . . . that some kind of observance of the seventh day existed prior to the Mosaic law."[1] He also claims that, "though the Mosaic law does not bind us, our moral obligations exist quite independent of that law,"[2] and that we find "the most ample evidence of the observance of the Lord's day as a Christian festival by the apostles and their immediate converts, whose example has been followed by all Christian churches down to this day."[3] The decalogue, then, is abolished only so far as it was a system of positive laws for the Jews. Its moral character, in which are its more essential elements, remains, and is obligatory on us. Even the positive nature of the ante=Mosaic Sabbath—as its septenary character—continues, because unaffected by the abolition or fulfilment of Judaism. All Jewish positive laws were based on moral principles; as, the command to offer the first=fruits, on the principle of thankful homage due the great Giver; and the requirement of sin=offerings, on the principle that there can be no forgiveness of sin without the shedding of blood—suffering. The positive laws may be temporary, while the principles are eternal.

Closing, now, this part of the discussion, we claim that a fair and full investigation shows that there was an ante=Mosaic sacred day, that the disbelievers in such a day fail to give a satisfactory account of the early septenary division of time, and modern researches in cuneiform inscriptions seem positively to confirm the other evidence of such a division, and

[1] Ibid., p. 161.   [2] Ibid., p. 161.   [3] Ibid., p. 163.

of a genuine Sabbath; that none have shown that the decalogue, or even the fourth commandment, is abrogated, or that either was given solely for the Jews; that the whole decalogue stands on a plane superior to that of the Jewish civil and ceremonial law; that the apostle Paul in teaching that the observance of the seventh day in the new dispensation was optional, as was that of other sacred days and seasons of the old dispensation, did nothing to undermine the moral elements of the fourth commandment; and that all moral elements are permanent and universal in their application. Thus we come out of the old dispensation with the moral, which are the chief, elements of the original Sabbath undiminished, untarnished, enforced upon us by both reason and Scripture, and, dissolved from their former positive ordinal element of time-reckoning, likely to assume some new relation in the new dispensation.

CHAPTER V.

THE CHANGE OF OBSERVANCE FROM THE SEVENTH TO THE LORD'S DAY.

Having considered the Sabbath of the old dispensation, it is intended now to consider whether there is divine authority for a change of the weekly sacred day in the new dispensation, and if there is, in what that authority consists.

1. The Lord's day has what is known in affairs of property as the right of possession, which should hold unless disproved. The Christian public generally, through many centuries have kept the first day sacred; and they should continue as they have been born and bred, unless they find reason for change. We observe the Fourth of July as that of the declaration of independence, not so much because we have individually examined history to see whether that is the true day, as because the example of our fathers has naturally led us to suppose it is the right one. For like reasons we observe the first day of the week as the Sabbath. But if thorough research should prove that the third of July and the seventh day of the week are the ones to be observed, we ought to change.

2. The change of institutions in the change from the old dispensation to the new was not sudden and

violent, but gradual and rational; the new institutions commencing, indeed, immediately, but the old ones disappearing gradually. The old institutions were not sinful, though the new had commenced, else they should have been at once abandoned. Hence time was taken for the people to think, and to change, not through force, but through principles. Baptism took the place, in a sense, pertaining to covenant, of circumcision. Baptism was commenced immediately; but circumcision was continued more or less by some of the Christians through many years. It was twenty years after the death of Christ—after the beginning of the new dispensation—that Paul circumcised Timothy. The Lord's supper took the place of the passover, and, instituted just as Christ was about to give his life for the world, it was intended to commemorate that act to the end of time. Yet the Christians did not immediately abandon the passover, but with some subsequent modifications, kept it several centuries. Christ's sacrifice took the place of the many temple sacrifices. But the Christians a long time continued to attend the temple services held in connection with the sacrifices, even until the temple was destroyed, and there was no more place for sacrifice. Immediately after the outpouring of the Holy Spirit at pentecost the believers were continually in the temple praising God (Acts ii. 46, 47). When Peter healed a lame man, as he and John were going to the temple at the hour of prayer, it was the evening hour for sacrifice. Twenty-seven years after the death of Christ we find Paul purifying himself, with four others that had a vow (Acts xxi. 26), and that ceremony involved offering sacrifice in the temple (Num.

vi. 3-18). While doing this, then, as a matter of prudence with the Jews, he adopted principles and practices that contributed to the final abandonment of all sacrifices. We must conclude that while the institutions of the new dispensation were commenced at its beginning, those of the old were not immediately forsaken. And by analogy, if we find that the apostles and primitive saints kept the first day, we shall also find that they did not at once give up all observance of the seventh day.

3 Our authority for the change from the institutions of the old dispensation to those of the new does not come so much by the explicit commands of the apostles as by their examples. We have Christ's distinct command to be baptized, but neither his nor his apostles' command to discontinue circumcision. Yet the apostles taught that circumcision was not necessary to salvation, and under that principle it ceased. We have no command from either Christ or apostles to cease the observance of the passover. Christ gave command to his apostles to observe the Lord's supper; but he did not give that command to all believers nor did his apostles. We infer the duty and privilege of all Christians to observe it from the example of the apostles in administering it to all Christians of their time, which indicates their understanding of Christ's original command to observe it. In such things apostolic example is equal to command. We have no inspired command to cease offering sacrifices; but from principles set forth in the Epistle to the Hebrews, and from the example of the apostles, and of the Christians under their instructions, in finally omitting sacrifices altogether, we conclude that it

would be wrong in us now to offer sacrifices as under the old dispensation. By parity of reasoning, if the first day takes the place of the seventh, we shall not find a command to cease observing the seventh, and shall find inspired *example* in keeping the first day, rather than distinct *command* to keep it. Whatever the apostles of Christ taught by example, while under inspiration, we are bound to observe. If they and the Christians with them carefully and steadily kept sacred the first day of the week, then, of course, the apostles gave instruction to those around them so to do; and that example and instruction are authoritative. We cannot think it right to go contrary to the universal apostolic instruction and example. From their example we get the light of duty.

4. A change of time for the sacred day from the seventh to the first day of the week is presumptively possible and probable. (1) So far as the original Sabbath pertained to the seventh day of the week, it admitted the possibility of a change. If changed, it would still read, "Remember the Sabbath day to keep it holy." So far as the day was *positive*, it was mutable. (2) Nothing in its nature forbade a change Its time was not different in kind from that of other days. It could as well be a blessing to man on the first as on the seventh day if the Lord changed it. (3) Exact identity in observance of time is, and ever has been, a practical impossibility never required. The world turns around; men do not keep the same time that we do either in Europe or California.* God

---

* When the late Czar of Russia died we heard immediately of it here in the morning of the day on which it occurred in the afternoon.

could therefore change the time without a violation of his own law in the constitution of the day. Traveling westward the days lengthen, and continuing around the globe in that direction, we should lose one day, and of necessity must make a change in order to be in accord with other Sabbath worshipers. Going north of the Arctic circle we should have but one day and one night in the year, if measured by the visibility of the sun, and could not have a Sabbath in unison with those nearer the equator. Two parties encircling the earth by going in different directions, east and west, will be two days apart when they meet at the point whence they started. An English ship touched at Pitcairn's Island in the Pacific on a Saturday, and found the islanders keeping Sunday. The explanation was in the fact that they had gone thither from the same home-land by sailing in opposite directions. Though differing one day in time, each party was in God's sight acceptably keeping the Lord's day, if either was; yet, continuing together, an adjustment so as to keep the same time would be important and proper. (4) The essential chief point in the fourth commandment is not keeping a particular seventh day, but devoting six days to the general purposes of labor, and one—a seventh—to holy rest;[1] and the seventh day might be termed the first, or the first the seventh. (5) The objects of rest could as well be secured on another day than the seventh, if God so direct. One of those objects is worship, which is not dependent on a particular time, though it should be conformed to the divine plan. Dr. Dale objects: "The law required rest; it did not

[1] Dr. Schaff, Apostolical Church, p. 556.

require worship."[1] And Professor Moses Stuart says: "There was no provision for social worship among the Hebrews on the Sabbath."[2] The truth is, a "holy convocation" for public worship was expressly appointed for the Sabbath before the Israelites broke up their encampment at Sinai (Lev. xxiii. 3).[3] Nor were they ignorant of holy convocations previous to that time. We find in Ex. xii. 16 that "an holy convocation" was appointed for both the first and the seventh days of the passover feast when it was instituted, before the Jews left Egypt. In their minds, doubtless, keeping the Sabbath "holy" implied a "holy convocation." (6) The command does not absolutely preclude a change of day; since it does not read, "Remember the seventh day," but "the Sabbath day, to keep it holy." Though on the seventh day then, it need not be always. The seventh was subsidiary to the Sabbath, and might, by divine appointment, give place to another day. (7) The seventh day was chosen to commemorate a particular event—the creation. A change might be made, to commemorate a greater event, on another day. (8) An event greater, in some aspects, has occurred—the resurrection of Jesus Christ—the climax of his redemptive work. "If Christ hath not been raised then is our preaching vain, your faith also is vain" (1 Cor. xv. 14). "I create new heavens and a new earth" (Isa. lxv. 17). The new creation is the beginning of the new dispensation. The original Sabbath commemorated the completion of the first creation; the Lord's day commemorates that of the second creation. Here are

---

[1] Ten Commandments, p. 99.
[2] Old Test. Canon, pp. 66, 67.
[3] See *in loc.* Kalisch, Lange, and Murphy.

two great events, and two special days commemorating them. But the events and the origin of the days are in different eras and dispensations; yet both days pertain to weekly time. As the latter dispensation takes the place of the former, it might be expected that the commemorative day of the latter would take the place of that of the former. (9) Yet the change of time, while specially commemorating the new event,—the Redeemer's resurrection,—would not wholly discard the commemoration of the original event—the creation. For still there would be the six days' labor in memory of God's creative work, and the one day of rest in memory of his rest. (10) The original Sabbath having been given in part to develop and sanctify man's religious nature, and the Lord's day being better fitted now in the new dispensation to accomplish the same purpose, it might be expected that it would be put in the place of the original day. (11) The fact that Christ, as Lord of the Sabbath, absolved himself and followers from Jewish Sabbatic perversions, and from slavery to the letter of Sabbatic law, without abolishing the Sabbath, suggests the probability that he will change the time of the sacred day if sufficient reasons for it should arise. (12) The fact that through several centuries previous to the coming of Christ many Jews perverted the Sabbath, and in its name bound upon themselves and others many burdens grievious to be borne, suggests that the Lord of the Sabbath *may* change the time of the sacred day to relieve it from those multiform abuses, and to give his new church a new and free day for its most precious religious festivals. the commemoration of Christ's death, by the Lord's supper, and that of his resurrection, the completion of his redemption, by the new day itself.

CHAPTER VI.

"THE FIRST DAY" BECOMES THE SACRED WEEKLY DAY AMONG THE EARLY CHRISTIANS.

In the chapter next preceding on the Sabbath we have seen that there was a possibility, and even probability, of a change of observance from the seventh to some other day of the week. We now resume and proceed with the discussion.

1. The Lord's day in the new dispensation was the chief of all days with the apostles and early Christians, and was their special day for rest and worship.

(1). The Lord's day during the Apostolic age. (*a*) Christ, in the first instance, gave great significance and emphasis to his resurrection day, by appearing five different times to his disciples during its hours. —to Mary Magdalene (John xx. 14-17), to the other women (Matt. xxviii. 9, 10), to the two disciples on the road to Emmaus (Luke xxiv. 13-31; Mark xvi. 12), to the apostle Peter separately (1 Cor. xv. 5), and to ten of the apostles collected together (Mark xvi. 14; Luke xxiv. 36-49; John xx. 19-23). In respect to power, he might just as well have risen on the seventh day. Why did he not do it, and give it the more honor? But simply appearing so many times on the day that he rose might not in itself have made it a sacred festival. either weekly, monthly, or annual

Yet *much* more notice of it in its weekly round, either by himself or his apostles, would be nearly certain to make it a noted day, and sacred to the Christians.

Objection: These admitted facts of Christ's appearance on the day that he rose do not prove a change of sacred time. *Reply:* Seventh-day authors are profuse in their representations that First-day keepers adduce Christ's several manifestations of himself on his resurrection day as proof that that day in its weekly recurrence should be kept holy, and the seventh day be spent as secular. Thus they mislead tens of thousands of their readers and adherents.[1] First-day observers claim this: that the occurrences on the day in the morning of which Christ rose, constitute the *beginning* of a series of events, which soon led to the universal keeping by Christians of the first day of the week as sacred; and that that early observance and its causes have made the first day chief and holy in nearly the whole militant church in all subsequent ages.

(*b*) But, Christ, while not appearing again, so far as we learn, during the next six days after that of his resurrection, not even on the Sabbath embraced in that number, did appear on the next *first* day, at least to the eleven, and in commemoration, it would seem, of his resurrection, as well as mercifully to convince the doubting Thomas (John xx. 24-29). For some reasons, a portion of which apparently do not appear, the disciples, and especially the sacred writers, at once came to regard the first day of the week as

---

[1] Andrews, Hist. Sab., p. 143; also, Examination of Seven Reasons for Sunday-keeping, pp. 8, 9.

sacred and honored. There it stands, with them a marked and remarkable day.

Objection First: Christ and his disciples did not keep the day on which he rose as sacred and holy; he and two disciples traveled to Emmaus on that day and returned; the women went to embalm his body, which they would not have done on the [1] Sabbath. *Reply:* It is not claimed that there was a constitutional change in the time of the first day, nor admitted that the *Sabbath's* hours were different in *nature* from the time of other days, nor was it intended that the first day should be observed before its purport was understood; neither does any divine law prescribe how far it is proper to walk or ride on the Sabbath or the Lord's day.

Objection Second: The "eight days"[2] after the resurrection of Christ, when he appeared unto the eleven, were a day more than a week, and consequently the time was on our Monday.[3] *Reply:* By the Hebrew reckoning it *was* at the *beginning* of the eighth day from Christ's resurrection. Just seven days from that event was the *first day morning*, and the following evening after sunset was the beginning of the Jewish eighth day—the close of the Roman seventh day—what we call Sunday evening. There was just a week between the two appearances of Christ to his apostles, or perhaps a few hours more than a week. The Jews were accustomed to speak of "eight days" when the eighth had been only commenced, not completed. The circumcision of Christ occurred "when eight days were accomplished"

---

[1] W. H. Littlejohn, Constitutional Amendment, pp. 34-36.
[2] John xx. 26.   [3] Andrews, Hist. Sab., pp. 147, 148.

(Luke ii. 21), which was when the eighth day had been reached, not ended.[1] For, the law was, that "in the eighth day" of the child's life the rite of circumcision should be observed (Lev. xii. 3); and in the case of John the Baptist, "on the eighth day they came to circumcise the child" (Luke i. 59). Therefore, since the phrase "when eight days were accomplished" means only after the eighth day was begun, the phrase, "after eight days" (John xx. 26) does not necessarily mean any more. And since "the same day" (John xx. 19) reckoned from was the day, and not the later evening of the day, on which Christ rose, it was near the beginning of the eighth day from his resurrection when he appeared the second time to his assembled apostles, Thomas being with them. And therefore the time was the evening of Sunday, and *not* of Monday, as the seventh=day Sabbatarians claim.

Further, the terms "first day" and "eighth day" were interchangeable by common usage. They evidently meant the same, and the writings of the early Fathers show such use. Justin says, "The first day after the Sabbath, remaining the first of all the days, is called, however, the eighth."[2] It was, therefore, natural to speak of the second "first," or "eighth," day as "eight days" after the first, the two extreme days being counted. Such method of reckoning was common in that age, as also that of excluding the two extremes. In Luke ix. 28 is a case of the inclusive method, and in Matt. xvii. 1 and Mark ix. 2 a case of the exclusive, both cases pertaining to the

---

[1] See Townsend's Notes on Luke ii. 21.
[2] Dialogue with Trypho, chap. xli.; Aut. Nic. Lib., Vol. ii. p. 139.

same event—the transfiguration of Christ. Both modes of computing were occasionally employed by the same writer. In Tacitus' History, chapter xxix., Piso speaks of himself as Caesar—within the extremes of—six days; and in chapter xlviii. Piso is described as Caesar during four days.[1]

Still further, though the Jews in Christ's time in some respects used the Hebrew chronology, they evidently often reckoned days by the number of different times the sun appeared. At evening, after sunset, and during the night, they would speak of the next morning as the "morrow," just as we do, though by the Hebrew reckoning it was the same day. Paul preached at Troas in the night time, "ready to depart on the morrow" (Acts xx. 7), at the next sun, the next day; yet, by Hebrew chronology it was really *not* the "morrow," but the same day. One man said to another, "The day groweth to an end, lodge here . . . and to-morrow get you early on your way" (Judges xix. 9). He did not mean after sunset, but after the next sun came. If it were already after sunset, he would have said the same. "Her judges are evening wolves; they gnaw not the bones till the morrow" (Zeph. iii. 3). Wolves prowl in darkness; yet the next sun was called the "morrow," though strictly, by Hebrew reckoning, the morrow was not till after the next sun had set.[2] When Paul "continued his speech until midnight," it was reckoned as the same day. He left Troas "at break of day" the next morning, and that was counted as "on the mor-

---

[1] See Webster and Wilkinson's Com. on Luke ix. 28.
[2] See also, Ex. xxxii. 5, 6; Lev. vii. 15, 16; Josh. vii. 13. 14; 2 Chron. xx. 16. 17, 20; James iv. 13, 14.

row" (Acts xx. 7, 11). The night and the next morning were counted as parts of two different days. So, when Jesus was with his apostles during the evening next following his resurrection, it was a part of one day; and the next morning was a part of another day. Reckoning thus is strictly Biblical, and counting thus, the next Sunday, even in the morning, was "eight days" after.

(c) Some suppose that Christ's *ascension* was on the first day of the week, making their inference from a passage in the epistle of Barnabas, as follows: "We celebrate the eighth with joyfulness, on which Jesus rose from the dead, and when he had manifested himself he ascended into the heavens."[1] Hefele, also Gebhardt, Harnack, and Zahn, editors of the latest edition of the Apostolic Fathers,[2] reading the passage with only a comma, instead of a period, after the word "dead," suppose it teaches that Christ both rose and ascended on the eighth day. This view does not seem to be sufficiently well founded.

(d) Whatever admissible rendering be given to Acts ii. 1, it is apparent that the descent of the Holy Spirit was on the day of Pentecost, and the general learned opinion now is, and the ancient Christian tradition was, that the day of pentecost occurred on the first day of the week, our Sunday. The reckoning which results in that conclusion is this: The preparation for Christ's last paschal supper (Matt. xxvi. 17; Mark xiv. 12; Luke xxii. 8) was made near

---

[1] Ant. Nic. Lib.; Vol. i. p. 128; see also, "The Apostolic Fathers," translated by Rev. G. A. Jackson, and edited by Prof. G. P. Fisher, p. 97.

[2] Patrum Apostolicorum opera, Vol. i. p. 57.

the close of Thursday, the fifth day of the week, the fourteenth of the month Nisan, at which time the passover lamb among all the Jews at Jerusalem was slain. Jesus ate the passover meal at the usual time, the beginning of the sixth day, their Friday, our Thursday evening; and at that time the feast of unleavened bread commenced. He was crucified on the sixth day, after the night succeeding Thursday. The wave offering was made on the seventh day, Saturday, the Jewish Sabbath, which was the second day of the feast, and the sixteenth of Nisan; and fifty days from that (Lev. xxiii. 15, 16) was the pentecost, on the first day of the week. According to this, the evidence is that the Redeemer again put special honor upon the day of his resurrection, by fulfilling his promise in the descent of the Holy Ghost on the seventh first day after that on which he rose from the dead,—seeming thus to require the continued observance of the sacred week of seven days, and to appoint the first day, instead of the seventh, as the honored and especially religious one henceforth. That was the complete opening of the new dispensation, and the first day was then made the "birthday of the Christian Church."[1] Such significance already given the first day by divine acts, together with the effusion of the Holy Spirit at Pentecost, suggests the probability, that further and definite instruction was given by the Savior in person before his ascension, or by his Spirit afterwards, concerning the continued observance of that day, which instruction was well

---

[1] Schaff, Church History, Vol. i. p. 61; also, Dr. Smith's Old Test. Hist., p. 265.

understood by the apostles, and communicated by them to the Christians of their time, though not recorded for our reading.

Objection: "It is generally supposed that this pentecost . . . fell on the Jewish Sabbath, our Saturday."[1] *Reply:* 1. We think it now generally supposed that this pentecost fell on our Sunday. But we seek truth, not merely the opinion of the majority. 2. The date of this pentecost depends on certain dates connected with the Jewish passover, and on the date of Christ's last paschal supper, and of his death. It is, therefore, involved in difficulties. Dr. Schaff speaks of it as an "intricate question,"[2] and Alford as "extremely difficult."[3] Some authors, however, have added to the inherent difficulties by their own errors. Professor Hackett and Dr. William Smith, for example, agree in fixing upon Friday, the fifteenth of Nisan, as the first day of the feast of unleavened bread, and as that of Christ's death, and upon Saturday, the Jewish Sabbath, as the time fifty days after which (Lev. xxiii. 15, 16) the day of Pentecost occurred.[4] And yet Professor Hackett infers that pentecost that year "fell on the Jewish Sabbath, our Saturday," and Dr. Smith that it "fell on Sunday." The cause of this discrepancy must be this: The former reckons Saturday, the second day of the feast, as the first of the fifty days, and the latter reckons the day following as the first of the fifty. Who reckons

---

[1] Hackett, Com. on Acts ii. 1.
[2] Lange's Com. Matt. p. 454, note.
[3] Com., Matt. xxvi. 17–19.
[4] New Test. Hist., pp. 314, 380.

scripturally? Probably Dr. Smith, as we shall hereafter attempt to show.[1]

But if Professor Hackett and others err in their manner of counting, Dr. Lange seems to err in the counting itself. He assumes correctly, we suppose, that the second day of the passover or feast of unleavened bread that year was Saturday, and that the fifty days were to be counted from that. But in the same paragraph he obliges himself to reckon that Saturday as the first of the fifty, by saying, "This feast of [seven] weeks was celebrated on the fiftieth day after the first day of the passover festival."[2] Reckoning Saturday, the Jewish Sabbath, as the first of the fifty, inevitably makes pentecost come on Saturday. But Dr. Lange says it came that year "on our Sunday." His general knowledge of the subject seems to bring him to a right conclusion; but his reasoning would lead to a wrong one.

Olshausen says: "It was from Friday evening at six o'clock that the fifty days began to be counted,"[3] committing thus the same error in dating that Professor Hackett does. He also agrees with him in the conclusion that the fiftieth day fell upon Saturday. Yet on the same page he virtually contradicts himself, by saying that "Pentecost in the year of our

---

[1] We have more recently found that Dr. Smith in his Old Testament History, p. 264, has this: "From the sixteenth of Nisan seven weeks were reckoned *inclusively*." He includes the sixteenth, the Sabbath; doing that, his deduction in his New Testament History, p. 380, note, is incorrect. He is inconsistent with himself, or has changed his opinion. Beginning with Saturday and counting seven weeks brings us to the eighth Saturday; and does not include it, and that Saturday is the fiftieth day. [2] Com., Acts ii. 1, p. 26. [3] Com. Acts ii. 1; Vol. iii. p. 191.

Lord's death fell upon Saturday; but it began at six o'clock in the evening, when the Sabbath was at a close, and it lasted till six o'clock on Sunday evening." That is saying that it came on Sunday, when he had before said it came on Saturday. Beginning with Saturday and closing on Sunday would give fifty-one days. We do not find that these discrepancies and errors in counting have heretofore been noticed. We therefore conclude that by them the real difficulties of the subject may have been unduly magnified in the minds of many.

3. It seems to be a certainty that the early Christians regarded the event of the outpouring of the Spirit—that is, pentecost—in the year in which Christ died, as occurring on the first day of the week. And ever since the primitive era the Christian world in general have conceived of Whitsuntide as commemorative of the descent of the Holy Spirit at pentecost. Neander speaks of the feast of pentecost as the equivalent of Whitsuntide, observed in remembrance of Christ risen and glorified, and of the effusion of the Holy Spirit.[1] Dr. Schaff says: "The church always celebrated pentecost on Sunday, the fiftieth day after Easter."[2] Olshausen says: "The whole church, so far as we can trace the history of pentecost, have celebrated the feast on Sunday."[3] Wieseler supposes that the Western church changed the celebration of pentecost from the seventh to the first day in conformity with her observance of Easter on that day.[4] But his supposition is not confirmed

---

[1] Hist. Ch., Vol. i. p. 300 (Torrey's Trans.).
[2] Hist. Apost. Church, p. 194, note.   [3] Com., Acts ii. 1.
[4] Alford, New Test. for English Readers, Acts ii. 1-4.

by proof; and if it were, it would not account for the celebration on the first day by the church in general. The Syriac New Testament was found divided into lessons to be read in public worship, and in the list of Sundays is the "Sunday of Pentecost."[1] The Peshito Syriac version dates back, as the learned agree, to the close of the second, or beginning of the third, century, and some suppose to the close of the first or beginning of the second. So much evidence of belief in the primitive church that pentecost came on Sunday could hardly exist, unless it were founded on truth. And such general belief is entitled to much weight in discussing the question before us.

Among the fixed data on this subject are the following: Christ was crucified on Friday, and rose the next Sunday.[1] The preparation for the passover, including the killing of the paschal lamb, was to be made on the afternoon of the fourteenth of Nisan (Ex. xii. 6, 18; Num. ix. 3; xxviii. 16), and the passover was to be eaten just after, at evening, near the beginning of the fifteenth (Lev. xxiii. 5). With the fifteenth the feast of unleavened bread, or passover, was to commence, and on that day was to be held a holy convocation (Lev. xxiii. 6, 7). The feast of first-fruits, including the wave offering, was to be observed during passover week, on the morrow after the

[1] Dr. Gustav Seyffarth holds the view that Christ died on Thursday, not Friday. See Lange on Matthew, Dr. Schaff's note, p. 454, note, and p. 457. Rev. J. K. Aldrich holds the same theory, and presents a strong, yet not satisfactory argument in its favor. See Bibliotheca Sacra, Vol. xxvii., July, 1870. But as they both regard Friday as the fifteenth, their view in respect to the day of pentecost need not be inharmonious with the one advocated in these pages.

Sabbath (Lev. xxiii. 10, 11), and fifty days from that, inclusive or exclusive, was to be the day of pentecost (Lev. xxiii. 15, 16). Among the unsettled data are these: Was the Friday of that year on which Christ was crucified the fourteenth or fifteenth of Nisan? Was the Sunday on which he rose from the dead the sixteenth or seventeenth of Nisan? Did Jesus eat the passover meal at the usual Jewish time, or one day previous, i. e. at the beginning of the fourteenth or of the fifteenth of the month? Was the Sabbath on the morrow after which the wave offering was to be made the regular weekly Sabbath (Lev. xxiii. 11), or the first day of convocation in the passover week? Did the fifty days reckoned from the morrow after the Sabbath (Lev. xxiii. 15, 16) embrace the morrow itself?

We know, from the evangelists, that Christ rose from the grave on the first day of the week, and that the day preceding was the Sabbath, and that Christ was crucified on the day preceding the Sabbath—Friday. And according to the first three evangelists we know that Jesus ate the passover meal at evening, the beginning of Friday, apparently at the usual time. That usual time was certainly at the beginning of the fifteenth of Nisan (Lev. xxiii. 9; Num. xxviii. 17); and later in the day, it would seem, Christ was crucified. This reckoning makes Friday the fifteenth, and not the fourteenth, of Nisan, in the year of Christ's death. Nothing would make it seem otherwise, except this: The apostle John speaks of the Jews as on Friday forenoon yet to eat the passover (xviii. 28). If they had not already partaken of the first and chief passover meal, and were to do it the following evening, then this Friday was the fourteenth, and not the fifteenth of the month.

We need to determine the meaning of the phrase, "But that they might eat the passover" (John xviii. 28) In the New Testament the word "passover" *Πάσχα*, has three significations. (1) It means the paschal *lamb*, as, "And the first day of unleavened bread, when they *killed the passover*" (Mark xiv. 12).[1] There is the same use of the Hebrew word for passover in the Old Testament (Ex. xii. 21; Deut. xvi. 2, 5, 6). There is the same use of the Greek word in Josephus.[2] (2) It also means the one meal called the paschal supper, the first in the week of unleavened bread; as, "I will keep the passover at thy house . . . . And they made ready the passover" (Matt. xxvi. 18, 19).[3] The Old Testament has like use of the word, and the Septuagint translates the Hebrew by the Greek word for passover (Ex. xii. 48; Num. ix. 4, 5). With this meaning Josephus also employs the word.[4] (3) It means, further, the passover *festival* itself, or the feast of unleavened bread, lasting seven days; as, "Now the feast of unleavened bread drew nigh, which is called the passover" (Luke xxii. 1).[5] And Josephus says of the feast of unleavened bread, the seven days, "And is by the Jews called the passover."[6] Nothing forbids this third meaning of the word "passover" in John xviii. 28, unless the word "eat" confines it to the meaning of paschal supper.

---

[1] See also, Luke xxii. 7; 1 Cor. v. 7.
[2] Ant. b. iii. ch. x. sec. 5.   [3] See Luke xxii. 8, 13; Heb. xi. 28.
[4] Ant., b. ii. ch. xiv. sec. 6.
[5] See Luke ii. 41, 43; Matt. xxvi. 2; John ii. 13; vi. 4.
[6] Wars, b. ii. ch. i. sec. 3.

But such limitation is not always given by that expression. The word "eat" is employed in the sense of celebrate, and that in reference to this same festival: "And they did eat the festival seven days" (2 Chron. xxx. 22). Such is the literal rendering.[1] The word "eat" seems to have been used in preference to the word "keep," because the act of eating unleavened bread was prominent. Therefore the passage in question (John xviii. 28) does not necessarily imply that the Jews at the time of Christ's trial and crucifixion had not eaten the first passover meal the evening previous. They may have had in prospect their voluntary peace-offerings, and the eating therewith, which were observed by private individuals and families, particularly on the first day of the passover week. Such offerings were provided for by Jewish law (Lev. vii. 15, 16; Num. x. 10).

The foregoing conclusion is strengthened by chronological calculations, which show, that in the year of Rome 783, of Christ, 30 (really 34), the year of his crucifixion, the fifteenth of Nisan fell on Friday.[2] And such seems now to be the trend of discussion. Dr. Schaff in his "Apostolic Church," published in 1853, said, "While this Friday, according to the synoptical Gospels, seems to have been the fifteenth of Nisan, an unbiased interpretation of several passages in the Gospel of John would make it the fourteenth."[3] But in Lange on Matthew[4] he in one sentence favors the opposite view, and in Lange on

---

[1] Apostolic Church, p 193, note.   [2] Ibid., pp. 455, 456, note.
[3] See Robinson's Eng. Harmony, notes, p. 201.
[4] Wiesler in Hertzog's Encyc. xxi. p. 550, quoted by Dr. Schaff, Lange's Com., John, p. 563.

John, published in 1875, he still more favors it.[1] This is doubtless a change in the right direction.

Did the fifty days reckoned "from the morrow after the Sabbath" (Lev. xxiii. 15, 16), include the morrow itself? In respect to this question, we have seen, that different men have reckoned differently,[2] but we do not find that they themselves have noticed the difference. The direction is, "And ye shall count unto you from the morrow after the Sabbath, from the day that ye brought the sheaf of the wave-offering; seven Sabbaths shall be complete; even unto the morrow after the seventh Sabbath shall ye number fifty days" (Lev. xxiii. 15, 16). The Septuagint reads, "Ye shall number to yourselves from the day after the Sabbath, from the day on which ye shall offer the sheaf of the heave offering, seven full weeks; unto the morrow after the last week ye shall number fifty days." Does this language mean "from" in the sense of *after* the day on which the wave-offering was made, or from in the sense of *with*, or inclusive of the day for that offering? We think the language is not decisive of that question in either the Hebrew or the Septuagint. We have in this Article seen instances of both the inclusive and exclusive.[3] Still, the Scripture phrase seven sabbaths shall be complete," meaning, or at least implying, seven *weeks*, seems decidedly to favor there being seven complete weeks after the wave-offering, and before the pentecost; seven weeks exclusive of both extreme days. The Targum has the following; "And number to you after the first feast day of Pascha, from the day when you brought the sheaf for the elevation, seven weeks;

---

[1] Ibid., pp. 562, 563.   [2] See pp. 90, 91.   [3] See p. 86.

complete shall they be. Until the day after the seventh week you shall number fifty days." The phrase, "until the day after the seventh week," shows that pentecost, at one extreme was not to be included; and we may well infer, it would seem, that the day for the feast of first-fruits, at the other extreme was also not to be included. And the phrase, "complete shall they be," still further seems to indicate, that the seven weeks were to be complete without either of the two feast-days standing at the extremes of the weeks. Turning to Josephus, we get additional light. He speaks of the festival of first-fruits, of the wave-offering, and says, "When a week of weeks has passed over after this sacrifice (which weeks contain forty and nine days), on the fiftieth day, which is pentecost, etc."[1] The phrase "*after* this sacrifice" favors *excluding* the day of the wave offering in numbering fifty days. Dr. Robinson says that pentecost was "seven weeks after the sixteenth day of Nisan;"[2] by which we understand him, that seven weeks were completed after that day, and then came pentecost; seven full weeks intervening between the first day of passover week and pentecost. Dr Robinson held that Christ's crucifixion was on the fifteenth of Nisan,[3] and, that being Friday, by his view pentecost was on Sunday. The sixteenth of Nisan in the year of Christ's death being the day of the wave-offering (Lev. xxiii. 6-11), and being also

---

[1] Ant., b. iii. ch. x. sec. 6. [2] Greek and English Lexicon, Πεντη-χοστή.

[3] Harmony of Gospels, notes; also Bib. Sac. Vol. ii., Aug. 1845.

Saturday, the Jewish Sabbath, counting fifty days after that day we come to Sunday as the day of pentecost.

If Friday, the day of crucifixon, was the *fourteenth* of Nisan, as some hold, and the first day of unleavened bread was Saturday, the fifteenth, and the wave-offering, it being the second day of the feast, was on Sunday, the sixteenth, then numbering fifty days *inclusive* of the day of the wave-offering, would bring the day of pentecost on Sunday. We think the *former* reckoning the true one, but either is possibly correct. We feel bound to have in mind the fact that the primitive Christians said the day of pentecost was on Sunday. And we are aiming to show that, notwithstanding all disagreements in the reckoning made by different scholars, nothing proves the primitive testimony untrue.

All theories having any probability in their favor seem to be adjustable to the assertion of primitive church history, that the day of pentecost in the year of Christ's death came on Sunday, and was ever after observed by the Christians on that day. It is a very noteworthy fact in the series of first-day events, that the new dispensation, so far as can be decided, opened on Sunday, and not on Saturday.

(c) We have thus far considered events which occurred within less than fifty days after Christ's resurrection. We have no more in their immediate vicinity of time concerning the first day. We must wait to see whether those we already have, in connection with others unknown, will work any particular change of observance in sacred days, or whether those events, having passed by, will stand in history as isolated facts, without any special sequence. But we eagerly pass to the earliest date of apostolic or evangelistic writings, to see whether we discover any indications of change. The first three, or the synoptic Gospels, are the first writings of that kind which we may expect to find. They were written between about twenty-five and thirty-five years after Jesus' resurrection, and John's Gospel, fifty years or more after that event. We have been speaking of the "first day of the week;" but we do not find any such expression coming from the Saviour's lips, or from any of his disciples at the time of his death. He had foretold his death and resurrection; but the latter he spoke of as to occur on the "third day." Each of the three synoptic Gospels make record of it; Matthew (xx. 19) and Luke (xviii. 33) each once, and Mark three times (viii. 31; ix. 31; x. 34). The Scribes and Pharisees heard of that prophecy of his the next day after his crucifixion, and made it the basis of their request of Pilate for a guard to be stationed at his tomb in readiness for the third day morning (Matt. xxvii. 62-66). The angels repeated the prophecy to the women at the sepulchre on the morning of the resurrection (Luke xxiv. 7). The two disciples going to Emmaus reminded the Saviour of the "third day" on which he was to rise again (Luke xxiv. 21); and he spoke of it himself to his apostles assembled on the evening of the "third day" (Luke xxiv. 46). Nine several times the evangelists make some record respecting that "third day." That was the current phraseology, then, concerning the day of Christ's resurrection. It was the "third day," not "first day." But when from twenty-five to fifty years have witnessed the inauguration of the Christian dispensation, what do we find? Each of the four evangelists, in his account of Christ's resurrection, says that he rose on the "first day of the week," and Mark and John employ that term twice each (Matt. xxviii. 1; Mark xvi. 2, 9; Luke xxiv. 1; (John xx. 1, 19). Luke in his Gospel four times mentions the prophecy that Christ would rise the "third day"; yet, from twenty-five to thirty years after that frequent expression used at the time of the resurrection, he, in both his Gospel and treatise on the Acts of the Apostles (Acts xx. 7), speaks of the "first day" as though it were a phrase in common use, and dedicated to that one event. And about twenty-five years subsequent to Christ's death the apostle Paul uses the same term, "first day" (1 Cor. xvi. 2), as though not only it had peculiar significance, but was in some way specially observed at that time. The only way to account for this change of historic phrase, from "third day" to "first day" and for this occasional, yet incidental, mention of it by different inspired writers, is to suppose that it was already a noted day among all Christians, and was well understood to be such. And the term "first day" seems to imply some contrast in the ordinary conceptions of the people between that and "seventh day"; as though the two days may have been observed by different classes in some special manner.

(f) When, therefore, we come to read, "upon the first day of the week, when we were gathered together to break bread, Paul discoursed with them" (Acts xx. 7), we are prepared to accept the natural implication of the language, that on the "first day" the disciples customarily observed the Lord's supper, and held other religious services. That inference receives additional force from the fact that, as recorded in the previous verse, the apostle and his companions, having come to Troas, "tarried seven days"; as though they had waited for the usual time for assembling. We find no intimation that the disciples were called together for a special occasion.

The evangelists were not careful always to mention the same things. But in regard to so important an event as Christ's resurrection no one is silent. And no one fails to state that he rose on the "first day of the week." There must be meaning in that fact. And just about then when they record it, one of them also records that the latest of the apostles holds a meeting with the disciples on a "first day of the week." He does not speak of it as though it were an unusual event. At that meeting a sacrament is observed, which was instituted in that series of events which culminated in Jesus' resurrection. The intent seems to be to bind into a close union the sacred commemoration of his sufferings and death, and the celebration of his victory over the grave. The one is placed in the hours of the other. The ordinance is sacred; the day seems to be sacred. And we find this fact in a line of events all of which conspire to give note and peculiarity to the "first day of the week."

Objection: The "first day of the week" could not have been regarded as sacred or religious, because Paul set out upon a journey on that day. Conybeare and Howson tell us that the meeting at Troas was on " the evening which succeeded the Jewish Sabbath."[1] Dr. George B. Bacon[2] and many others have expressed the same opinion. *Reply:* (1) But Conybeare and Howson admit that the opposite view may be correct, and quote Greswell, who "supposes that they sailed from Assos on the Monday." (2) The question whether Paul and his companions journeyed from Troas on Sunday or Monday depends upon whether Luke reckoned by Jewish chronology, or by Roman, or Babylonian. The Jewish commenced and closed the day at sunset; the Roman, at midnight;[3] the Babylonian and Persian, at sunrise.[4] If the reckoning was either Roman or Babylonian, the evening in question belonged to the first day of the week, and the morrow to Monday. The highest authorities affirm that in the time of Christ, Jewish chronology had become modified by the Roman.[5] In some things it was the one; in others, the other. It had also become affected by the Babylonian.[6] Passages in the Old Testament show that by the Jewish reckoning there were only three watches in the night: the first, or "beginning of the watches" (Lam. ii. 19), the "middle watch" (Judg. vii. 19), and the "morning watch" (Ex. xiv. 24; 1 Sam. xi. 11). But in the New Testament Matthew speaks of the "fourth watch" (xiv. 25), and the Saviour, of four sections or watches (Mark xiii. 35). Therefore Christ and the apostolic writers, in respect to night-watches, used

[1] Life and Epistles of St. Paul, Vol ii. p. 206.
[2] Sabbath Question, p. 105.
[3] Hegewisch's Introduction, Chronology, p. 18.
[4] Ibid., pp. 17, 71.
[5] Smith's Bible Dic., "Chronology, Day," p. 313; Horne's Introduction, Vol. iii. p. 162.
[6] Hegewisch's Introduction to Chronology, pp. 17, 71.

Roman chronology; for the Romans had four watches.[1]

But some will object that the Jews, on one occasion, brought their sick to Christ for healing on the Sabbath, as the "sun was setting," or had set (Luke iv. 40; Mark i. 32; Matt. viii. 16). This they would not have done on the Sabbath itself; therefore they kept Jewish time, and closed the day with sunset.[2] *Reply:* First, they may have been only the more rigid Pharisaic Jews that would not bring their sick to be healed on the Sabbath. Secondly, though the Jews of Christ's time did close the Sabbath with sunset, that does not prove that the evangelists, twenty-five or fifty years afterwards, reckoned the day in the same manner, when writing for Christians, chiefly converts from the Gentiles, who reckoned the day by the Roman method.

A mixed chronology prevailed in that age, especially among the Jews. Though they originally commenced the day of twenty-four hours with sunset, they had now partly adopted the Babylonian method, and spoke of the lesser, the daylight day, as commencing at sunrise, or six in the morning. "Jesus answered, Are there not twelve hours in the day" (John xi. 9)? The evangelists use the same natural day in speaking of the hours "third," "sixth," "ninth" (Matt. xxvii. 45; Mark xv. 25; Luke xxiii. 44; John xix. 14) when Christ's crucifixion occurred. And the Greeks and Romans also often reckoned by the lesser day of twelve hours, extending from sunrise

---

[1] Smith and Barnum, Bible Dic., p. 1175.
[2] Rev. W. A. Littlejohn, Constitutional Amendment, p. 176.

to sunset.[1] With such reckoning, it was natural to speak of the later or dusky evening as part of the daylight day which had just preceded it. A convenient, though varied, chronology was in the ascendency.

Did Luke use Roman chronology in his account of Paul's visit to Troas? The following reasons indicate that he did: (*a*) He wrote mainly of and for Gentile Christian congregations in the Roman empire, and would be likely to use their chronology, which was Roman. (*β*) The meeting at Troas was held upon, or continued into, the later evening of that day; the day had already some signs of being more or less sacred; by Jewish reckoning the later evening ruled the next "morrow"; Paul and his Christian companions did not spend that morrow sacredly; therefore the evening previous did not belong to the morrow; and the chronology was not Jewish. The signs of sacredness in the first day already found are, the distinction given to it by Christ, by his evangelists, by Luke in this case under consideration. To which should be added—what occurred even earlier—Paul's direction to have certain sacred gifts decided upon and set aside on the "first day" (1 Cor. xvi. 2). That by Hebrew reckoning the later evening ruled the morrow, and made it sacred, if itself were sacred, is shown in the case of the yearly passover supper. That occurred after sunset, and was the beginning of the first day of the feast of unleavened bread (Lev. xxiii. 5, 6); Deut. xvi. 6-8). "The evening and the morning were the first day" (Gen. i. 5). Therefore, if the time of the meeting at Troas

---

[1] Lange on John i. 39, p. 93, 1st col.

were at all sacred, Luke in this record did not use Jewish chronology. (γ) The series of noted events that occurred during the day of Christ's resurrection commenced in the morning, and not in the evening. If it were, as some claim, the evening next following the Jewish Sabbath that the meeting was held in Troas, then the apostles celebrated that wonderful event the night preceding the morrow or day of the week on which it occurred. That is altogether improbable. They would wait, at least, until the glad morning came; they would not wish to commemorate the day of his rising from the tomb and appearing to so many at so many different times, while they would yet have to say that the weekly day was not till the "morrow";[1] and therefore, doubtless, the evening of that meeting belonged to the daylight day preceding it, and not to the one following it; and the chronology used was Roman; and the next morrow was Monday, and not Sunday. (δ) The apostle John probably used Roman chronology in describing a similar meeting subsequent to Christ's resurrection, and doubtless while writing more for Jewish Christians than Luke did in the Acts of the Apostles; and therefore it is nearly or quite certain that Luke employed Roman, and not Jewish chronology in the case now under consideration. John, having in his Gospel, recorded the fact of Christ's resurrection, says that he came and stood in the midst of his assembled disciples, "the same day at evening, being the first day of the week" (John xx. 19). It was the evening of the "first day of the week" (xx. 1). Was it the evening of the first day

---

[1] See Discussion on "Morrow," pp. 86, 87.

by Jewish or Roman chronology? The answer will depend, in part, upon whether that evening was before or after sunset. It was after sunset; First, because, as the doors were shut "for fear of the Jews" (vs. 19), it is altogether probable that they had sought shelter under the shades of evening. Secondly, because the two disciples who that day went to Emmaus, and communed with Christ on the way, had there, "toward evening . . . sat at meat" with him (Luke xxiv. 29, 30), then had travelled to Jerusalem, and there had found the disciples, before Jesus stood in the midst of them (Mark xvi. 12-14). It cannot reasonably be supposed that all this was done previous to sunset. Thirdly, because the disciples at Jerusalem were "at meat," at their evening meal, when Christ appeared among them (Mark xvi. 14). And the Jews' evening meal was not usually taken until their day's work was done, which was at sunset. And on this day, so full of strange events, the disciples, in fear because of the Jews, would be likely to take their evening meal later than the usual time, rather than earlier. Fourthly, it was after sunset, the later evening, because the apostle John expressly says it was ὀψίας *late*, the late evening (xx. 19), when Jesus appeared among his disciples.

Objection: The word ὀψίας is sometimes applied to hours in the afternoon previous to evening; as, when Christ was about to feed five thousand, we read, "When it was evening" (Matt. xiv. 15). And it could not have been as late as sunset, or night-fall; for the people were in a desert place, and returned to their homes the same day, after being fed. *Reply:*

The word, in Greek or English, is used relatively; and when the five thousand were fed it was, no doubt, late, as compared with the forenoon; the latter part of the afternoon had commenced. In the same passage (vs. 23) the same Greek word is used again, sigfying the time when Jesus was alone, the people having departed, and he having gone into a mountain to pray. The idea of *late*, in whatever language expressed, unlimited and undefined by anything in the connection, would signify a time near or after sunset, or later still. Such is its acknowledged general meaning. In the case when the Saviour appeared to his apostles on the evening of his resurrection, instead of any circumstances indicating that it was only about the middle of the afternoon, there are several showing that it was as late as what all nations naturally understand by the full evening.

By Jewish computation there were two evenings— one, between three in the afternoon and sunset, or about six o'clock; and one after sunset. By *late*, ὀψίας the later evening would certainly be meant, unless something in the connection confined it to the earlier. And all Greek linguists seem to agree that in this instance the later evening is the one indicated; as Robinson, Lange, Alford. The terms "earlier" and "later" are used relative to each other; though by Jewish chronology they belonged to two different days. The earlier evening would not be after sunset, at the beginning of the Jewish day, and the later one in the afternoon, at the close of the Jewish day, but just the reverse; the two evenings that touched each other at six o'clock being compared with each other, and the one coming last being the late one.

When Jesus manifested himself to his disciples John says it was "the same day at evening [later evening], being the first day of the week" (John xx. 19). The later evening, belonging to the first day, by Jewish reckoning was the evening preceding, Saturday evening, that following the Jewish Sabbath. Therefore, if Jewish chronology is used, this meeting of Christ with his disciples was the evening before his resurrection, while yet his body lay in the tomb. That conclusion is absurd. Therefore the inevitable inference is, that not the Jewish, but the Roman or Babylonian, chronology is employed in this narrative; and the evening of the first day was the same as our Sunday evening; and the morrow after that evening was Monday, and not Sunday.

In this meeting of Christ with his apostles at Jerusalem, we have a key of interpretation in the case of the meeting at Troas. John using Roman chronology to describe an event at Jerusalem which occurred just after the Redeemer's resurrection, there is no good reason to suppose that Luke employed Jewish chronology to describe an event thirty years after at Troas, far towards Rome from Jerusalem. The meeting at Troas was certainly in the evening of "the first day of the week," (Acts xx. 7), or was continued into the evening and until after midnight. By the Roman reckoning, that evening belonged to the daylight day preceding; the next day, or morrow was the second day of the week or Monday. Paul and his companions travelled from Troas towards Assos, not on Sunday, but on Monday, and that first day of the week at Troas was apparently and, so far as appears, wholly devoted to religious services; it would seem, according to the usual custom. It follows that this passage in Acts xx. 7 presents a strong front against both the seventh-day Sabbatarians, on the one hand, and those who hold that the apostles and their contemporaries did not religiously observe the first day, but practiced secularity upon it, on the other.

(*g*) The next notice we find in the sacred record respecting the "first day" is Paul's direction to the church at Corinth: "Upon the first day of the week let each one of you lay by him in store as he may prosper, that no collections be made when I come" (1 Cor. xvi. 2). It was a "collection for the saints" (vs. 1), persecuted and poor, at Jerusalem. It was in part a return for the noble acts of the Christians there, who, during the protracted continuance of pentecost, to supply the "need" of those who had come from far, freely sold their lands and houses, and brought the "prices and laid them at the apostles feet," in the sacred cause of Christian benevolence (Acts iv. 31-37). Equally sacred was the act enjoined upon the saints, and all the saints at Corinth. This was no mere secular call or business transaction. Each one was directed to decide upon and set aside the amount of his gift at home, or by himself, on the "first day." Yet there were to be "gatherings," and that before he came. This implies collections, and some one place of deposit,—a church treasury. When were those "gatherings" most naturally made? "Upon the first day of the week; when we were gathered together to break bread" (Acts xx. 7). This is rendered nearly or quite certain, by the testimony of

Justin Martyr, born only about forty years after this writing of the apostle Paul. In his account of the religious services held by Christians on Sunday, in connection with that part relating to the Lord's supper, he says: "They who are well to do, and willing, give what each thinks fit; and what is collected is deposited with the president, who succors the orphans and widows, and those who through sickness or any other cause are in want, and those who are in bonds, and the stranger sojourning among us, and, in a word, takes care of all who are in want."[1] Paul's injunction and Justin's record evidently refer to the same practice, and help interpret each other. Paul says, "Upon the first day of the week"; Justin describes what occurred "upon the first day of the week," Sunday. Paul prescribes for the need of the afflicted saints; Justin tells what was done for such. Paul says, "Let every one of you lay by him in store," judging for himself; Justin say, "They who are well to do, and willing, give what each thinks fit;" Paul speaks of "gatherings" of the gifts; Justin of "what is collected." Paul implies that there was some depository of the contributions; Justin says that contributions were "deposited with the president." Paul's direction, or a similar one given by all the apostles, probably gave birth to the practice recorded by Justin; and since in Justin's time the gifts were "collected" on Sunday, so doubtless they were in Paul's time.

(*h*) Justin's record, and Paul's injunction taken together, would lead us to expect allusions, at least, to collections for the poor in other New Testament

[1] Ant. Nic. Lib., Vol. ii. pp. 65, 66.

churches. Accordingly, we find that the apostle gave the same "order to the churches of Galatia" (1 Cor. xvi. 1). They were "churches," more than one; Galatia was a large region. The injunction to the church at Corinth began thus: "Upon the first day of the week." Surely, the "fore-front" of it was not omitted in the "order to the churches of Galatia." They, too, were to attend to this " upon the first day of the week."

Further, the apostle commended the example of the Corinthians in this thing to the believers in Macedonia (2 Cor. ix. 1, 2), and that not in vain, for their zeal "stirred up very many." And he commended the example of both the Corinthians and Macedonians to the saints at Rome (Rom. xv. 26). In all these instances the contributions were, as he says, "for the poor among the saints that are at Jerusalem." All for the same object, they were unquestionably all to be taken by substantially the same measures. A specific direction that the money be laid aside in one case "upon the first day of the week," was no doubt repeated and deemed important in all cases. It was a part of their religious service, just as it was in Justin's day. We do not hear of any who determined to do it on the seventh day instead of the first. The facts increase in number, which show that the first was a noted and special day throughout all the Christian churches of Asia; and if there, everywhere.

Objection: The observance of the first day of the week in the primitive Christian church, arose from the spontaneous feelings and judgment of the early Gentile churches while under apostolic supervision, and did not commence first at Jerusalem, or with Jewish Christians. *Reply:* Why, then, do we not hear of some difference of opinion on this point between Jewish and Gentile converts? Not a breath of it appears. If Sunday-keeping arose far off among the Gentiles, should we not hear of some dissent from it at Jerusalem? Some Judean professed believers, hearing of the work among the Gentiles, went down to them from Jerusalem teaching that circumcision "after the custom of Moses" (Acts xv. 1) was necessary to salvation. If the keeping of the Lord's day was first commenced there contrary to custom at Jerusalem, would not these same Jewish teachers have hastened down to administer correction? The question concerning circumcision was respectfully sent back from the region of the Gentiles that it might be decided by the church, apostles, and elders, at the great religious centre. If the Lord's day were not already observed at Jerusalem, would not a similar question respecting it have been sent there from the Gentile Christians for decision? At Jerusalem Jesus rose from the dead; at Jerusalem appeared to so many on the day that he rose; at Jerusalem appeared to the eleven on the next return of the "first day of the week"; at Jerusalem on the day of pentecost, on the Lord's day, fulfilled his promise to send the Holy Spirit. At Jerusalem the great foundation facts occured on which is based the observance of Sunday at all. And the cheering and fruitful idea of making that a day of sacred commemoration, did it arise not at Jerusalem, but far away among the Gentiles? It is certain that the words "first-day of the week" became consecrated phraseology in the apostolic churches. Yet the apostle and evangelist Matthew uses that language (xxviii. 1); and his Gospel was first written of the four, and was written especially for Jewish converts in Palestine, and he, according to tradition, resided in Jerusalem fifteen years after the resurrection of Christ, and wrote his Gospel at about the time that Paul and Peter were founding the church at Rome. It appears that of all writings extant, his was the first to contain the expression, "first day of the week," as applied to our Lord's resurrection. Which is the more probable: that the early church used that phrase as synonymous with Lord's day, and the latter term as in some sense sacred, contrary to the view and practice of Matthew, or in accordance with them? And if after leaving Jerusalem he preached the gospel for a period in other parts, as tradition states, and was thus laboring when Paul met the disciples at Troas on the "first day of the week," and gave direction to the church at Corinth to set aside their gifts for the poor on the "first day of the week," is it at all probable that the idea of keeping the first day sacred was new or unacceptable to the apostle Matthew, or to Christians with him? What! did Paul give strict instructions to various Gentile churches to decide upon, and set apart their contributions for the poor saints at Jerusalem, "upon the first day of the week," and those saints themselves know nothing about observing that first day, or receive the suggestion first from their Gentile brethren? Did Paul and Barnabas carry up the new project of keeping sacred the first day, when they went from the Gentile churches to Jerusalem? If so, strange that we do not hear about it! Professor Stuart says that the early Christians "all agreed to keep holy" the first day of the week,[1] and we have yet to learn that any real evidence to the contrary anywhere appears. It will not be wise to assume or suppose that there is such evidence until it is produced.

Objection: Jerome, one of the fathers, seems to sanction visiting the tombs of martyrs, and the making of garments on Sunday. *Reply:* Jerome lived nearly three centuries after the apostles, and what was approved by him, or practised by some in his day, cannot be considered as having apostolic sanction. Visiting martyrs' tombs was certainly not gross desecration of the Lord's day; the making of garments may have been in stress of circumstances for the poor or those in bonds, and not a usual practice; these things may have been only in Jeromes' locality, and a laxness in observing the day may have prevailed in that age which was not known in the apostolic period. This does not constitute proof that the early Christians were disagreed about keeping the first day sacred. Dr. Hessey,[2] who quotes Jerome on this point, admits that the testimony of that Father is affirmative and positive respecting the religious observance of the Lord's day in the early centuries of the Christian era.

Objection Second: Macknight says, the practice of abstaining from labor on the first day was condemned by the Council of Laodicea, A. D. 364, as Sabbatizing.[3] Many others have followed him in the statement.

[1] Com., Gal. iv. 10.
[2] Sunday, p. 74.
[3] Com., Col. ii. 16, p. 389.

Reply: This objection seems to have arisen from an error in reading. What the Council of Laodicea did condemn was Judaizing on the seventh day. In consequence they decided that the New Testament Scriptures as well as the Old ought to be read at religious services whenever held on the seventh day, and that labor ought not to be wholly abstained from on that day. Their decision in substance was just the opposite of Macknight's statement. Authority for this representation is given by Neander,[1] Eadie,[2] and the act of the Council itself.[3]

(*i*) The instance at Troas is the first mention of the first day of the week in connection with a Gentile congregation. Other instances are those relating to the church at Corinth, to the churches of Galatia, Macedonia and Rome. The Christian Gentiles, having Christ's resurrection as the foundation of their hope and joy, and his resurrection day as the time for many, at least, of their religious assemblies, and not having had the custom of observing the Jewish Sabbath, it is nearly or quite certain that their one sacred festival day was the first of the week. This occasion at Troas was about twenty-five years after the resurrection of Christ. And the Pauline instructions to the churches of Galatia, Achaia, Macedonia and Rome, were at about the same period. All evidence bearing on the subject is, that the disciples then regularly met on the first day; and since it is known that the inspired teachers exhorted and commanded regu-

---

[1] Church Hist. (London ed.) Vol. iii. p. 422.

[2] Com., Col. ii. 16.

[3] Canon, xxix. Morris's Lib. Fathers, St. Ephrem, p. 391. note.

lar attendance on stated worship (Heb. x. 25), the time for it in general, with the Gentiles at least, must have been on that day. One of the strongest evidences that the first day of the week was then observed by the Christians through some divine authority, is this: The Gentile believers had been unaccustomed to the sacred observance of a septenary division of time, and now, for some reason, clearly seem to have been wont to attend the Lord's supper. and to set aside aside sacred gifts, "on the first day of the week." No ordinary cause could have produced such a revolution. And with inspired men for their religious teachers, how they could have made such a change without supposed divine authority is incomprehensible. Further, their religious teachers being known to them as having wrought miracles, and as professedly speaking by divine inspiration, how those Christians could have been led to suppose that they had divine authority for keeping the first day, unless they really had it, is equally incomprehensible.

Objection: "The Lord instructed his disciples that the Sabbath would exist at least forty years after his death; since he taught them to pray continually that their flight at the destruction of Jerusalem, which occurred A. D. 70, might not take place on that day" (Matt. xxiv. 20).[1] *Reply:* First, the gates of all cities were closed on at least the weekly Sabbath, and travelling on those days could be only with the greatest difficulty. Hence the prayer that their flight might not be in such unfavorable circumstances. Secondly, if travelling on the Sab-

[1] W. H. Littlejohn, Constitutional Amendment, p. 65.

bath were in all circumstances inherently wrong, the Saviour would not have given conditional permission for it by enjoining prayer that if possible it might be prevented. Thirdly, the Jewish Sabbath did exist at the destruction of Jerusalem, though among Christians chiefly superseded by the first day, and strict Jews and Jewish authorities still in power would interpose many obstacles to the flight of Christians or others on the seventh day.

(j) Tracing the course and instructions of the apostle, we find that the Christians of his time had special religious services of their own, separate from those of the Jews. Giving directions respecting the incestuous person, the apostle Paul says: "Ye being gathered together" (1 Cor. v. 4). Speaking of abuses that had crept into the observance of the Lord's supper by the church at Corinth,—certainly a meeting separate from the Jews,—he says: "Ye come together not for the better . . . When ye come together in the church . . . When, therefore, ye assemble yourselves together in one place" (1 Cor. xi. 17, 18, 20). Writing concerning the exercise of spiritual gifts, he remarks: "In the church I had rather speak five words with my understanding . . . If therefore the whole church be assembled together . . . When ye come together . . . If there be no interpreter, let him keep silence in the church" (1. Cor. xiv. 19, 23, 26, 28). Speaking of women, he says: "Let your women keep silence in the churches . . . It is a shame for a woman to speak in the church" (1 Cor. xiv. 34, 35). In all these instances they must have been Christian, and not Jewish, assemblies. The apostles ordained elders in the churches (Acts xiv. 23), which must have been in Christian, and not Jewish, assemblies. Apostles and Christians met for consultation and advice (Acts xv. 4, 6, 23; xx. 17, 28), which must have been in meetings by themselves. Each church was regarded as a "flock" (1 Pet. v. 2, 3), a company, and they could not have been without meetings distinctively their own. They must have had their assemblies or synagogues of worshippers, under the superintendence of their own church officers (James ii. 2, 3). In the nature of the case, these meetings of Christians could not have been held ordinarily at the time of Jewish asssemblies for the Christians frequently attended the latter (Acts v. 42; xviii. 4: xix. 8), and desired the Jews to attend their religious services (1 Cor. xiv. 23).

When, therefore, were these distinctively Christian meetings held? We have no trace that one of them was held on the seventh day. We have positive evidence that one or more were held on the first day, with many probabilities that that was the chief day for all Christian assemblies (Acts xx. 7; 1 Cor. xvi. 2, etc). The only day named in the New Testament for the observance of the Lord's supper after its institution is the first day of the week. Contributions for the poor were determined upon and set aside, and probably collected on that day. Naturally, even if not by command, the chief Christian assemblies would cluster upon some one day of the week. Those distinctive assemblies must have been numerous, and all the probabilities are that their special day was the first, and not the seventh, of the week.

CHAPTER VII.

THE "LORD'S DAY" COMES TO BE THE CHRISTIAN SABBATH.

Within about thirty or thirty-five years after the date of Luke's treatise on the Acts of the Apostles, and of Paul's first Epistle to the church at Corinth, the first day of the week, as we learn from the apostle John (Rev. i. 10), had come to have a distinctive and sacred title,—the " Lord's day,"—just as the commemorations of the sufferings and death of Christ had come to have the sacred title of " Lord's supper" (1 Cor. xi. 20). It was the Lord's supper, because he gave it, and it commemorated his propitiatory death; it was the Lord's day because he gave it, and it commemorated his triumph over death and hell. He gave the supper in person, before his death; he evidently gave the day in person, after his death, by rising upon it, by appearing so much upon it, by producing in some way such an impression that the apostles and disciples immediately began to observe it, and appointed the most precious of all their religious services, the Lord's supper, upon it.

Objection: By the Lord's day may have been meant Easter-day, on which the Lord's resurrection was annually celebrated. *Reply:* None of the early fathers use the phrase with that meaning; and, since the day in the year for Easter was a long time in question, the apostle John did not refer to a doubtful day in addressing the churches on so important a matter.

Objection second: The apostle may have been speaking of the Sabbath, and may have given it a designation similar to that in Isa. lviii. 13: "my holy day."[1] *Reply*: If John meant the Sabbath, he would doubtless have called it by its usual name. The early fathers used the term "Lord's day" for the first day of the week, copying, no doubt, from the apostle. They also were careful to distinguish between Sabbath and Lord's day; and we should not expect that their teacher, the apostle, would use a term of confusion, as he did if by Lord's day he meant the Sabbath. Besides, the phraseology for Lord's day, in this case, is peculiar to itself, as we shall see. It is never used elsewhere for the seventh-day Sabbath, either in the Greek of the Old Testament or that of the new. It is mere groundless assumption to say that it here means the Sabbath.

Objection third: By the Lord's day the apostle meant the day of judgment, often designated "the day of our Lord" (1 Cor. i. 8), "the day of the Lord" (1 Cor. v. 5; 1 Thess. v. 2; 2 Pet. iii. 10), "the day of the Lord" (2 Thess. ii. 2). *Reply:* John evidently speaks of a literal day; Peter and Paul, quite as evidently, of a great event, occupying more than a common day. The latter speak of a day in the unknown future; while John speaks of one in the known past. If Peter and Paul referred to the destruction of Jerusalem,—which is nearly impossible,—that does not an-

[1] Andrews' History of the Sabbath, pp. 188-192.

swer to the day which John had for meditation and visions. Moreover the phraseology of John is, Κυριακῇ 'Ημέρᾳ; while that of the other apostles is, 'Ημέρα Κυρίου, or the like; the adjective form, Κυριακῇ, being used in the former instance, and never in the latter in Scripture, pertaining to day, except in this case; which distinction the fathers also carefully observe.

On "the Lord's day" John was "in the Spirit" (Rev. i. 10), as if there were some similarity between that and the outpouring of the Spirit on the day of pentecost. On that day the Lord appeared to the beloved apostle, and spake to him (Rev. i. 10–18), much as he appeared to Mary Magdalene and the other women, to the two that went to Emmaus, to Cephas and to the ten, on the original first day; but more gloriously to John alone, the last of the twelve on earth. On that day the Savior communicated to the apostle much or all of the book known as the Revelation by John, thus still more signalizing the first day of the week. Neander, referring to the early "special observance of Sunday in place of the Sabbath," says: "The first intimation of this change is in Acts xx. 7, where by the Lord's day can hardly be understood the day of judgment."[1]

That the Lord's day was one in special honor to Christ the Lord is indicated by usage in similar cases. The phrase "Lord's supper" (1 Cor. xi. 20) indicates a special supper in memory and honor of the Lord; the phrase "Table of the Lord" (1 Cor. x. 21) indicates a table spread to his honor; that of "apostles of Christ" means apostles devoted to his service and

---

[1] Church History, Vol. i. p. 295.

honor; that of "Lord's house" (Ps. cxvi. 19) means a house dedicated to his glory: that of "feasts of the Lord" (Lev. xxiii. 4) implies the same honor to him; and "Lord's day" (Rev. i. 10) must mean a day in special honor of the Lord.

We have in these various citations from Scripture incontestible evidence that the first day of the week was at least one of special and sacred significance and observance to the apostles, and to Christians contemporary with them. What Christian having knowledge of these facts could consent not to keep the Lord's day? If to some not enough seems to be said on the subject in the New Testament, let them recall how little is said in the apostolic writings on baptism and the Lord's supper. The latter institutions are brought down to us in a connected chain of Christian example from the apostles themselves, and not less so the sacred Lord's day. The evidence acquires much strength from the fact that nowhere among the Christians immediately succeeding the apostles appears any doubt or neglect about observing the first day of the week.

Objection: The apostle Paul gives countenance to the theory and practice of not observing one day more than another. He says: "One man esteemeth one day above another; another esteemeth every day alike. Let each man be fully assured in his own mind" (Rom. xiv. 5). *Reply:* The reference is to Jewish days and ceremonies, and not the least to the Lord's day. For, just preceding (vs. 1), doubtful disputations are spoken of, and no evidence appears that there was any disputation about keeping the Lord's day. Next (vs. 2, 3), questions about eating "herbs" and eating "all things" are spoken of; and those were Jewish questions, and not Christian, except as it was important that the Christian conscience should get released from superstitions concerning them. Then the observing of days is classed with eating or not eating, and both were Jewish. The passage teaches that the observing of such Jewish ceremonies and days is optional. But Alford says: "I therefore infer that sabbatical obligation to keep any day, whether seventh or first, was not recognized in apostolic times."[1] Yet he does not disclaim all obligation to observe the Lord's day. But concerning the claim that Rom. xiv, 5 refers to Jewish days only, he declares that it is "a quibble of the poorest kind." We need not be moved by this assertion; since the more accurate Ellicott, referring to Alford's remark, says: "It, however, can scarcely be considered exegetically exact to urge this verse against any theory of a Christian Sabbath, when the apostle is only speaking of legal and Judaizing observances."[2]

The attempt has been made by modern review writers, as also hy Bishop Hooper more than three centuries ago,[3] to render the Greek phrase εἰς μίαν σαββάτων (Matt. xxviii. 1, and in parallel passages) "on one of the Sabbaths"; thence inferring that the New Testament writers recognized as a Sabbath the first, as well as the seventh, day of the week. That construction ignores Hebraistic usage, which was to date each day of the week from the Sabbath; and read, for our Sunday, first day after the Sabbath,

---

[1] New Test. for English Readers, Rom. xiv. 5.
[2] Com. Gal. iv. 10.
[3] Early Writings, p. 342.

or between the Sabbaths; for our Monday, second day after the Sabbath; and so on through the six days. This attempt to find the first day of the week recognized by the New Testament writers as one of the Sabbaths is defeated by the fact that Jewish writers, as in the Talmud, uniformly designate the first, second, etc., day of the week by giving the required numeral, and following it the word for Sabbath, as in the Greek phrase before us.¹ They seem to have had no other way for specifying any day of the week, except the Sabbath. The fact that the plural for Sabbath is used indicates either the two Sabbaths at the two extremes of the six days, or a transfer of the Aramaean form, or a plural of distinction, after the analogy of the names of festivals.¹ The plural is certainly sometimes used when only one Sabbath is referred to (Matt. xii. 1; Luke iv. 16; See 13:10). The foregoing Jewish method of designating the days of the week seems to have prevailed long before Christ came and by his resurrection signalized the first day of the week. Previous to that the first day could not have been thought of as a Sabbath. A passage illustrating the ancient usage occurs in Justin Martyr's Dialogue with Trypho. Justin speaks of Christ's resurrection as occurring on the first day after the Sabbath, $\mu\iota\alpha\ \tau\tilde{\omega}\nu\ \sigma\alpha\beta\beta\acute{\alpha}\tau\tau\omega\nu$.³ If we render this "in one of the Sabbaths," as some would, we are in immediate difficulty. Justin is endeavoring to tell on what day the resurrection oc-

---

[1] See Lightfoot's Horae Heb. et Tal. on Matt. xxviii. 1.

[2] Winer's New Test. Grammar, pp. 176, 177.

[3] Patrologiae, Tom. vi. p. 566. Dialogus cum Tryphone Judaeo, c. 41; Ant. Nic. Lib., Vol. ii. p. 139.

curred, and by that rendering he simply says it was on one of two days. Besides, in the next sentence he repeats the same phrase, and adds concerning the day, remaining (μένουρα) the first or chief (πρώτη). If he means, "one of the Sabbaths," which one? If he means the first after the Sabbath, that is intelligible. That he did mean the first after the Sabbath, is proved by the fact that he immediately says, "It is called, however, the eighth (ὀγδόη)." Justin must have written this within less than a century after the Gospels were written, only forty or fifty years after the apostle John's death, and the passage makes the usage of that time very evident. Besides, the meaning cannot be one Sabbath of the Sabbaths, because σαββάτων is neuter, and μία feminine. It must be one day (ἡμέρα) of the Sabbaths, which is awkward and improbable; or else one day after the Sabbath, or the first between the Sabbaths, either of which is natural and probable.

We now turn to ask, What were the example and precept of the apostles respecting the seventh day? Their continuing for a time after pentecost to attend meetings of the Jews on that day is no proof that they regarded, and would continue to regard, the seventh as the more sacred in the new dispensation. The fact that no record appears of their holding a distinctively Christian service on the seventh day, while it does appear that they held such services on the first day, indicates that there was probably a change in respect to the sacredness of the two days; and we may well look for some evidence that the seventh day had lost its strong hold upon the intelligent and unbiased Christian mind.

Does such evidence appear? Turn to Col. ii. 16: "Let no man therefore judge you in meat, or in drink, or in respect of a feast day, or of a new moon, or of a Sabbath day." Much depends upon the meaning of this one verse. Two quite different classes unite in holding that the word "Sabbaths" (σαββάτων) does not refer to the seventh-day Sabbath, but to other Jewish festivals. They are, first, the seventh-day Sabbatarians, who contend that their Sabbath cannot be meant; and secondly, those who sacredly observe the Lord's day under the impression that if in the New Testament any release is given from observing the day there called "Sabbaths," it negatives all argument to show that the first day of the week is the Christian Sabbath. A third class hinge much on this verse, to show that the fourth commandment is abrogated. We deem all three classes wrong. Whoever may be wrong, and whatever the true interpretation, this passage is the Rosetta stone of the new dispensation on the Sabbath question. It has not a tri= lingual inscription, like the Egyptian stone found at Rosetta, but receives a tri=lingual application. And as that ancient stone contained the elements of a key to the hieroglyphics in Egypt, so this text, by its true meaning, has a key to the right understanding of the Scriptures pertaining to the Sabbath. Some seventh=day Sabbatarians acknowledge that if the word "Sabbaths" in this verse does refer to the seventh day, then that settles the case against them. And all non=Sabbath Lord's day men might well acknowledge that if this verse does not teach that the fourth commandment is abolished, then the case is settled against them. If its help is denied them, they cannot sustain their opinion.

Andrews[1] and other seventh day Sabbatarian authors, in their endeavor to show that "Sabbaths" means Hebrew festivals other than the weekly Sabbath, are, unfortunately for the truth, we think, able to ally important names to their cause. There do join them eminent Lord's day Sabbath advocates. These scholars vary in the degree of positiveness with which they hold their opinions on this point; but among those who more or less entertain them are the following: Albert Barnes,[2] Dr. Justin Edwards,[3] Dr. Pond,[4] President Timothy Dwight,[5] Professor Moses Stuart,[6] and apparently Dr. Charles Hodge.[7] And it is no small item in the conception of the seventh-day Sabbatarians that two noted publishing societies come to the aid of their opinions on this question: the American Tract Society, in two publications,[8] and the Congregational Publishing Society.[9]

If the interpretation of the foregoing authors is correct, then where is there aught in the New Testament to release us from observing the seventh day still, even though we also keep the Lord's day? That they are not correct,—that the word σαββάτων in Col.

[1] Hist. Sab. pp. 87, 138, 159.
[2] Com., Col. ii. 16. pp. 306, 307.
[3] Com. Fam. Test., p. 328; Sab. Manual, pp. 135, 136.
[4] Christian Theology, p. 631.
[5] Theology, Vol. iii. p. 258.
[6] Com., Rom. xiv. 5.
[7] Systematic Theology, Vol. iii. p. 332.
[8] Family Test., with notes, Col. ii. 16; New Test., with notes, Col. ii. 16.
[9] Dr. Pond's Theology, p. 631.

ii. 16 does not refer to ceremonial feast days, but to the weekly Sabbath,—seems to be certain for the following reasons: 1. Another word in the verse, that for "feast day" (ἑορτή) means feast; is in numerous instances used to signify feast; is applied to the Jewish ceremonial feasts (to the passover, Luke ii. 41; John xiii. 1; to the feast of tabernacles, John vii. 2, 8, 10, 11, 14, 37; feasts not specified, Matt. xxvi. 5; xxvii. 15; Mark xiv 2; xv. 6; Luke xxiii. 17; John iv. 45); is translated "feast" in the twenty-seven instances of its occurrence in the New Testament, except in this one case of Col. ii. 16, and ought to be so translated here and is in the revised version. The Lord seems not to have inspired men to use two words with precisely the same meaning in the same catalogue of ceremonial days or other objects, and inspired men seem not to have done it. 2. The word σαββάτων, though frequently occurring, does not in any other instance in the New Testament mean Jewish ceremonial days, and the natural inference is that it does not here. The common reader, and all readers, would naturally suppose that it means here what it does everywhere else. 3. The ceremonial feast days of the Jews, though often spoken of in the New Testament, never take the name, nature, or entire observance of the weekly Sabbath. Each has its own distinctive name and character, and never has occasion to take "Sabbath" for its name. There is no gleam of evidence that the Jews of the apostles' time, or any of the people to whom he wrote, had ever heard the feast days called "Sabbaths." He would not in one epistle originate a new name for them. 4. None of those feast days are ever called Sabbaths in the Old Testament Hebrew, save the day of atonement in two instances (Lev. xvi. 31; xxiii. 32), and possibly the first day of convocation in the passover feast in one passage (Lev. xxiii. 11, 15). In the latter case, however, there can be no positive proof that the convocation day is called a "Sabbath,"[1] and in either case it was not to give the day the name "Sabbath," but to indicate that it, was to be more sacredly kept than other ceremonial feast days. That difference seems to have been simply between doing no work, and no *servile* work. The single word שַׁבָּת (Shabbath), used to designate the seventh day, or Sabbath, in the fourth commandment, is not even applied to the day of atonement without the qualifying or defining word שַׁבָּתוֹן (Shabbathon) accompanying it. 5. In the single instance where the feast of trumpets is in the English acccepted version called a "Sabbath" (Lev. xxiii. 24), and in the one verse where the feast of tabernacles is twice called a "Sabbath" (Lev. xxiii. 39), there is a mistranslation. The revised version reads "solemn rest." The Hebrew for "Sabbath" is *Shabbath* or *Shabbath Shabbathon*. The day of atonement is given the latter, the double name, *rest of resting*. But the feasts of trumpets and tabernacles are called merely *Shabbathon*, a Sabbatism, a partial rest day. 6. This difference is very clearly noted in the Septuagint, where the seventh day, the day of atonement, and the seventh year are termed *Sabbaths*, and the two feast days merely *rest days;* the former being translated by the Greek σαββάτων, and the latter by ἀνάπαυσις, *rest.* Therefore there is no authority for calling those two feast days ceremon-

[1] Subject discussed, p. 368. Bib. Sac.

ial Sabbaths. They were called Sabbatisms merely to describe them as days to be kept in *part* like the weekly Sabbath. 7. The translations of the Pentateuch into the Chaldee language, which are called Targums, make the same distinctions that the Septuagint does between Sabbaths and Sabbatisms, or mere *rest* days, showing that the ancient Jews never called their ordinary feast days by the name "Sabbath." 8. So far as English, Greek, and Hebrew concordances reveal the use of the word "Sabbath," or "Sabbaths," it is always applied to the seventh-day Sabbath, in both the Old and New Testaments, outside of one chapter in the book of Leviticus (xxiii), and one verse in a second chapter (xvi. 31)—referring to Sabbath and day of atonement—with the exception of the Sabbatic *year*, and the application to the year seems to be confined to Leviticus, and a single verse elsewhere (2 Chron. xxxvi. 21). The single verse now under discussion (Col. ii. 16), is, of course, excepted. With a use of the word "Sabbath," applied to feast days, so very limited, is it probable that a single other case,—removed from the former by more than fifteen hundred years in time, and by nearly all the books in the Bible,—is an exception to the great rule of usage? We think not. 9. In Col. ii. 16 the phraseology, "Of a feast, or of a new moon, or of a Sabbath day," is, in substance, a copy of Ezek. xlv. 17, where we read, "In the feasts, and in the new moons, and in the Sabbaths." The difference in the English accepted version is between "holy day," in the former instance, and "feasts" in the latter. But we have seen that "holy day" should have been rendered "feast." Besides, "holy day" often really means ceremonial "feast," as in Neh. viii. 9-11, where the feast of tabernacles is spoken of. Six other instances occur in the Old Testament, besides this in Ezekiel, where the word "Sabbaths" is joined to those of "feasts" and "new moon." And in each of these seven cases the word for "Sabbath" or "Sabbaths" is not the Hebrew for *Sabbatism*, or mere *rest day*, but is that for the weekly Sabbath. Now, it is nearly or quite certain that the apostle borrowed his phrase in Col. ii. 16, from the like phrases in the Old Testament, and also that he meant by the word "Sabbaths" what is meant by it whence he borrowed—the seventh-day Sabbath. 10. The word "Sabbath" or "Sabbaths" in the New Testament, Greek or English (Col. ii. 16 aside), being never applied to feast days, is, nevertheless, applied to the seventh day at least fifty-nine times. Is it not arbitrary and unreasonable to take the word in the sixtieth instance, and declare that it means feast days! Is it not an error to even *suppose* that it means feast days? 11. There are only two instances in the whole Bible where the word "Sabbath" is certainly applied to a ceremonial feast day, the day of atonement, which was a *fast* day, not feast day, when the people were to afflict their souls. and even there not unqualified; and there are nearly one hundred and fifty instances where the word "Sabbath" or "Sabbath-day," singular or plural, is applied to the weekly seventh day. One hundred and fifty against two. The day of atonement occurred once, while the weekly Sabbath occurred fifty-two times in the year. In respect to passages, one hundred and fifty against two, and in respect to days in the year, fifty-two against one! What! on this basis, say that in the one lone passage left, the word "Sabbaths" means ceremonial feast days, and does not mean the weekly Sabbath! This seems like doing violence to the word of God. Can Christian men longer consent to do it, when they consider the facts of the case? No preconceived or cherished opinions can justify us in holding any doctrine inconsistent with light that comes from the sacred page. "Let no man, therefore, judge you . . . in respect of . . . a Sabbath day." It is ageeed by all that this makes it optional with us whether or not to keep the "Sabbath days." If the term means seventh-day Sabbaths, then it is left to our choice, and there is no obligation upon us to keep them. This being the apostolic teaching and example enjoining us to sacredly regard the Lord's day, it inevitably follows that we have here evidence of a change of the sacred weekly day in early Christianity. The evidence may have come suddenly upon us, we may have found it where we least expected it, but, unless there is essential defect in the foregoing data and reasoning, we have come to proof of a change of observance in the sacred weekly day under the apostolic supervision. The example, as well as the instructions, of the apostles, on such a question, must be ample authority to all those who accept them as inspired teachers sent from God.*

We must conclude that Christ first, and his apostles following him, gave absolute authority for the universal special observance among Christians of

---

*Another marked difference between feast days and Sabbaths was this: On feast days "no servile work" should be done, while on Sabbaths "no *manner* of work" should be done. Lev. xxiii.

the first day of the week, at least to some extent. That the apostles had full authority from their Lord to direct on this subject, is unquestionable. They had delegated power to bind and to loose, in affairs of the church (Matt. xviii. 18). They could remit sins, and were sent by Christ, as he was sent of the Father (John xx. 21-23). The Holy Ghost would teach them and bring all things to their remembrance (John xiv. 26). They were authorized to pronounce men accursed (Gal. i. 8); under their ministry Ananias and Sapphira were smitten dead (Acts v. 5, 10); Hymeneus and Alexander for their heresy were delivered unto Satan (1 Tim. i. 20). The apostles gave direction as to discipline in the church (1 Cor. v. 13); they corrected abuses that crept into the observance of her ordinances (1 Cor. xi. 20-30); they absolved Christian converts from ceremonial observances of the law (Acts xv. 24, 29); and surely they had authority to say whether in the Christian dispensation, the seventh or the first day of the week was to be kept sacred.

(*o*) Next comes one of the most fundamental of all questions pertaining to the whole subject. Does the apostolic authority releasing from obligation to keep the seventh-day Sabbath, abolish the fourth commandment, or render it inapplicable to the Lord's day? This we have heretofore discussed, when considering whether the apostles taught that the Decalogue, or even the fourth commandment, has been abrogated. We may here give an outline of the view there presented, with some addition. First, the command to keep the seventh day is not exactly the same with the fourth commandment; therefore, the one may be set aside without wholly annulling the other. The command pertained to the seventh day; but we have shown that there might be a change of day without abrogating the command. We have found a new weekly day observed, at least to some extent, called the "Lord's day." We need to observe the distinction between proportional and ordinal. We have, in the new dispensation, a proportional seventh of time to be held as sacred. We have not the ordinal seventh. The former is by far the greater. It holds in itself all the *moral elements* of the command. The seventh ordinal was continued until the first ordinal was instituted. No matter whether the primitive saints and the apostles understood all this. The apostles in due time knew and taught that the Lord's day was thenceforth to be the best of all days; and that the seventh day must retire from the chief position.

Dr. Joseph Cook says; "The whole scope of the Sermon on the Mount shows that the moral spirit of the whole Decalogue is re=instituted. This is as true of the fourth commandment as of the fifth, sixth, or seventh."[1] This is not enough to meet those who say that the Decalogue or the fourth commandment is abolished; for they say it was abolished with Christ's death. Nor was it intended distinctively for them. Where is the evidence that Christ ever "re=instituted" the moral part of any portion of God's word? He recognized it; that is enough; it stands by his own first fiat. But the men who claim

[1] Boston Lectures.

the abolition of the fourth commandment, or of the Decalogue, say that nothing of these now stand save what the apostles "re=instituted." Where is the evidence that *they* re=instituted the law? They, too, recognized much; yet nothing of the law stands by virtue of their recognition, but by its original enactment. Their recognition confirms the original enactment; that is our blessing. Mr. Cook says, again, "The teaching and example of the apostles and our Lord substituted for the seventh the first day of the week." True; but we must say more to those who claim that nothing of the moral law stands except what the apostles "re=instituted." We must deny that the moral law was ever abolished. Then we must demand proof that the apostles ever speak as though they were "re=instituting" any divine moral laws. Christ gave a new commandment (John xiii. 34), and the apostles rehearsed it (1 John iii. 23), but not as re=instituting it. Just so they repeated the commands of the Decalogue, not as re=enacting them, but as appealing to them for divine authority. That the apostles held to the binding and permanent nature of the Decalogue, is evident from the following: Paul, in Rom. xiii. 9, teaches the obligation to observe the last five commandments, naming the subject of each; and James teaches the same by one comprehensive declaration (ii. 8), and specifies the sixth and seventh (ii. 11). Paul, in Eph. vi. 2, teaches the duty of keeping the fifth commandment; and James (v. 12) specifically teaches the obligation to observe the third commandment; and Paul again, in 1 Cor. vi. 9, and viii. 4-6 shows the duty of obeying the second, and in Rom. i. 18-25, that of obeying the first commandment. Concerning the fourth, Paul teaches exemption from the former seventh-day Sabbath (Col. ii. 16) but he, and the whole history of the church subsequent to Christ's resurrection, so far as given in the New Testament, teach both the privilege and duty to keep sacred a new seventh day, in commemoration of that resurrection, the completion of redemption. Now, in respect to the abolition of the seventh day as of binding nature, Paul does speak as if giving a new message (Col. ii. 16); and also in respect to the first day (1 Cor. xvi. 2). But how is it with reference to the other commands? Paul refers to the "law" and the "commandment," given of old, as existing still (Rom. xiii. 8, 9; Eph. vi. 2), and James speaks more emphatically of the "royal law according to the Scripture" (ii. 8), and of the "duty to keep the whole law" (ii. 10), and of the great Sovereign who gave the law, as, "he that said" (ii. 11), implying that as he commanded, so it should be done, and so the law would remain. Dr. Hessey tells us that "we are nowhere told that we are to obey the commandments called moral *because* they are contained in the Decalogue,"[1] What telling would he have besides these repeated appeals to the Decalogue by two inspired apostles.

Further, that the moral law is nowhere, and in no part, abrogated, may be inferred from the apparent fact that no holiness, or state of mind, on the part of any human beings, is ever acceptable to God, unless in it is embraced the spirit of full obedience by the active powers, by which we do not mean

[1] Sunday, p. 152.

full sanctification, nor, necessarily obedience with the greatest possible strength; yet, without any conscious disobedience or known reservation. "The righteousness of the righteous shall not deliver him in the day of his transgression" (Ezek. xxxiii. 12); "Blessed are they that keep his testimonies and that seek him with the whole heart. Yea, they do no unrighteousness (Ps. cxix. 2, 3); "Ye cannot serve God and mammon" (Matt. vi. 24); "Whosoever shall keep the whole law, and yet stumble in one point, he is become guilty of all" (Jas. ii. 10); "Thou that art of purer eyes than to behold evil, and that canst not look on perverseness" (Hab. i. 13); "Wheresoever our heart condemn us, God is greater than our heart, and knoweth all things" (1 John iii. 20). The Old and New Testament are agreed on this point. Able men have so understood the Scriptures in regard to it. Calvin, commenting on Matt. vi. 24, says: "Since God everywhere commends sincerity, while a double heart is abominable, all those are deceived who think he will be contented with half of their heart."[1] President Edwards says: "If there be a full compliance of will, the person has done his duty."[2] "If a man, in the state and acts of his will and inclination, does properly and directly fall in with these duties, he therein performs them."[3] This assumes that full obedience of the will is necessary to true virtue and acceptance with God. The Westminster Confession of Faith says: "The moral law

---

[1] Com., *in loc.*
[2] Works, Vol. ii. p. 104; Freedom of the Will, Part iii. sec. iv.
[3] Ibid., p. 105, sec. v.

doth forever bind all, as well justified persons as others, to the obedience thereof . . . Neither doth Christ in the gospel anyway dissolve, but much strengthen, this obligation."[1] The modern doctrine that Christ by his death, or by his apostles, "abolished," as Robertson and others say, the moral law, or Decalogue, or that he both abolished it and renewed it, as some say, would have seemed a strange opinion to those Westminster divines. Baxter said, "If you would be truly converted, be sure that you make an absolute resignation of yourselves and all that you have, to God."[2] President Edwards says, of the surrender in conversion: "Giving up ourselves with all that we have, wholly and forever unto Christ, without keeping back anything or making any reserve."[3] The Assembly's Larger Catechism says of the penitent: "He so grieves for, and hates his sins, as that he turns from them all to God, purposing and endeavoring constantly to walk with him in all the ways of new obedience."[4] Such is evangelical preaching everywhere. But can we be fully accepted with God after conversion with less obedience than at conversion? Impossible! God is not changeable. He always requires what Edwards calls "a full compliance of will," in the sense of full obedience of will to his will, to his moral law. Without that "full compliance," we cannot be fully accepted with him. It was so in the old dispensation and is so in the new.

[1] Chap. xix. sec. v.
[2] Orme's Life of Baxter, Vol. ii. p. 82. See, also, Prof. Morgan on "The Holiness acceptable to God," p. 66, etc.
[3] Works, Vol. iii. p. 189; Religious Affections, Twelfth Sign.
[4] Ques. 76, Ans.; see also Westminster Con. of Faith, chap. xv. sec. ii.

But, has that will of God, that moral law, been once interrupted by its abolition? What cause for its abrogation could there have been in Christ's death? And what proof is there that there was such a cause or such a fact? But this moral will and law of God is much of it revealed in the Old Testament, the once Jewish Scriptures. What occassion is there, therefore, to say, with Dr. Dale, that "the Jewish revelation has become obselete;"[1] or with Dr. G. B. Bacon, that "Christianity superseded the whole of the Jewish law;"[2] or even with Dr. Thomas Arnold, to question whether "The law itself be done away in Christ."[3]

When Paul changed the fifth commandment, by extending its reward beyond long life in Canaan to long life "on the earth" (Eph. vi. 2, 3), he did not revoke the duty to honor father and mother. When he and the other apostles, under the guidance of their Saviour, instituted an order of services in the apostolic churches, which made the first or Lord's day sacred, and left the observance of the seventh day optional, they did by no means revoke anything in the fourth commandment which did not pertain to the seventh day in its ordinal sense. So far as we know, they never uttered one word against the fourth commandment, nor even assumed that they set it aside. We know very well that all they who now reject the seventh and keep the first day, and with that simple change, endeavor strictly to obey the fourth commandment, do find something of that

---
[1] Ten Commandments (Fourth), p. 93.
[2] Sabbath Question, p. 101.
[3] Works, Vol. iii. p. 257: Sermon xxii., The Lord's day.

commandment left to them. Therefore it would seem that there is something in the fourth commandment besides the ordinal element of the seventh day. The sacredness of the seventh day is separable from the rest; and therefore, when Paul, and doubtless all the apostles previously, formally released men from keeping holy the seventh day, he did not annul or proclaim annulled, the whole fourth commandment. What is separable in practice is in theory separable. Assume it as a fact, that when Paul announced release from the obligation to observe the seventh day, the Christians were actually devoting the first day to religious services, and to religious joy on account of Christ's resurrection, were they not in effect, keeping the fourth commandment with the exception of the ordinal seventh=day feature of it? Then who has the right to say, that when the apostle gave his direction in Col. ii. 16, he substantially revoked the fourth commandment? The Christians were in substance keeping the greater part of it. That Paul did not cite it and say that in the main it was binding still, does not justify the assumption that it was all annulled. It was to stand until repealed. When the Lord, through the apostle Paul, released the whole Christian world thereafter from the obligation to observe the seventh day, did he at the same time revoke the command, "Six days shalt thou labor and do all thy work" (Ex. xx. 9)? Who will say he did, and give us proof of it? No proof can be given. But what about the remaining part of the fourth command? We find the church under the apostolic supervision released from the ordinal seventh=day feature, and we find that at least a few years previous to that, the first day with them was noted, and devoted in part to religious purposes, with no evidence that the whole of it was not held sacred. From these premises sound reasoning will not justify the inference, that the whole of the fourth commandment is made null and void. And if not, then are we not driven to the conclusion, that by divine authority, through inspired men, a change has been made in the time, in the ordinal religious element, of the weekly religious day? We can not say that the new is to be kept as was the old in all particulars. For, while apostles supervised still, we find the Sabbatic sacrifices in the temple not transferred to the Lord's day, and we find observed on that day the Lord's supper, which did not pertain to any commemorations or transactions of the seventh-day Sabbath. The clause in the command which requires us to restrain our children and servants from labor during more than six days in seven, is that, too, annulled? Are we left without a "Thus saith the Lord" for our own benefit and that of our families in respect to the time for labor? No, we are not thus left. Releasing from the ordinal seventh day observance does not release from this part of the command. But, why not keep the command precisely as it reads? Because we find another day taking in substance the place of the former one in this new dispensation.

In all this the Lord's-day Sabbath advocates are not usurping authority to change the fourth commandment; but they are taking care not to change it, or unlawfully to announce it abolished, or no longer in force. It is not a question whether devoted

Christians would observe the Lord's day if there were no fourth commandment. But it is a question whether Christians of little experience and knowledge, and those of small devotion, will faithfully observe it, if they understand that no real authority can be brought from the Decalogue enjoining the observance of the Lord's day. It is a question whether the world must reel and totter and fall into ruin, because it has no such law as the fourth commandment contains. Long enough some have tried the method of having no law for the Sabbath, nothing but the good instincts and principles of the partially sanctified, and the prudence of self-interest, and the vain conceits and the godless notions of an impenitent world. The Christian spirit in our land is shivering and shuddering at the prospect and fear of the coming of the Continental sabbath, the fruit of unsound Sabbatic doctrine. Hence, the strongest obligation rests upon all Christians to yield no inch of ground to error on this subject, to tenaciously hold every element and thought of truth pertaining to one sacred day in seven.

Objection: We cannot distinguish in the fourth commandment both moral and positive elements, and properly claim permanence and authority for the former and not for the latter, and yet include in the former the requirement to suspend all labor one day in seven. *Reply:* We admit that one part of the septenary feature in the fourth command is positive; but we are not to assume that *all* of the positive in the command is repealed. The ordinal septenary element is repealed, according to Paul's inspired word (Col. ii. 16). The proportional septenary element is not repealed, because the primitive church, while under apostolic supervision, did, at least to some extent, sacredly regard the first day, which is as truly septenary in the proportional as the seventh day, and no evidence appears that they did not regard it as wholly sacred. That there are moral elements in the fourth commandment pertaining to rest, worship, spiritual culture, and holiness, it would seem that no thoughtful person can deny. Its *company* in the Decalogue is a guarantee for its moral nature in part. If it were wholly positive, we should have no right to assume its abolition without divine instruction to that end. If we knew it was wholly both positive and transient, we should not look for it where it is. But its moral elements existed before even the formal command itself. They were combined and crystallized in it.

Bishop Butler says: "Moral duties arise out of the nature of the case itself, prior to external command."[1] Those moral elements are also permanent. Archbishop Whately says, that moral precepts are binding on all in all ages.[2] It is not needful to make a very studied division between the moral and positive in this command, because revelation comes to our aid. It tells us, and subsequent evidence tells us, that the primitive church, under the guidance of the apostles, while they were under the guidance of Christ, changed their chief weekly sacred day from the seventh to the first of the week. We are not left simply to take the moral elements, and be guided by them as well as we may. We are blessed by the in-

[1] Complete Works, p. 176.
[2] Difficulties in Writings of St. Paul, p. 159.

spired singling out for us of other positive elements, and the locating of them in the Lord's day.

In all of the chief institutions of the old and new dispensations, there are certain underlying moral principles that unite them. And wherever these moral principles appear, they have, as Whately implies, a binding force on us. There was the principle of a covenant with God, entered into by Abel, by Noah (Gen. ix. 9), especially developed in Abraham (Gen. xvii. 2), made anew and amplified in the new dispensation (Heb. viii. 6). But the constituent elements of it on God's part are everlasting. Wherever it appears in the divine word, it makes an obligatory injunction on us, and that because of its moral and eternal nature. The articles of that covenant are distinctly declared to be the Ten Commandments (Deut. iv. 13). They were very conspicuously promulgated. Their nature is such that all moral beings must be bound by them in general. A slight change in them to adapt them to the world, instead of to the Jews merely, has been made. But that does not render them inapplicable to us. The fourth, where the chief change has been made, is still applicable and obligatory as it stands changed, because the covenant in its elementary part is everlasting. The principle of sacrifice is another great underlying bond, uniting the two dispensations. It took the form of animal, symbolic sacrifices in the old, and was perfected and finished on God's part by Christ's sacrifice in the new. It remains for believers ever to hold him as their sacrifice (1 Cor. v. 7) before the Father, and to be themselves a "living sacrifice, holy, acceptable unto God" (Rom. xii. 1). So, the law of the Sabbath has certain moral constituent parts, joining the two hemispheres of the world's redemptive history. It appeared in the seventh day previous to the Decologue, and held its course all the way until in Christ Jesus it was made anew. Its inner nature even unites the two worlds, present and future; its rest here being a symbol of the rest that remaineth to the people of God (Heb. iv. 9). It has not sunken from human sight, for we find the substance of it in the Lord's day now. Its moral elements, along with those of the other commands, were codified and chiseled into tables of stone, that they might forever be written in human hearts. The importance is too great, and it is now too late, to suppose that they have become inoperative or have been abolished.

Rev. Newman Smyth, D.D., is understood in one volume to sanction the view that the fourth commandment is abolished. He says: " His [Christ's] word, 'the Sabbath was made for man,' finally makes the glorious Christian privilege break loose from the restraints of the law."[1] Mr. Smyth's own words convict him of error. He says: " A wonderful revolution was wrought in the transference of the sanctity of their Sabbath to the Lord's day."[2] Transference is not abolition. The "moral leadership of the Bible," "moral good," "moral progress," are with him favorite thoughts.[3] He says again: "Man's moral sentiments, and their growth, come from the Father of lights, or all is darkness."[4] He evidently

---
[1] Old Faiths in New Lights, p. 85.
[2] Ibid., p. 354.
[3] Ibid., pp. 76, 78, 80; 67, 73.
[4] Ibid., p. 69.

believes that moral truth is eternal. He cannot, then, consistently believe that the moral element, "the sanctity" of the fourth commandment, is abrogated; or, that men can legitimately, "break loose from the restraints of the [moral] law."

CHAPTER VIII.

THE EARLY FATHERS CONFIRM THE TEACHINGS OF THE APOSTLES.

The proposition we are now seeking to establish is this: The first or Lord's day in the new dispensation was the chief of all days with the apostles and early Christians, and was their special day for rest and religious worship. In adducing evidence to sustain this proposition, we have devoted several chapters to a consideration of, First, The Lord's Day during Apostolic Age. We now consider:

Secondly, The Lord's day during the Four Centuries next subsequent to the Era of the Apostles. In prosecuting this investigation, we expect to find evidence that overthrows the peculiar tenets on this subject of the following classes; the Seventh-day Sabbatarians, who hold that the observance of Sunday as the Sabbath was a corruption that came into the church not until some time after the earliest of the fathers who succeeded the apostles; the non-Sabbath Lord's-day men, who hold that we cannot found the observance of the Lord's day on the fourth commandment, and hence that it is abrogated; the large class who believe that the sacred observance of the Lord's day was not established during the apostolic period, but by the church subsequently; and the Christian Sabbatarians, who fail to reinforce their own arguments for a Christian Sabbath from the passage in Col. ii. 16—holding, as they do, that the word "sabbaths" there does not refer to the Jewish seventh-day Sabbath.

If the testimony of the early fathers is really at variance with the peculiar sabbatic views of all the foregoing classes, then the way of faith on the Sabbath question is made very clear; and if that way shall obtain general credence in the church, it will certainly lead to a far better observance of the Lord's day than now exists. Such understanding of the patristic testimony, if it can be confirmed. fully sustains the view heretofore taken in these chapters concerning the Lord's day during the apostolic age.

The early fathers—those nearly or quite contemporary with, and those soon succeeding, the apostles—speak definitely of the first or Lord's day as religiously kept by themselves and their fellow-Christians. Respecting their testimony, it is not here claimed that it is exceedingly valuable in doctrine or wisdom, but that it has peculiar importance in respect to the history of customs and practices in the religious life of the early Christians. As Dr. Hessey says, "Those whose exegesis of Scripture is indifferent may be admitted as witnesses to matter of fact."[1] It is not of chief consequence to know that these patristical writings were by the authors whose names they bear, but that they date in the early Christian era, and are historically trustworthy.

The Epistle of Barnabas, though probably not written by Paul's noted companion of that name, was certainly in existence in the early part of the second

[1] Sunday, p. 41.

century—Hilgenfeld says at the close of the first,[1]— and therefore dated in the apostle John's time, or at least within twenty or thirty years of his death. Writing in behalf of Christians, the author of that epistle says: "We keep the eighth day with joyfulness, the day also on which Jesus rose again from the dead."[2] The first day the patristic writers sometimes called the eighth, because it comes next after the seventh. We see that the eighth was the first, because it commemorated the resurrection of Christ. This positive declaration of the keeping of Jesus' resurrection day, made while the apostle John yet lived, or within a few years after his decease, would in that early time have been contradicted if it were untrue. But no such denial appears. If Christians had been divided in respect to keeping the first day, Barnabas's declaration would not have been so universal.

Objection: This epistle was not written by the Barnabas of Scripture, and is therefore a forgery and fraud.[3] *Reply:* It may have been written by another Barnabas, or by one who from respect to that name assumed it as a *nom de plume*. In either case, it is not a forgery. It has won historic confidence by being found carefully preserved with the Codex Sinaiticus of the Scriptures; and that copy of the epistle restored the first four and a half chapters of the Greek text, which part was previously known to the learned only in an ancient Latin version. It

[1] Ante Nicene Library, Vol. i. p. 100.

[2] Ibid., p. 128.—Bishop Lightfoot says, previous to the year 80.

[3] Andrews, Hist. Sab., pp. 211, 242; Littlejohn, Constitutional Amendment, p. 248.

were folly now, after the most eminent scholars in patristic lore have scanned and accepted this epistle, to deny its genuineness, or the force of this passage concerning Christ's resurrection day.

The Epistle to the Magnesians (shorter recension), ascribed to Ignatius, contemporary of the apostle John, is now by the more reliable scholars regarded as genuine. Even Professor J. B. Lightfoot, who held that the three epistles in Syriac discovered by Dr. Cureton were only an abstract of the genuine,[1] has changed his opinion, and now accepts the shorter recension of the Greek. He holds that this epistle to the Magnesians, even if it were not actually written by Ignatius, may be safely regarded as having been composed by some competent and authoritative person as early as the middle of the second century.[2] It has been found in the early Greek, Armenian, and Latin. The shorter recension has the following: "If, therefore, those that were brought up in the ancient order of things have come to the possession of a new hope, no longer observing the Sabbath, but living in the observance of the Lord's day; on which also our life has sprung up again by him and by his death."[3] The word "day" is in question, some supposing it should be "life"—Lord's life. Drs. Roberts and Donaldson, the latest English editors, accept the word "day"; and Zahn, editor of the latest edition of the Ignatian epistles, says $\sigma\alpha\beta\beta\alpha\tau i\zeta o\nu\tau\epsilon s$ in the

---

[1] Ant. Nic. Lib., Vol. i. p. 142.

[2] Apostolic Fathers (Jackson and Prof. G. P. Fisher eds.), pp. 68, 69.

[3] Ant. Nic. Lib., Vol. i. p. 180.

preceding clause determines that ἡμέραν should follow κυριακήν,[1] making it read "Lord's day."

Pliny the younger, contemporary of the earliest Fathers, as governor of Pontus and Bithynia, where persecution of the Christians had arisen, about A. D. 112, reports thus: "The Christians affirm the whole of their guilt or error to be, that they were accustomed to assemble together on a stated day, before it was light, and to sing hymns to Christ as a God, and to bind themselves by a *sacramentum*, not for any wicked purpose, but never to commit fraud, theft, or adultery; never to break their word, or to refuse, when called upon, to deliver up any trust; after which it was their custom to separate, and to assemble again to take a meal, but a general one, and without guilty purpose."[2] Andrews—with Böhmer and Gesner supporting—says, because the first day is not mentioned by Pliny, he "furnishes no support for Sunday observance."[3] But Pliny's stated day, hymns to Christ, *sacramentum*, and a meal together, are so similar to Luke's "first day of the week, when the disciples came together to break bread," and "Paul preached to them" (Acts xx. 7), that the two days will be regarded by nearly all as identical, especially in connection with other testimony now to be given.

[1] Patrum Apostolicorum, Opera, Vol. ii. p. 37. NOTE.—The numerous quotations we make from the fathers, we have verified by reference to the original Greek or Latin. But we make references here chiefly to the Ante Nicene Library, as far as that extends, because that is most accessible to the majority of our readers, and was so to us during the chief part of our examination of this subject.

[2] Hessey on Sunday, p. 42.
[3] Hist. Sab., p. 236.

The Christians had no other such day besides the first.

Justin Martyr unconsciously defines the phrase "stated day," about thirty or forty years later than Pliny's letter, when, speaking of Christians, he says, "On the day called Sunday all who live in cities or in the country gather together to one place; and the memoirs of the apostles or the writings of the prophets are read as long as time permits; then, when the reader has ceased, the president verbally instructs and exhorts to the imitation of these good things. Then we all rise together and pray, and, as we before said, when our prayer is ended bread and wine and water are brought and the president in like manner offers prayers and thanksgivings according to his ability; and the people assent, saying Amen; and there is a distribution to each, and a participation of that over which thanks have been given, and to those who are absent a portion is sent by the deacons; and they who are well to do and willing give what each thinks fit; and what is collected is deposited with the president, who succors the orphans and widows, and those who through sickness or any other cause are in want, and those who are in bonds, and the strangers sojourning among us; and, in a word, takes care of all who are in need. But Sunday is the day on which we all hold our common assembly, because it is the first day on which God, having wrought a change in the darkness and matter, made the world; and Jesus Christ our Saviour on the same day rose from the dead. For he was crucified on the day before that of Saturn [Saturday]; and on the day after that of Saturn, which is the day of the sun, having appeared to his apostles and disciples, he taught them these things, which we have submitted to you also for your consideration."[1] This seems to imply, among other things, that Jesus taught his apostles and disciples to hold their religious services and observe the Lord's supper on the first day, called Sunday. It at least shows that such services were held each first day of the week. Think of this whole passage as having been written by a noted man of the church and the times, at least only thirty or forty years after the death of the last of the apostles, and as having then no contradiction, but much confirmation. Thus early in the patristic age we find incontrovertible evidence that the first day of the week was regarded by the Christians as sacred to religious services. The custom of so observing it could not have arisen in so short a time subsequent to the days of the apostles, if contrary to their instructions and example.

Objection: Many writings ascribed to Justin are spurious.[1] *Reply:* The above testimony is from Justin's First Apology, well known to be genuine.

Objection Second: Justin did not mean the Lord's day, for he speaks of Sunday; and Lord's day may, therefore, mean the seventh, and not the first day.[2] *Reply:* The services he describes show that he meant the first day; and he says it was the day on which Christ " rose from the dead." Addressing the Roman emperor and senate, he naturally called the day by its secular name—Sunday—established by usage before Hadrian's death, which occured A. D.

---

[1] Ant. Nic. Lib., Vol. ii. pp. 65, 66; also, Apostolic Fathers (Jackson and Prof. Fisher eds.), p. 179.

138. The name *Lord's* day might have aroused Augustus's suspicions of Justin's loyalty. The Lord's day and Sunday are known to have been identical, as we shall soon see.

Along with other manuscripts in the Library of the monastery of the Most Holy Sepulchre in Constantinople found by Bryennios now Metropolitan of Nicomedia was the "Teaching of the twelve Apostles." Soon after being found it was translated into English in 1884. It is certain that it dates back to the middle of the second century or the last of the first century, making its time soon after the apostle John's death. In it is this passage fourteenth chapter: "Coming together on the Lord's day, break bread and give thanks, confessing your transgressions, that your sacrifice may be pure." This makes it sure that the Lord's day was observed at that early period.

Some thirty or forty years later, Dionysius, bishop of Corinth, A. D. 170, in a letter to the church at Rome, says: "To-day we have passed the Lord's holy day, in which we have read your epistle."[3]

Objection: Dionysius does not identify the Lord's day with the first day, and it may therefore have been the Sabbath.[4] *Reply:* The epistle must have been read to a Christian assembly, such assemblies customarily met on ths first day, or Sunday, Justin Martyr a short time previous described the assemblies of Sunday; on that day the latter was undoubtedly read, and these facts nearly identify Sunday with Lord's day.

Melito, bishop of Sardis, about A. D. 170, is credited by Eusebius with writing, among other works, one "On the Lord's-day."[5] The work itself is lost.

Objection: The discourse may have been about our Lord's *life*, the work ἡμέρα, day, not being in the Greek text.[5] *Reply:* Melito probably had the full title, and Eusebius omitted a part because ἡμέρα was so often understood after κυριακή. The latter word occurs only twice in the New Testament,— Lord's Supper (1 Cor. xi. 20), Lord's day (Rev. i. 10). It is a peculiar adjective form, originated, like some other adjectives, by the apostles,[1] and used here as a noun in the possessive. The word for Lord in general use is κύριος. But the Fathers so often used κυριακή followed by ἡμέρα, that the latter was sometimes omitted, because the former suggested it. In Heb. iv. 4, the adjective for *seventh* has the word for day understood.[2] Sophocles' Greek Lexicon gives examples of κυριακῇ ἡμέρᾳ in the Apocalyse (i. 10), and in the writings of Ignatius, Irenaeus, Clement of Alexandria, and of others. This adjective form for the name of our Lord is not nearly so much followed by any other word as by that for *day*. Hence, κυριακή suggests ἡμέρα. All noted students of the patristical writings give the title in full—"Lord's day"—to Melito's production now in question—as Routh, Laemmer, Hessey, Means, in Smith's Dictionary, Patrologiae Graecae. Moreover, a modern discovery, that of the manuscript in the Syrian convent in the desert of Nitria in the year 1843, has furnished the *Syriac* of Eusebius's list of Melito's works, and there this title is, "On the first day of the week," showing how the early translators into the Syriac understood

---

[1] Winer's New Testament Grammar, p. 236.

[2] Ibid., p. 590.

the title.¹ Melito was contemporary with Dionysius; doubtless they understood the meaning of "Lord's day" alike, and both as Justin did, and he as being identical with *first* day or Sunday.

Irenaeus, a martyr, bishop of Lyons; A. D. 178, is quoted by an early subsequent writer as saying: "This [custom] of not bending the knee upon Sunday is a symbol of the resurrection, through which which we have been set free, by the grace of Christ, from our sins and from death . . . and took its rise from apostolic times."² The writer speaks definitely of "the Lord's day" as the Sunday spoken of by Irenaeus, and he undoubtedly knew the bishop's meaning. A question early arose whether the close of the paschal fast should be on the fourteenth day of the moon, whatever day of the week it came, or on the Lord's day alone. The former was the practice of many Eastern churches, and the latter of the Western. The bishops of various districts issued epistles on the subject. Eusebius says that Irenaeus presided over the churches in Gaul, and the bishops there, as in other parts, unanimously communicated "that the mystery of our Lord's resurrection should be celebrated on no other day than the Lord's day; and that on this day alone we should observe the close of the paschal fasts."³ Andrews twice says that there is no instance where the term Lord's day is found in Irenaeus's works.⁴ The above is an instance reported by Eusebius.

¹ Spicilegium Syriacum, Cureton, p 57. See also, Apostolic Fathers: (Jackson and Prof. Fisher eds.), p. 190.
² Ant. Nic. Lib., Vol. ix. pp. 162,163.
³ Eccl. Hist., Vol. ii. p. 236.
⁴ Hist. Sab. pp. 217, 273.

Clement, made presbyter of the church at Alexandria about A. D. 189, quotes from Plato, where he says the philosopher all but predicts the economy of salvation, and also where he fancifully supposes Plato prophesies of the "Lord's day," under the name of "the eighth."[1] Andrews admits that Clement employs the term ', Lord's day," but says it is not certain that he means a *natural* day.[2] Yet, in the same paragraph Clement makes other quotations; four from Homer, one from Hesiod, and two from Callimachus, where the seventh day is named, plainly a natural day; and Clement therefore must have meant the literal Lord's day, a natural day, the first of the week. But if any doubt remains about this reference, another makes his testimony clear, where he speaks of the true Gnostic, by which he means the real Christian, as keeping "Lord's day" in commemoration of the Lord's resurrection."[3]

An important testimony—in a work quoted from by Eusebius, but discovered in full by Dr. Cureton, among the Nitrian MSS. in 1843,—is that of Bardesanes, who flourished near the close of the second century. Drs. Cureton and Hessey put the time about the middle of the second century; but they are doubtless in error as to the conquest of Arabia by the Romans to which Bardesanes refers as then recent. There were three such wars; one waged by Avidius Cassius, about A. D. 162-5; another by Septtimius Severus in A. D. 195-6, and the third

---

[1] Ant. Nic. Lib., Vol. xii. pp. 284, 285.

[2] Hist. Sab., p. 219.

[3] Ant. Nic. Lib., Vol. xii. p. 461.

by Macrinus, A. D. 217-18.[1] The second was the greatest, and probably the one referred to by Bardesanes. He discourses first of the Jewish Sabbath observance, and then says: "Wherever we be, all of us are called by the one name of the Messiah—Christians; and upon one day, which is the first of the week, we assemble ourselves together, and on the appointed days we abstain from food."[2] This evidence is indisputable.

Tertullian, reputed to have been converted to Christianity A. D. 185, speaks of "the sacred rites of the Lord's day in the church,"[3] distinctly implying that there was such a day, and that it was religiously observed. In one place he says: "We count fasting or kneeling in worship on the Lord's day to be unlawful ";[4] and in another: "We, however (just as we have received), only on the day of the Lord's resurrection ought to guard not only against kneeling," etc.[5] The two passages together show that by the Lord's day he meant the day of Christ's resurrection, and that day they kept joyfully, and not with fasting and other austerities; and the latter passage shows that they had received directions in regard to observing the Lord's day from those who had gone before them. In two passages he repels the charge of opposers that the Christians worshipped the sun; in one, saying: "We devote Sunday to rejoicing from a far different reason than sun-worship ";[6] and in the other, charging upon the pagans the naming of the

[1] Smith's Dic. Biog., Vol. i. p. 257.
[2] Spicilegium Syriacum, p. 32.
[3] Ant. Nic. Lib., Vol. xv. p. 428.   [4] Ibid., Vol. xi. p. 336.
[5] Ibid., p. 199.   [6] Ibid., p. 85.   [7] Ibid., pp. 449, 450.

first day of the week by the term Sunday, he says: "It is you, at all events, who have even admitted the sun into the calendar of the week."[7] In connection with this last passage he says: "We make Sunday a day of festivity," by which he meant religious joy, not secular festivity. In his essay on idolatry he speaks of the Christians as having "a festive day every eighth day," and of that as the Lord's day.[1] In his discourse on prayer he speaks of what is appropriate "on the day of the Lord's resurrection," and says, "Deferring even our business, lest we give any place to the devil"[2]; by which he implies that business on the Lord's day ought to be and was suspended. Neander regards this passage as "indicative of the transfer of the law of the Jewish Sabbath to Sunday," and of Tertullian's belief that attending to any business on Sunday is sinful.[3] Notice that in respect to some part of the keeping of the Lord's day Tertullian speaks of having received instruction from those who had gone before. Probably he had also in respect to omitting business. Mr. Andrews, the seventh=day Sabbatarian, implies that Tertullian uses the term "Lord's day" in only three instances of any moment.[4] We have given five, including two where it is called by the more explicit phrase "the day of the Lord's resurrection"; and seven, including two more where the term "Sunday" is used as equivalent to Lord's day. Another seventh=day author,[5] claiming Neander for authority, professedly quotes from him (Rose's translation): "The festival of Sun-

[1] Ant. Nic. Lib., Vol. xi. pp. 162, 163.   [2] Ibid., p. 199.
[3] Church History, Vol. i. pp. 295, 296.   [4] Hist. Sab., p. 222.
[5] W. H. Fahnestock, M. D. "Bible Sabbath."

day, like all other festivals, *was always only a human ordinance;* and it was far from the intention of the apostles to establish a divine command in this respect." If any such language ever escaped from Neander's pen, the seventh-day writers ought not to be allowed now to suppose that any such idea as it conveys was that historian's latest testimony. On the contrary, in the records which had his seal at his death, he cites Acts xx. 7 and Rev. i. 10 as apostolic intimations of a change among the early Christians from the seventh to the first day of the week; which latter, following the apostle John, he terms the "Lord's day." He also cites Barnabas and Ignatius, whom we have already quoted, as giving evidence to the same fact of change. He held, further, that the early churches "composed of Jewish Christians, though they admitted with the rest the festival of Sunday, yet retained also that of the Sabbath."[1] We have, then, Neander's sanction to our main deduction from not only Tertullian's testimony, but from that of Barnabas and Ignatius also.

It is certain that Tertullian used the names "Lord's day" and "Sunday" as equivalent. Undoubtedly, then, Justin by the word Sunday meant Lord's day; and Dionysius by Lord's day meant Sunday; and Melito, Irenaeus, Clement, and others before and after, used these names interchangeably. Seventh day Sabbatarian authors have positively declared that there is no early evidence that the term "Lord's day" meant the first day. But when we find from the distinguished Tertullian that they did in his time mean the same, and find no evidence of any other usage, we

[1] Church History, Vol. i. (Torrey's translation), pp. 295, 296.

may well conclude that the apostle John by the term "Lord's day" meant the first day of the week, which commemorated our Lord's resurrection, and that the meaning which he gave was ever after continued. So, also, we may well conclude that the sacredness ascribed to the Lord's day by Tertullian had from the first been known in the Christian church. Much evidence tends to that conclusion; no real evidence tends to the contrary. Shall we find this view corroborated by testimonies of later dates?

Minucius Felix, author of Octavius, about A. D. 166 or 198, said of the Christians, "On a solemn day they assemble at the feast."[1] The speaker in the dialogue from which this is taken refers to the Lord's day and supper. The character of the latter he misrepresents; but that does not weaken this evidence of the day's observance.

We have reviewed, up to this point, the first century after the apostle John's death, and we find in that time thirteen thoroughly credible witnesses concurring in the fact that the Christians of that era regarded and observed the first or Lord's day as the *chief* of all days; and we find no contemporay testimony to the contrary.

Cyprian, raised to the rank of presbyter A. D. 247,—one of the martyrs in Africa,—speaks of the Lord's day as sacred", and as at once the first and the eighth; and, by a play upon the ordinal, he recalls the fact of "the observance of the *eighth* day in the Jewish circumcision of the flesh."[2]

Origen, in his Commentary on Exodus, says the

[1] Ant. Nic. Lib., Vol. xiii. p. 464.
[2] Ant. Nic. Lib., Vol. viii. p. 198.

Lord's day is superior to the Jewish Sabbath;[1] and in his noted work against Celsus, the epicurean philosopher (A. D. 244-249), he acknowledges that he kept the Lord's day, and says, " The perfect Christian . . . is always keeping the Lord's day."[2] Origen was one of the most learned men of his time and must have known the views of the earlier Fathers; and had he disagreed with them and their fellow Christians respecting the Lord's day, it would somewhere appear.

Anatolius, bishop of Laodicea, A. D. 270, whom Eusebius ranks as superior to all of his time in science and learning,[3] in his Paschal Canon, speaks of the Lord's day by name at least ten different times. He says the Lord's resurrection took place upon it, and that "on the Lord's day was it that light was shown to us in the beginning, and now also in the end the comforts of all present and the tokens of all future blessings."[4]

Victorinus, martyr, bishop of Petabio, A. D. 270-290, speaks of the Lord's day as one of joy and thanksgiving.[5]

The Apostolic Constitutions, attributed to Clement of Rome, for the most part dating at least between A. D. 150 and 350, placed by Bunsen in the second or third century, and certainly referred to by Epiphanius, who died A. D. 402,—contains this: "On the day of the resurrection of the Lord, that is, the Lord's

---

[1] Patrologiae, Tom. xii. p. 345.
[2] Ant. Nic. Lib., Vol xxiii. p. 509.
[3] Eccl. Hist., Bk vii. chap. 32.
[4] Ant. Nic. Lib., Vol. xiv. pp. 420, 425.
[5] Ibid., Vol. xviii. p. 390.

day, assemble yourselves together, without fail, giving thanks to God, and praising him for those mercies God has bestowed upon you through Christ."[1]

Peter, a martyr and a bishop of Alexandria, A. D. 306, in a sermon on penitence said: "The Lord's day we celebrate as a day of joy, because on it He rose again; on which day we have received it for a custom not even to bow the knee. . . . On the Lord's day we ought not to fast, for it is a day of joy for the resurrection of our Lord."[2]

Eusebius, bishop of Cæsarea A. D. 315 (dying previous to 340), besides stating that Irenæus (bishop of Lyons A. D. 178) wrote an epistle on celebrating the mystery of Christ's resurrection on the day of the Lord only,[3] states twice that Constantine appointed the first and chief of all days, the day of the Lord, for prayer,[4]—not, however, that he originated it,—and says that he commanded all to assemble on the Lord's day for refreshment to the body, and for comfort and invigoration to the soul by divine precepts.[5] In his commentary on the ninety-second Psalm Eusebius speaks of the "saving Lord's day . . . in which the Savior of the world . . . obtained the victory over death."[6] Constantine's edict concerning the Lord's day, A. D. 321, would never have been issued, if previously the day had not long been observed by the Christians.

[1] Ant. Nic. Lib., Vol. xvii. p. 189.
[2] Ibid., Vol. xiv. p. 322.
[3] Eccl. Hist., Bk. v. Chap. xxiv. p. 239.
[4] Life Const., Bk. iv. chap. xviii. p. 189; Orat. Praise Const., chap. ix. p. 828.
[5] Ibid., chap. xvii. p. 378.
[6] Patrologiæ Græcæ, Tom. xxiii. p. 1170.

The Nicene Council, A. D. 325, assumed the existence and the customary observance by the Christians of the Lord's day, in their decision that as a rule prayer on that day should be offered standing, and not kneeling,[1] and that Easter should be celebrated on that day.[2]

Athanasius, bishop of Alexandria, A. D. 326, recognizes the Lord's day so much as to suppose that in the phrase "upon Sheminith,"—upon the *eighth*,—in the title of the sixth Psalm, there is a reference to that day;[3] and as to say, in comments on the phrase "This is the day which the Lord hath made," in Ps. cxvii. 24 (cxviii. our version), "The phrase signifies the resurrection day of our Savior, which is named from him, to-wit, the Lord's day." Elsewhere he speaks of the persecutions suffered by the Christians while they were at prayer on the Lord's day.[4]

Epiphanius, bishop of Constantia in Cyprus, A. D. 367, a man of extensive reading, speaks of the Lord's day *as established by the apostles;*[5] and if in his time that were not a conceded fact, we should probably find it contradicted.

Basil, bishop of Cæsarea, A. D. 370, exalts the day on which Christ arose and believers rose with him.[6]

Gregory, bishop of Nyssa, A. D. 372, magnifies the Lord's day as *the* day the Lord hath made, and as

[1] Christian Councils, Hefele, p. 434.
[2] Canon xx of Counc; Schaff's Hist. Ch, p. 376; also Ch. Hist., Vol. ii. p. 383.
[3] Opera, Tom. i. folio, Pars ii. p. 1014.
[4] Lib. of Fafh.,Hist. Tracts, p. 195.
[5] Opera, folio, Tom. i. p. 1104: chap. xxii. Exp. Eid. Cathol.
[6] Opera, (Paris ed.), Tom. ii. p. 123.

commemorating Christ's resurrection and the begining of creation.[1]

Ambrose, bishop of Milan, A. D. 374, speaks often of the Lord's day, implying that it was the day of His resurrection.[2]

Jerome, ordained presbyter A. D. 379, speaks often of the Lord's day, of its sacredness to Christians, of church attendance upon it, and of its distinction from Jewish sacred days.[3]

Gregory of Nazianzus, made bishop of Constantinople A. D. 380, refers often to the Lord's day and to the memory of his resurrection.[4]

Theophilus, bishop of Alexandria, A. D. 385, discourses of the Christians as honoring the Lord's day because of the blessing of his resurrection,[5]

Gaudentius, bishop of Brescia, A. D. 387, calls the first the Lord's day, and identifies it as that of His resurrection; and of the beginning of creation.[6]

Augustine, ordained bishop of Hippo A. D. 395, expresses his view of the Lord's day by saying to Faustus the Manichaean, "What you call Sunday, we call the Lord's day; and on it we do not worship the sun, but commemorate the Lord's resurrection."[7]

Chrysostom, elected archbishop of Constantinople A. D. 397, speaking of the Lord's day, says, " All the unutterable blessings, and that which is the root and

---

[1] In Christ, Res., Opera, fol. Colon. Agrip. p. 454.
[2] Opera, fol. Tom. ii. p. 883, C. Epist.
[3] Opera, Tom. iv. p. 272, in Epist. Gal. iv.10.
[4] Comm. Opera, fol. Tom. ii. p. 1094; Orat. xli.
[5] Biblioth. Veterum Patrnm, Vol. v. p. 860.
[6] Biblioth. Vererum Patrum, p. 945, De Paschæ, Tract i.
[7] Manichean Heresy (Edinburgh ed.), p. 324.

the beginning of our life, took place on this day.'[1]

Cyril, made bishop of Alexandria A. D. 412, in discoursing on the purposes of the Sabbath of the old dispensation, assumes often that the Lord's day is to be honored.[2]

Theodoret, made bishop of Cyrus A. D. 420 or 423, speaks of the Jews as observing the Sabbath, and of the Christians as keeping sacred the Lord's day.[3]

Socrates, the historian who flourished about A. D. 420, speaks of the Lord's day and of the Sabbath as occurring weekly.[4]

Sozomen, also an historian, and contemporary with Socrates, speaks of the Lord's day as that which the Jews called the first day of the week, and of Constantine's honoring the day because on it Christ arose from the dead.[5] His language implies that it was not made the Lord's day by Constantine, but that it was such before his edict.

Sedulius, presbyter and poet, who flourished about A. D. 450, in his Paschal Song, gives high honor to the Lord's day.[6]

Leo the Great, bishop of Rome A. D. 440-461, speaks of the day of our Lord's resurrection as sacred, and gives a summary of the reasons that make it so conspicuous.[7]

[1] Homil. 1 Cor. xvi. 2, Lib. Fathers (Oxford ed.), p. 606.
[2] De Adorat. in Spir. et Verit., Opera, fol., Vol. i. pp. 619, 620; de Fest. Paschal., Tom. vi. p. 82.
[3] De Fabulis Haer., Tom. iv. p. 219.
[4] Greek Eccl. Hist., Vol. iii. p. 436, Bk. vi. chap. viii.
[5] Ibid., Vol. iv. p. 16, Bk. 1. chap. viii.
[6] Biblioth. Vet. Patr., Tom. vi. p. 470, H. Lib. iv.
[7] Schaff's Hist. Christ. Church, Vol. ii. p. 385; Leon Epist. ix. ad Dioscurum Alex. Episc., chap. 1.

The Coucil of Eliberis, or Elvira (Hefele), A. D. 305 or 306, threatened with church suspension any one, living in town or city, who should absent himself from church three Lord's days.[1]

The Council of Laodicea, A. D. 363, voted that Christians should rest from labor on the Lord's day if they were able;[2] seeming to imply, as Dr. Heurtley suggests, that some of them had not always the command of their own time.[3]

The Council of Antioch, A. D. 340, ordained that refusal to partake of the communion, which was observed each Lord's day, should be visited with excommunication.[4]

The Council of Sardica, A. D. 347, adopted the action of the Council of Eliberis.[5]

The Council of Gangra, about the middle of the fourth century, condemned those who contemned the house of God.[6]

The First Council of Toledo, A. D. 400, decreed that those who refused to partake of the communion which was observed each Lord's day, should be excommunicated.[7]

The Fourth Council of Carthage, A. D. 436, added to the foregoing that if one left the church while the minister was preaching he should be anathematized.[8]

---

[1] Conc. Elib. Canon xxi. Labbi, Tom. ii. col. 9, p. 376.
[2] Conc. Laod. Canon xxix. Labbi, Tom. ii. col. 570; Neander's Church Hist., Vol. ii. p. 300.
[3] Hessey, Sunday, p. 316.
[4] Conc. Antioch, Canon ii. Labbi, Tom. ii. col. 1309.
[5] Conc. Sardica, Canon xi. Labbi, Tom. iii. col. 20.
[6] Conc. Gangra, Canon v. Labbi, Tom. ii. col. 1101.
[7] Conc. Toledo, i. Canon xiii. Labbi, Tom. iii. col. 1000.
[8] Conc. Carthag. iv. Canon xxiv. Labbi, Tom. iii. col. 953.

TESTIMONY OF THE EARLY FATHERS

In the case of each Council there is indicated a previous knowledge of the Lord's day and the church services on that day.

When Christianity came to assume control of *national* affairs, civil action was often taken in favor of the Lord's day. Constantine, A. D. 321, commanded the general observance of the Lord's day; granting to Christians leisure for religious services, and enjoining upon pagan soldiers prayer to God on that day;[1] also ordering the suspension of suits and courts of justice, yet granting civil action, on Sunday, for the emancipation of slaves.[2] Under Valentinian and Valens, A. D. 368, a law was enacted forbidding the exaction of taxes and collection of other dues on Sunday.[3] Theodosius I., A. D. 379 and 386, forbade civil proceedings and pagan spectacles or theatrical performances; and the latter Theodosius II. forbade, A. D. 425.[4] Leo and Anthemius, A. D. 469, forbade other secular amusements, and granted to Christians other immunities from civil annoyances and proceedings on the Lord's day.[5]

Such is the course of history through about four centuries succeeding the death of most of the apostles. From beginning to end it shows an unbroken chain of evidence that the Christians sacredly observed the Lord's day. No testimony to the con-

---

[1] Life Const., Bk. iv. chaps. 18, 19.

[2] Neander's Ch. Hist., Vol. ii. p. 300.

[3] Schaff's Church Hist., Vol ii. p. 381; Hessey, Sunday, pp. 83, 84.

[4] Ibid., also Robertson's Church Hist., Vol. i. p. 248; Hessey, Sunday, p. 83.

[5] Cod. Theod. xv. 5, 2, a 386; Hessey, Sunday, pp. 83, 84.

trary, or reference to it, anywhere appears. The proofs are doubled, and often more than quadrupled, all along the line; the earlier life of some witnesses continually overlapping the later of others. The seed of testimony, which we discover in the apostolic and earlier patristic days, develops into the lofty tree with wide-spreading branches after a few centuries have passed by. This universal observance of the Lord's day among the early Christians is proof that they regarded such observance an obligation as well as privilege, and that they believed the obligation had been imposed by divine authority. Such belief on the part of the apostles was equal to inspiration. Suppose the pilgrims had crossed the Atlantic to Plymouth Rock in the ship Neptune, and not in the Mayflower. Could subsequent history, through four hundred years, possibly state, repeat, and reiterate that they came in the Mayflower, with not the least dispute, or even allusion, to the contrary? Impossible! Suppose the Lord's day were *not* sacred and chief with the apostles and early Christians, could all subsequent history, through four centuries, represent and reiterate that it was sacred and chief, with no statement to the contrary? Equally impossible!

Objection: First-day authors rely on the phrase *Dominicum Servasti?* "Hast thou kept the Lord's day?" as a genuine question, put by the persecutors to the Christians in the primitive era, and as therefore showing that the first day was then kept sacred. We deny its genuineness, and the validity of the inference from it.[1] *Reply:* So far as appears to the present writer this objection is well founded. And

[1] Andrews, Hist. Sab., chap. xv.

the phrase in question has been so often adduced in the first-day argument as to justify calling attention to its probable lack of authority. Dr. Justin Edwards,[1] Gurney, the English author,[2] President Appleton of Bowdoin college,[3] Rev. A. A. Phelps,[4] Henry Wilkinson,[5] Gilfillan,[6] and the recently issued volume, "Sabbath Essays,"[7] all quote this language as reliable. In the ancient Christian writings *Dominicum* sometimes stands for Lord's supper, and for Lord's day and Lord's house; the word for supper, day, and house being understood, and inferable from the connection. McClintock and Strong cite a passage from Cyprian where they say *Dominicum* means both Lord's supper and Lord's house in the same paragraph.[8] But their translation would not be accepted by many, is certainly not necessitated, and is contrary to that given by the Ante Nicene Library, which renders the word "Lord's supper" in both instances.[9] The sufferings of many early Christians led to a volume entitled " *Acta Martyrum,*" of which there have been several editions, Ruinart's being apparently the most valuable, and in it the word *Dominicum* often occurs. But, so far as we learn, no one has found it there joined to the word *servasti* with *diem* either

[1] Sabbath Manual, p. 120.
[2] Hist. Authen., and Use, Sab., pp. 87, 88.
[3] Works, Vol. ii. p. 219.
[4] Perpet. Sab. 141.
[5] Formerly Principal Magdalen Hall, Oxford, quoted by Pres. Appleton.
[6] The Sabbath, p. 7.
[7] Sabbath Essays, p. 249.
[8] Bib. Theo. Eccl. Cyc., Vol. ii. p. 859.
[9] Ant. Nic. Lib., Vol. xiii. p. 11.

expressed or understood. Bishop Andrewes, of Winchester, born A. D. 1555, seems to have first given this quotation from the *Acta Martyrum*, and he gave it erroneously, probably by some mistake of memory or copying. From him the error, if it be such, has come down through centuries, no first=day Sabbatarian author taking pains to verify the quotation, or to attempt it. But no dependence need be placed on the dialogue introduced by the question, *Dominicum servasti?* The verified quotations from the Fathers are of themselves sufficient to show that the early Christians observed the first day of the week as the most sacred of the seven.

We now consider:

Thirdly, how the *seventh* day was regarded by the Christians during the three centuries next succeeding the apostles. If we find evidence that it was as strictly observed by them, as by themselves and their fathers before the new dispensation commenced, then we must conclude that the primitive Christians kept equally sacred two days in the week, and that the Lord's day was not intended to take the place of the seventh=day Sabbath.

After the destruction of Jerusalem, at least, the Christians began to omit more than ever the observance of the seventh day, and to regard it as no longer binding. The temple destroyed, the sacrifices having ceased, the holy place no more,—then, if not before, began to dawn upon the common Christian mind the fact that the Jewish economy was abrogated, and that Judaic rites and ceremonies were no longer required by the Lord. Yielding the seventh day was one of the last steps in breaking off from the old order of things, and Judaizing Christians continued long to observe both the seventh day and the first. But as might have been expected, the observance of the two days by Christians in general was not permanently practiced. The earlier Gentile Christians embraced their new faith in connection with worship in Jewish synagogues; and therefore, probably, with the Jews, more or less observed the seventh day for a season. But we know not when the observance of the first day of the week was commenced, unless as early as the day of pentecost, or earlier. And doubtless quite early many Gentiles and many Jewish Christians began to avail themselves of the apostolic privilege of omitting the strict religious observance of the seventh day—a privilege embraced in such sayings as that of Paul: "Let no man therefore judge you . . . in respect of . . . the sabbath-days" (Col. ii. 16).

Yet the historical part of the New Testament is too early to give much light respecting the omission to keep the seventh day sacred. Appeal must be made again to the early fathers, whose views doubtless were directly, in some cases, in most indirectly, received from the apostles. Here we are at issue with the Sabbatarians, who advocate the seventh day as still the Sabbath. They contend that the fathers of the second century at least did not sanction the neglect to keep holy the seventh day. We maintain that while they did not deem it sinful to keep both days, and regarded it as impossible for a Christian to neglect the first day, they strenuously opposed binding the consciences of believers to the observance of the seventh.

Ignatius, contempory of the apostle John, by the shorter recension, speaks of Christians as "no longer observing the sabbath "—seventh day; and, by the longer recension, exhorts to the spiritual observance of the seventh, but deprecates the " Jewish " formal method.[1] The epistle of Barnabas, while commending the eighth (first) day, speaks of the Lord as abolishing Jewish sacrifices, new moons, and Sabbaths;[2] and as saying, " Your present Sabbaths are not acceptable to me."[3] Justin Martyr implies that the Christians did not feel obligated to keep the seventh day, by saying " We, too, would observe the fleshly circumcision, and the Sabbaths, and, in short, all the feasts, if we did not know for what reason they were enjoined you." Also, " How is it, Trypho, that we would not observe those rites which do not harm us,—I speak of fleshly circumcisions, and Sabbaths, and feasts."[4] Irenaeus treating of symbolic signs, says that sacrifices suggested the " true sacrifice," " circumcision after the flesh typified that after the spirit," and " Sabbaths taught that we should continue day by day in God's service," implying that all these had passed away.[5] Be it observed that the fathers did not regard the seventh-day Sabbath as the whole of the fourth commandment. Not once can we find in their writings the statement that the fourth commandment is abolished. But we do find there the strongest affirmations that the decalogue is unrepealed and yet in force, and even also that the fourth commandment is not abolished. Those specific testimonies we consider hereafter.

[1] Ant. Nic. Lib; Vol. i. p. 150.
[2] Ibid; p. 103.
[3] Ibid; p. 128.
[4] Ibid; Vol. ii p. 109.
[5] Ant. Nic. Lib; Vol. v. pp. 427, 422.

Tertullian, exhorting Christians not to mingle in heathen festivals, since they would not in the Jewish, says, "By us, to whom Sabbaths are strange, and the new moons, and festivals formerly beloved of God."[1] More explicitly he says, "The observance of the Sabbath is being demonstrated to have been temporary."[2] Bardesanes contrasts the observance of the seventh day by the Jews with that of the first by the Christians, implying that the latter did not regard the seventh as sacred.[3] Origen gives a list of the sacred days he was accustomed to observe, without including the Sabbath,[4] and speaks of the Lord of the Sabbath as having changed it.[5] Victorinus says, "Lest we should appear to observe any Sabbath with the Jews, which Christ himself, the Lord of the Sabbath, says by his prophets that his soul hateth, which Sabbath he in his body abolished."[6] Anatolius, A. D. 270, speaks often of the Lord's day and its celebration, but not of the seventh as having any honor in comparison with the first.[7] Eusebius speaks of the Sabbath, meaning the seventh day, as a Mosaic institution, and of the Lord's day as "more honorable than the Jewish Sabbath."[8] Athanasius speaks emphatically of the Sabbath, seventh day, as having passed.[9] Cyril, archbishop of Jerusalem, elected presbyter A. D.

[1] Ibid, Vol. xi. p. 162.
[2] Ibid, xviii. p. 211.
[3] Spicilegium, Syriacum. pp. 31, 32.
[4] Ant. Nic. Lib., Vol. xxiii. p. 509.
[5] Com. in Matt. Opera, Tom. iii. 543 E.
[6] Ant. Nic. Lib., Vol. xviii. p. 390.
[7] Ibid., xiv. p. 425.
[8] Comm. on Ps. xcii.
[9] De Sab. et Cir. Opera, Tom. ii. fol. p. 55.

345, says, "Nor throw thyself into the assemblies of the heathen spectacles . . . . And fall not into Judaism . . . Abstain from all observance of Sabbaths, and from calling any indifferent meat common or unclean."[1] Hilary, elected bishop of Poitiers, about A. D. 350, speaks of the first day as much superior to the seventh, and as the one observed by Christians.[2] Epiphanius speaks of the great Sabbath, rest, in Christ, to which the smaller or original one was introductory.[3] Ambrose speaks of the Lord's day as preferred over other divine works,[4] and of the Sabbath, seventh day, as secondary to it.[5] Gregory of Nyssa speaks of the Sabbath, seventh day, as though it pertained to the former Jewish institutions.[6] Jerome, contrasting Jewish with Christian institutions, places the Sabbath with the former.[7] Augustine says, "The rest of the Sabbath we consider no longer binding as an observance."[8]

Thus we find a stream of evidence adverse to the observance of the seventh-day Sabbath among Christians, running through three centuries, and having its source among the Fathers nearest the apostles, and among the apostles themselves. Paul condemns binding the conscience to Sabbaths; Ignatius says, Christians no longer observe that day as chief, but the Lord's day; and. three centuries after, Augustine says, Christians

[1] Lib. of Fathers, Cyril, p. 51; Lec. iv. sec. 37.
[2] Prol. in Lib. Psal. Opera, col. 8.
[3] Adv. Haer. Opera, fol. Tom. i. p. 159.
[4] Enarratio in Ps. xliii. Opera, Tom. i. col. 887 E.
[5] Enar. in Ps. xlvii. Opera, Tom. i. col. 936. D.
[6] In Chris. Resur., Opera, fol. p. 456.
[7] Expl. Ps. cxviii.; Hessey., Sun., p. 306.
[8] Reply to Faustus, Bk. vi. sec. 4. p. 172.

consider Sabbath-keeping no longer binding. But note should be taken that when the Fathers taught that the seventh day need not be observed, they also taught that the first should be observed; that when the seventh lost its sacredness, the first received a sacredness in the universal Christian esteem. Nearly every patristic writer who teaches that it is not a duty to observe the seventh day teaches equally that it is the duty, or practice, of Christians to observe the Lord's day. The two days were not observed in exactly the same manner. Sunday had nothing of the sacrifices, or shew-bread, or fasts of the seventh day; and it had the Lord's supper, and rejoicing over Christ's resurrection, and its glorious assurances, which the seventh day had only in symbols. Yet, both days had convocations, Scripture reading, praise, prayer, and omission of the usual secular duties; as though the Lord's day had absorbed all the moral elements of the original Sabbath, and left the positive, to most of which the Judaizers still clung with much tenacity. This reveiw of the patristic writings confirms the testimony and impressions given by the New Testament in various respects. It shows that the first day of the week was celebrated by the apostles and early Christians in commemoration of Christ's resurrection; that it was the distinctive Christian day for sacred regard; that the chief and regular Christian assemblies were held upon it; that no evidence appears in the patristic writings, as none does in the New Testament, of Christians assembling as such on the seventh day, as the chief of all days; that the early fathers certainly used the term "Lord's day" as synonymous with "first day," and doubtless in imitation of the apostle John's language; that according to apostolic authority, Christians are released from the obligation to observe the seventh day, and are bound to observe the first; that the statement of Roman Catholic writers that Protestants are indebted to that church for authority to keep the Lord's day[1] is unfounded, since we trace the observance to the apostles; and that we ought to accept inspired example and instruction, though without express command, as authority for change of observance from the seventh to the first day, or else, in consistency, continue sacrifices, circumcision, and the passover, since they are revoked in the new dispensation by example and instruction rather than by command. The testimony of the fathers is utterly irreconcilable with any theory of New Testament teaching on this subject, except that the apostles and contemporary Christians regarded the first day of the week as the chief of all days, held on it their chief religious services, and believed it to be sacred.

And according to this showing from Scripture and the early patristic writings, those who observe the seventh day as now the chief day in the week, to be carefully kept sacred, have no basis for their peculiar theory and practice. It follows that the reason for their increase of numbers during these later years has been the misinformation on this subject disseminated by their publications and living teachers. We have shown from the Scriptures that the apostles and early Christians observed the first or Lord's day as chief and sacred. We have commenced with the fathers contemporary with and immediately succeed-

[1] Bib. Sac., Vol. xxxvi. p. 731.

ing the last of the apostles, and traced their testimony through the next succeeding four centuries. And we find in that space a long line of nearly fifty human witnesses, whose united testimony concentrates upon this, that the religious observance of the Lord's day was begun in the days of the apostles, and under their sanction. There arises no one note of dissonance in the whole troop of men, nor anywhere around them. This would not and could not be true unless our main proposition were true, that the Lord's day in all that time were first and chief. Nor is there simply a single utterance from each of these many witnesses, but some seventy-five different passages give their concurrent voice, and still more could be cited. And yet, in this long lapse of nearly fifteen hundred years, the writings of these fifty men have nearly all perished. And in the three centuries next succeeding the apostle John we have found and named nearly twenty men who directly, or indirectly, testify that in all that time the seventh-day Sabbath took a quite inferior place, at least in the Christian heart, as compared with the Lord's day. And their number, and the number of their testimonies, could both be much increased. This concurrent testimony respecting the first and seventh days is just what might be expected. The Lord's day coming forward to the chief place, the seventh day would retire to a quite inferior one. And yet all this is proved to be the fruit of apostolic instruction and example, and therefore the result of the word and act of Jesus Christ, who by it all is the more glorified.

In view of the facts ascertained or collected in this discussion, we see no occasion for any first day Sabbatarians to "confess to a consciousness of obscurity" in regard to the "authoritative change" from the seventh to the Lord's day, whether the latter be strictly a Sabbath or not; nor even for any to affirm that the change is a "difficult point to establish."[1] We have not precisely mathematical demonstration for the change, but we have the highest probabilities that our Lord in some way has given the first day of the week to be kept sacred in the new dispensation. And on the highest probabilities in all moral questions men are at liberty, and are bound, to believe and to act.

For equally strong, or stronger, reasons there is no real basis for what Dr. Hessey calls the "ecclesiastical theory" respecting the Lord's day:[2] the view that the sacred observance of the first day has no authority except in the history of the church since the apostolic era. For we obtain New Testament evidence that in the apostles' time the first day was religiously observed, and the obligations to keep holy the seventh day were cancelled. Further, we get evidence from the fathers, beginning with those contemporary with the last of the apostles, that they understood the apostles to authorize the keeping of the first day sacred, and to release from keeping the seventh as the Sabbath, and that the apostles authoritatively acted in this under instruction from their divine Master.

And again, according to this discussion, the view of some even American evangelical ministers, that the early Christians were disagreed on the question of keeping the first day in a religious manner, is entirely

[1] Sabbath Essays; Mass. Sab. Conventions, p. 149.
[2] Sunday, pp. 8, 132.

wrong. Not the least evidence of such disagreement appears in the New Testament, and positive evidence of agreement on that point appears in the patristic writings. Some early Christians held to more obligation to keep the seventh day than others did, but all agreed in the obligation to keep the first day.

CHAPTER IX.

THE EARLY FATHERS ON THE CEREMONIAL AND MORAL LAWS.

Having shown from the apostolic and succeeding fathers of the primitive era that the Christians of their time kept sacred the first day of the week, and did not regard the seventh day as binding for holy observance, we come to a third and more difficult question: Did the early fathers teach that setting aside the seventh day involves, in form or in substance, the abrogation of the fourth commandment? Two parties in opinion here come distinctly before us. One party is made up of two divisions, of which one says that the fourth commandment is in form abolished; that the Scriptures so teach, and the fathers also. The other division, not going so far, says that the early fathers did not found the observance of the first day on the fourth commandment, and we cannot; and that in substance that command is not in force, except analogically by its principle;—there was a sacred seventh day in the old dispensation, and there is another in the new. The second party holds that we properly *can* base the observance of the Lord's day on the fourth commandment; but are disposed to confess that we have to do it despite the views and testimony of the early fathers. They in consequence claim that the patristical writings on this subject are not trustworthy, since they stand adverse, as they think, to the doctrine of the Christian Sabbath as depending on the fourth command. They confess, even many of the most intelligent men on the Sabbath question confess, that in this one respect of patristical evidence, the cause of a sacred Sabbath is weak. The two parties understand the fathers alike in this respect, as wholly rejecting any sacred day based on the fourth commandment. But, while one party so understands them to the detriment of the command, the other understands them to the detriment of the fathers themselves. We do not fully agree with either party, but believe that the true apprehension of the language of the father's casts no detriment on either themselves or the command, *and is entirely consistent with a Christian Sabbath founded on both the command and the teaching and example of the apostles, which is the teaching of Jesus Christ.*

Dr. Hessey says, " The early church never appealed to the fourth commandment as a ground for observing Sunday."[1] Again, he says that none of the " early fathers " " refer to the fourth commandment, or to God's rest after the creation, for the sanction of the Lord's day."[2] Dr. Hopkins, of Auburn Theological Seminary, says, "neither Christ nor his apostles, nor the primitive fathers taught that the fourth commandment was of moral and permanent obligation."[3] In the volume, entitled " Sabbath Essays," of the Massachusetts Sabbath Conventions,

---
[1] Sunday, p. 203.
[2] Ibid., pp. 53, 54.
[3] Pittsburgh Evangelical Alliance Address.

Prof. E. C. Smyth, D. D., of Andover, says: "Paul, I think, we must believe, gave his pagan converts no command to keep the first day of the week as a sabbath of the law. Nor is it put in any such relation, so far as I am aware, by any teacher of the Christian church in the early centuries."[1] *Reply:* These statements, even though wholly true, are only negatives. Any number of these would fail to equal one positive. These authors do not affirm that the early fathers declared the fourth commandment abolished, yet they lean towards that conclusion. They imply, at least the first two authors imply, that since the fathers did not undertake to found the Christian Sabbath on the fourth commandment, we may not. But that conclusion we think is not warranted. The fathers may not have brought this precise point under their investigation, except a few of them in isolated instances. Their circumstances may not have led them to do so. They may not have known as much on this particular question as we ought to know. The author of the article in "Sabbath Essays" just referred to, wisely says of the fathers: "We are in a better position than were they to see the true relations of the new economy to the old."[2] In consequence of this truth we claim that we may base the observance of the Lord's day on the fourth commandment, though the Christian teachers of the early centuries did not. We expect to show that it would have been unnatural for them to do so, though natural for us.

But some go farther, and say that the fathers

[1] Sabbath Essays, p. 227.
[2] Sabbath Essays, p. 230.

taught that the fourth commandment is actually abolished. Dr. Hopkins says: "The universal sentiment of the early Christian church was that the fourth commandment had been abrogated as a law, together with the rest of the Jewish ritual to which it belonged."[1] From this we dissent, and expect to prove it to be an error. We therefore attempt to show:

The early fathers, in rejecting the seventh-day sabbath of their time did not discard the moral elements or the original Sabbath, nor the septenary proportional positive element, but only the septenary *ordinal* positive time element.[2] That is, their question of debate was, whether the seventh day or the first should be kept sacred. Yet, not so much whether the first should be, for that was in general assumed and declared, but whether the seventh was still binding. Now, it were possible for them to have that simple question in mind,—what really pertained to the ordinal time element,—without at the same time discussing whether one tenth part of the decalogue was abolished. They might even, in appealing or referring to the fourth commandment, do so merely to show that it did not require unalterable observance of the seventh day; that God was not inconsistent with himself in causing the seventh day to be set aside and the first to be kept; that the sacredness of the seventh day was not such that it could not be cancelled. They might discuss that question without discussing whether the whole fourth commandment in its entire length and breadth were abrogated; and that we claim was the phase of the discussion.

[1] Pittsburgh Address.
[2] See Bib. Sac., Vol. xxxvii. pp. 164, 430, 431, 434, 435.

Had they contended that the fourth commandment was abolished they would have had far more opposition than they did, and the discussions preserved to us, and even the mere allusions to the subject would show it. The Christians of that age, holding to the sacredness of the Old Testament as they did, could not have maintained themselves against the Jews and Judaizing Christians if they had been understood to hold and teach that one-tenth part of the decalogue was stricken out.

But many of the allusions to this subject by the early fathers occur in their addresses to pagan rulers and philosophers, in which they speak of the Christian custom and rule of keeping Sunday as the Lord's day. And in all that was said to *them* there was no occasion to involve more than the ordinal time element. They had with the pagans no reason to go farther back for their authority than to the apostles and Christ. And that same authority, so near at hand, and so thoroughly accepted by even all Judaizing Christians, was their all-sufficient appeal. Jesus had risen from the dead; thenceforth the day was sacred; that was enough; there was no occasion in their minds to get authority from the decalogue. Hence, their references to the fourth commandment were in rebutting objections, and were generally or always to this point—the obligation to keep the seventh day can be remitted. And that simple question touches only the *ordinal* time element, and does not involve the question whether what God gave as his law on Mount Sinai, written in tables of stone, were in one tenth part effaced. With us it is quite different. The early fathers looked back only a few years for their authority. One or more of them had touched the hands of an apostle; with others there was only one between themselves and him. But we at the best must look back nearly two thousand years. Looking thus more than half way to Sinai, our minds inevitably demand that we look to Sinai itself. Having no visible personal authority, as the earlier of the fathers had, nor any with only one or two generations between them and it, as others of the fathers had, and being obliged to rest on written testimony and authority, we necessarily demand all that can be had. And therefore Christians of this day summon not only Christ's resurrection and the apostles' teaching and example, but they instinctively demand also Sinai's law. Besides, they cannot bear to admit that the moral law given by Jehovah, in any of its elements wherever found, is abolished. Times and seasons and dispensations may change, but the intuitive feeling is, that a moral truth or law is never repealed. These things we say, not to be accepted without proofs, but as preparatory to a right understanding of the fathers on the question whether in discarding the seventh day they discarded also the fourth commandment.

It was assumed by all the early Christians, that their first or Lord's day was to come as often as the seventh day had. In effect they assumed that the septenary *proportional* time element was to remain. This came by intuitive deductions and divine assumptions, and therefore was not debated. They also assumed that their sacred day was to be devoted to sacred, or devotional and sacred, commemorative purposes. The modern view of some, that keeping every day alike (Rom. xiv. 5) involved no special observance of the Lord's day not only had no favor, but seems to have had scarcely a thought from the fathers. The more reliable commentators, as Ellicott,[1] Meyer,[2] Lightfoot,[3] agree that the Pauline reference in Romans, to which we have just referred, pertains only to Judaistic ceremonial days. And since the fathers, as far back as the apostolic era, as we have shown, undividedly agree as to the observance of the Lord's day, they could have had no sympathy with the thought of keeping no day at all, or all days the same.

No adequate conception of this subject can be obtained without a view of the seventh-day Sabbath as it was generally regarded and observed by the Jews in the patristic era. Jesus made various corrections of abuses of the Sabbath, but we are not to understand that those reforms widely prevailed among the Jewish people of that age, or that the Christians, even, so far adopted them as to have all their false notions and practices immediately corrected.

The Rabbinical doctors still taught, and the people still believed, the strangest absurdities respecting Sabbath desecration. The Rabbins enumerated thirty-nine principal prohibited works, each having its long list of secondary or subordinate works, performing any one of which was a violation of the Sabbath. The principal were such as ploughing, sowing, reaping, threshing, grinding, healing, hunting, bearing burdens, etc. Hence, teachers and people in general still believed it unlawful to heal a sick man

---

[1] Com. Gal. iv. 10 (Am. ed.).   [2] Com. Rom. xiv. 5.
[3] Com. Gal. iv. 10, and his reference to Origen.

(John v. 16) or to loose a crippled woman from her bonds (Luke xiii. 14) on the Sabbath; unlawful for the healed one to carry a light cushion on which he had been resting, as he went to his home (John v. 10); unlawful on the Sabbath to pick a head of wheat and shell it in the hand to appease hunger, for that would be both reaping and threshing; unlawful to walk on the grass, for the bruising of the tender leaves would be a kind of grinding;[1] unlawful to wear shoes with nails in them, for that would be bearing a burden, and so be a violation, they said, of the divine precept in Neh. xiii. 10; unlawful to carry *any* burden, except upon *both* shoulders instead of upon one, the former rendering the task so light that it would not really be a burden; unlawful to carry water to any animal, for that would be bearing a burden, though *lawful* to fill a trough with water and lead the animal to watering (Luke xiii. 15), for then the animal would carry the water; unlawful to put an ointment or plaster on a diseased eye for the purpose of healing it, though allowable to do it to allay the pain; unlawful, as the Essenes held, to remove a dish or any vessel out of its place;[2] or, as one class of Samaritans held, to remove one's self on the seventh day from the place or posture in which sunset found him on the sixth day.[3]

Other superstitious notions were subsequently added, some of them in the time of the fathers; as, an animal fallen into a ditch should not be removed on

---

[1] Jennings Jewish Antiquities, Vol. ii. p. 157.
[2] Heylin's Hist. Sab. Part i. chap. 8. sec. 2.
[3] Smith's Bible Dict., p, 2759; also, Farrar's Life of Christ, Vol. 1. p. 432.

the Sabbath, though some nourishment might be thrown to it, no one might whistle a tune or play on an instrument; no Jew might milk his kine on the Sabbath day, but might get another to do it, and then purchase the milk; the lame might use a staff on the Sabbath, but the blind might not; no one might carry money in his purse or pocket; no one should knock at a door with a ring or hammer; no one might walk through a stream on stilts, for he would carry the stilts; a tailor must not go out on Friday afternoon with his needle fastened to his raiment, lest he forget it and carry that burden on the Sabbath; a cock must not have a ribbon on its leg, for that would be carrying a burden; a physician must not be sent for on the Sabbath; one suffering from rheumatism, must not have the afflicted part rubbed or fomented, for that would be labor; no one must wear a false tooth, for that might necessitate labor;[1] no one catch a flea while it hopped about, for that would be a kind of hunting; and still other strictures were put upon the Sabbath-life, too trivial or too offensive to mention.

Such was the Sabbath known to both Jews and Christian converts from Judaism in the early Christian era; such the Pharisaic Jews insisted should be observed, and the Judaizing Christians complained of

---

[1] Respecting "a false tooth and a tooth of gold," there were two rulings given in a passage relating to women; one by a Rabbi *allowing* a person to wear such tooth; the other made by his superiors, — the wise men, —*forbidding* a woman to wear it on going out of her house on the Sabbath, because there would be a possibility of its falling out of her mouth; in which case she would be obliged to resort to *labor* in order to restore it. — Mishna, Sabbath, chap. vi. 5, Rev. Selah Merrill, D. D.

their Christian brethren if they did not observe it In these circumstances it were preposterous to suppose that the Jewish Sabbath, as known to the fathers in the early Christian era was identical with that of the fourth commandment. It was rather like the 'Sabbaths which God could not away with' in the prophet's time (Isa. i. 13); it was the Jewish *positive* and did not contain the moral and holy elements which the Lord placed in the Sabbath of the decalogue. In such associations even the *name* "Sabbath" had lost much of the sweetness it was originally designed always to have. The early Christians turned with pleasure to the new name, and new institution in part, the Lord's day. The existing Jewish Sabbath had become a reproach; and after Christ and his apostles had given such significance to the first day, it were easy for earnest and simple believers to transfer to it their affections for the one sacred day. Especially so, when the current of their thoughts and feelings was turning from types to the antitype, and the Jews and Judaizing nominal Christians were more or less absorbed, and wished to absorb others, with the mere outward and ceremonial of the Sabbath, and of other Jewish institutions. The fathers did not stop to philosophize on what they did, in some respects they knew not what they did; yet, emphatically, it was not the Sabbath as an institution that they fully rejected, but the Sabbath as an ordinal day, the Jewish seventh-day.

Though the fathers did not attempt to philosophize on this subject, there was a philosophy in their conduct. They engaged in the practical question of protecting the churches against Judaism, against the efforts of some to impose on the Christian conscience Rabbinic superstitions, and Judaic institutions that had accomplished their end and passed away. The chief of these were sacrifice, circumcision, Judaic feasts, and the Jewish Sabbath of that time. But neither apostles nor fathers said aught against these until for animal sacrifice was substituted the blood of Christ; for circumcision of the flesh that of the heart, and for baptism in respect to the seal of the covenant; for the Passover feast, the Lord's supper, and for the Jewish or seventh-day Sabbath, the Lord's day. The apostolic and patristic aim was to bring Christians away from the old to the new. Clearly, they were only Jewish institutions which they sought to displace. If there are other sabbatic elements than the merely Jewish—and we have seen that there are—of those the fathers did not treat. All principles and institutions that are *common to man* they left untouched. They opposed sabbatizing only as they opposed Judaizing. Their testimony bears at this day only against Saturday sabbatarianism, not against the Lord's-day Sabbath. Even Robertson, who says that Paul declared the Sabbath "abbrogated,"[1] says also of the apostle Paul's teaching: "To urge the observance of the Sabbath as indispensable to salvation, was, according to him, to Judaize; 'to turn again to the weak and beggarly elements, wherewith they desire to be in bondage.'"[2] Of course the Christian fathers rejected *such* observance of the seventh-day Sabbath; but in that rejection they did *not* embrace

[1] Sermons (Second Series), pp. 201, 202, 209; also (First Series), pp. 116, 118.
[2] Ibid. (Second Series), p. 204.

the rejection of the whole fourth commandment. We must examine in detail.

One writer, to sustain his theory of "the emancipation of Christians from the fourth commandment as a law,"[1] refers to Barnabas. This is the passage from which he quotes: "Furthermore, he saith unto them, 'Your new moons and Sabbaths I cannot away with.' Look ye how he saith, 'Your present Sabbaths are not acceptable unto me, but the Sabbath which I have made, in the which, when I have finished all things, I will make the beginning of the eighth day, which is the beginning of the new world.' Wherefore, also, we keep the eighth day unto gladness, in the which Jesus also rose from the dead, and, after that he had been manifested, ascended into the heavens."[2] One inference drawn from this by Prof. Hopkins is,—"That as an outward ceremonial observance God rejected it" [the Sabbath]. *Reply:* 1. He did reject the mere formal Sabbath in Isaiah's time (Isa. i. 13), 2, The argument of Barnabas is to the point, that God rejected the formal Jewish Sabbaths in his own time. What he says makes no decision on the true Sabbath of the fourth commandment, except by implication that the seventh day was not to be kept by Christians.

Another inference made is, "That even under the Old Testament it [the Sabbath] was to be kept holy chiefly as a symbol of future good." *Reply:* 1. The Lord's day taking substantially the place of the Sabbath, might also be a symbol of future good, even of

---

[1] Prof. S. M. Hopkins, Pittsburgh Alliance Address.

[2] Apostolic Fathers (Jackson and Fisher's ed.), p. 97; see also, Ant. Nic. Lib. Vol. i, p. 128.

the heavenly rest. 2. Barnabas seems to have a conception that the Lord's day, "the eighth day," is a kind of Sabbath. He says: "But the Sabbath which I have made," as Jackson and Fisher translate. Although the word "Sabbath" is not expressed in the original, it seems clearly to be implied, and to have some relation to the "eighth day." as though that took the place of the Sabbath in the new dispensation. A third inference by Prof. Hopkins is, — Barnabas teaches that the import of the Sabbath of the old dispensation "was realized in the blessings of the gospel." *Reply:* Not realized without one sacred day in seven; "Wherefore also we keep the eighth day." From all this we conclude, that since the formal Sabbaths of Isaiah's time did not emancipate the Jews from the real Sabbath of the fourth commandment, the Jewish Sabbath of Barnabas's time did not emancipate Christians from that command, except from the observance of the seventh-day. All other principles in that command stand unchanged. The direction concerning the "six days" is untouched The observance of a proportional seventh part of time is unaffected, because that is had in the keeping of the "eighth day." The element of "convocation" remains, for Justin Martyr particularly tells us of the public services held by Christians on "Sunday." The date of Barnabas's epistle is conceded by late and able editors to have been within the first quarter of the second century.[1] The writer must have been living when the apostle John died. His conception of the Jewish Sabbath of that time probably accorded with the one then current among

---

[1] Apostolic Fathers (Jackson and Fisher's ed.), p. 88.

Christians. Therefore, his view is initial and representative, and as a key it may assist in understanding others of the fathers.

Prof. Smyth has cited Ignatius in favor of the view that the fourth commandment was "limited as a statute" to the old dispensation; is "no longer literally binding," "no longer formally prescriptive," "not for us an outward ordinance." Yet, he does not go as far as some. He holds that the fourth commandment is "a revelation to us of a creative counsel and purpose of God in which we have a part as well as the chosen people," that it "suggests universal maxims," "is still directory," "discloses permanent and authoritative prnciples, to be conscientiously applied as *principles*."[1] *Reply:* 1. We think there is an inconsistency in saying that the fourth commandment was "limited as a statute" "to the old dispensation," and "is still directory" under the new. For whatever is divinely directory, is it not substantially a statute? There is also an inconsistency in saying that that command is "no longer literally binding," and yet has, or "discloses, permanent and authoritative principles, to be conscientiously applied." Where are the principles to be thus applied, except in itself? And are not those principles moral elements? And if to be conscientiously applied, are they not "literally binding"?

The passage which he quotes from Ignatius is this: "Be not deceived with strange doctrines, nor with old fables which are unprofitable. For if we still live according to Jewish law we acknowledge that we have not received grace: for the divinest prophets

[1] Sabbath Essays, pp. 235, 236.

lived according to Jesus Christ. . . . If, then they who were conversant with ancient things came to newness of hope, no longer sabbatizing, but living according to the Lord's [day], on which also our life sprang up by him and his death, . . . how can we live without him. . . . Therefore, having become his disciples, let us learn to live according to Christianity. . . . For Christianity did not believe into Judaism, but Judaism into Christianity."[1] *Reply:* 1. The part bearing distinctly on our subject is this phrase: "No longer sabbatizing." It was the Jewish sabbatizing of that age; for that it was which Ignatius opposed. That sabbatizing did not involve the whole of the fourth commandment. It was simply the keeping of the seventh day after the Jewish manner of that time. The two were not the same any more than a vitiated part is the whole of a genuine and pure thing. Therefore the passage, we think, does not teach any thing detrimental to the fourth commandment, except that the seventh day is not to be kept now that we are to live "according to the Lord's day." 2. Ignatius opposes the keeping of the Lord's day to the keeping of the seventh day: "No longer sabbatizing, but living according to the Lord's [day]." That fact emphatically suggests that the first day takes the place of the seventh. And as the Jewish vitiated seventh day of that time did not absorb the whole of the fourth commandment,—far from it,—the Lord's day must and does fall into the place left vacant by the apostolic striking out of the ordinal seventh part.

---

[1] Sabbath Essays, pp. 227, 228; Ant. Nic. Lib., Vol. i. pp. 179, 180, 181, 182; 183.

The same author in "Sabbath Essays," cites Justin Martyr, and says that he "nowhere alludes to the Lord's day as a fulfilment of the Sabbath."[1] *Reply:* 1. It was not a fulfilment of the original Sabbath in all respects. It had not the same ordinal time, *nor the Jewish ceremonial observances* which in the Jewish economy were added after the decalogue was given. But, 2. The question is not what Justin did *not* teach, but what he did teach. Did he teach that the fourth commandment is made void, as some say, or made void except as to "principles," as this author believes? He taught neither; unless the "principles," which are not revoked, embrace all but the ordinal seventh=day part. He did teach that the seventh day was no longer binding, and that the first day was. He did not analyze the elements as we now may; but what he actually did was,—he taught that the seventh day which the Jews held that the Christians, and all, ought to keep, was no longer in force, as it was under the old dispensation. This he might teach without saying or holding that the fourth commandment was revoked, or revoked except some "principles." What we wish to know is, whether in *this our* day we may appeal to the fourth commandment. We fail to see that Justin taught that we cannot.

3. Consider how Justin approached Christianity and biblical truth. His father and grandfather seem to have been Romans.[2] In customs he seems to have been a Greek.[3] He evidently had no early instructions in the Scriptures. He studied various philoso-

---
[1] Sabbath Essays, p. 228.
[2] Address of First Apology; Ant. Nic. Lib., Vol. ii. p. 7.
[3] Discourse to Greeks; Ant. Nic. Lib., Vol. ii. p. 279.

phies, found them unsatisfactory, learned of Christ and the prophesies concerning him, and there found rest,[1] without coming into the Christian faith as we now generally do through the moral law. As a philosopher he begins to preach Christ. His most vigorous and learned opponents are Jews, and questions about the law he gets from them. He encounters Trypho, either in fact or in imagination, and debates with him. At the outset, Trypho, counselling him, begins thus: "If, then, you are willing to listen to me . . . first be circumcised, then observe what ordinances have been enacted with respect to the Sabbath, and the feasts, and the new moons of God; and, in a word, do all things which have been written in the law; and then perhaps you shall obtain mercy from "God."[2] What Sabbath did Trypho mean? Plainly, that which the unbelieving Jews then kept, and which the Christians did not consider themselves bound to keep. Did Justin have any conception of it as the equivalent of the fourth commandment? It were violence to suppose it. See another jut of evidence that it was the Jewish ceremonial day. Justin says to Trypho, " think it not strange that we drink hot water on the Sabbath,"[3] indicating that the Christians did not regard the ritual law forbidding fires on the Sabbath, as still binding. The Sabbath that Justin had in mind all through this discussion is that which the Jews would impose upon him. And that was no more the real Sabbath of the command than that formal and false one of apostate Jews in Isaiah's day.

---

[1] Dialogue with Trypho; Ibid., p. 96.
[2] Ant. Nic. Lib., Vol. ii. p. 97.
[3] Ibid., p. 123.

And what was the law which Trypho had in mind in the foregoing passage? Clearly it was the ritual law: "Observe what ordinances have been enacted with respect to the Sabbath, and the feasts, and the new moons." If he had in mind the fourth commandment at all, it was the seventh-day part of it, which the Christians regarded as set aside, or which as Paul said should with each one be optional (Col. ii. 16). As the apostle joined feasts and new moons and Sabbaths in the same list, so repeatedly did Trypho and Justin,[1] and with like meaning, that of rites and ceremonies, and not of the decalogue. The only blame which Trypho casts upon the Christians is, as Justin says: "That we do not live after the law, and are not circumcised in the flesh as your forefathers were, and do not observe Sabbaths as you do."[2] And Trypho puts the same in this form: "And do not alter your mode of living from the nations, in that you observe no festivals or Sabbaths, and do not have the rite of circumcision; and further, resting your hopes on a man that was crucified, you yet expect to obtain some good thing from God, while you do not obey his commandments. Have you not read that that soul shall be cut off from his people who shall not have been circumcised on the eighth day?"[3] By both Justin's and Trypho's representations, living "after the law" was being circumcised, keeping feasts, and keeping Sabbaths; and that according to Trypho, was obeying God's "commandments." It was indeed true with the Jews of that day, in practice and widely in

[1] Ant. Nic. Lib., Vol. ii. pp. 97, 99, 109, 115.
[2] Ibid., p. 98.
[3] Ibid., p. 99.

theory, that obeying the law was observing rites and ceremonies, and not the ten commandments. "Ye tithe mint and anise and cummin, and have left undone the weightier matters of the law" (Matt. xxiii. 23). Trypho, referring to circumcision on the eighth day, continues: "But you despising this covenant, rashly reject the consequent duties," the duties implied by the covenant of circumcision. Continuing in this strain he adds: "you do not observe the law," by which he means the ritual law. In the next chapter Justin replies, and sets forth the "new covenant," which takes the place of the old one, and quotes from Jeremiah (xxxi. 31, 32) the passage which the writer in Hebrews (viii. 8, 9) also quotes, in expounding the Scriptures concerning the covenant of the new dispensation. In the same chapter he speaks of a "final law," which "placed against law has abrogated that which is before it," and he calls Christ "the new law, and the new covenant."[1] The law against which Christ as the "eternal and final law" is placed, is only the ritual and ceremonial; never is he placed against the moral, or anything moral in the ten commandments. Justin says: "The law promulgated on Horeb is now old, and belongs to yourselves alone," by which he means the ritual, and not the moral law; because he afterwards indicates that Christ's summary of the ten commandments was for all, and is still obligatory: "I think that our Lord and Saviour Jesus Christ spoke well when he summed up all righteousness and piety in two commandments."[2] When Christ made that summary the fourth com-

[1] Ant. Nic. Lib., Vol. ii. p. 100.
[2] Ibid., d. 217.

mandment stood unchanged; and so it did in Justin's opinion when he wrote, except that he said in substance that the Jewish seventh day was no longer binding. But in his first apology he represents the Sunday services to be full as many and sacred as ever were those of the seventh day; and in his Dialogue with Trypho he shows that the day itself was sacred, because he calls it "the first of all the days."[1] He also speaks of it as "the first day after the Sabbath," apparently as though in his mind it in some sense took the place of the Sabbath, or seventh day in the commandment. Condemning the idea of fulfilling the law of God by eating unleavened bread, and of being pious by being idle on the Sabbath,[2] he speaks of keeping "perpetual Sabbath," and indicates that the office of the real Sabbath was to breathe sacred influence and induce a genuine holiness that would last through all the week. Then, all sin repented of and put away, there would be "kept the sweet and true Sabbath of God." The new dispensation is not devoid of such a Sabbath, for it is better than the old; and the "perpetual Sabbath," which Justin says "the new law requires" us to keep, is not, as we have seen, destitute of a weekly sacred day.

Referring to Justin's statement that the prophets taught the keeping of Sabbaths as truly as did Moses, Prof. Smyth in "Sabbath Essays" says: "It is clear that he had no idea that the Sabbath was hallowed in the worship offered by Christians on the Lord's day."[3] *Reply;* He had no idea that the

[1] Ibid., p. 139.
[2] Ibid., p. 101.
[3] Sabbath Essays, p. 229.

Jewish seventh day and the ritual Sabbath was hallowed on the Lord's day. But the fourth commandment has nothing about offering sacrifices, or renewing shewbread, or not building fires on the seventh day. Setting those all aside, and coming to the very spirit of worship and praise and to the keeping of sacred time—whether the seventh day or "the first of all the days,"—and what difference is there between the two weekly seasons of hallowed time? Very little, or none. Having the latter now, what do we have but in substance all the moral, and one or more of the positive elements of the fourth commandment? Dr. Hessey, in commenting on Justin Martyr's writings on this theme, says that he "speaks of the whole of a Christian's life being a perpetual Sabbath," speaks also of Sunday being held in especial honor. It is obvious, that as holy scripture does, he is in the one case spiritualizing the now defunct Jewish law, and in the other mentioning a Christian ordinance on its own independent grounds."[1] *Reply*; We have shown that when Justin speaks of the Sabbath with reference to law, he speaks of the "defunct" Jewish ritual law, and not of the moral law. Of course, Sunday has "its own independent grounds," in respect to the ordinal time-element, as compared with the seventh-day Sabbath. But that does not imply that they have not both a common substratum of sacred religious purposes, and of proportional time-element, and of connection in the same commandment that gives injunction concerning the other six days of the week.

Dr. Hessey elsewhere has this remark; "No Isra-

[1] Sunday, pp. 43, 44.

elite could observe the fourth commandment independently of its development in the remainder of the books of Moses."[1] *Reply;* With equal truth he might have added, that we in the Christian dispensation can observe Sunday in all the unaltered elements of the fourth commandment, independently of the ritual additions of any of the laws of Moses, and in accordance with all the new services given to the weekly sacred day in the new era of the church.

Professor Hopkins, in commenting on the name "Sunday," given by Justin to the Christian sacred day, and on the reasons which Justin assigns for observing it, says; "The explicit rejection here not only of the Jewish term 'Sabbath,' but of the reasons on which the law of the Sabbath in the decalogue was founded, are highly significant."[2] *Reply:* 1. Christ rose from the dead on the first day of the week. The Roman name for the first day of the week at that time was "Sunday." Justin in his account of Sunday, on which Professor Hopkins comments, addresses the Roman Emperor, and two philosophers, one the son, and the other the adopted son of the Roman emperor, and also the Roman senate "with the whole people of the Romans." In such circumstances it was the most natural for him to use the Roman name, Sunday, for the Christians' sacred weekly day. And that he used the Roman name, we contend, is no good reason for supposing that Justin considered the fourth commandment abrogated. 2. With such controversy between the Jews and the Christians, and so much perse-

[1] Sunday, p. 117.
[2] Pittsburgh Evangelical Alliance Address.

cution by the former against the latter, the Christians would be likely to take a new name for their Sacred day. 3. The Jewish superstitious and trivial notions respecting the day called the Sabbath, would inevitably tend to the use of another name among Christians for the weekly sacred day. And the use of such a name would not necessarily or probably imply that they had set aside the fourth commandment in all its parts. 4. God had given them the name "Lord's day," which was far dearer then than the name "Sabbath," and therefore they would not be likely to retain the name "Sabbath." 5 The reason for the Lord's day was Christ's resurrection. And that, so near the event, was reason enough. Subsequently, the fathers attempted to link the Lord's day also to the creation, as a part of its reason. The occasion was sufficient for a new day and a new name, but we fail to see that both together are enough to justify us in the conclusion that one whole command was blotted out; especially when the new day so well adjusts itself to the place once filled by the old—the seventh day. We contend that these writers fail to show that Justin held that the fourth commandment is abrogated, or abrogated in form, while some "principles" are left. He teaches on this point only this: that the seventh=day sabbath is not binding, and that the first day, or Sunday, is.

Dr. Hessey, referring to Tertullian's testimony concerning the Lord's day, says: "I find in it nothing Sabbatarian."[1] *Reply:* Of course he finds

[1] Sunday, p. 46.

nothing in it of the merely Jewish elements of the Sabbath at that time, but that does not prove that there was nothing of the fourth commandment in the Lord's day. In the Lord's day there were certainly some elements of the fourth commandment, or those so far like them as to make them identical.

Another writer, Prof.[1] Smyth, concurring with Dr. Hessey, refers to this statement of Tertullian: "The Scriptures designate a Sabbath eternal and a Sabbath temporal."[2] The writer infers that the temporal Sabbath was that enjoined in the fourth commandment in every respect. *Reply:* 1. If that were a just inference, then Tertullian's testimony were in effect, not that the *whole* of the fourth commandment is abolished,—for that pertaining to *six* days would remain,—but that all the elements and parts of the Sabbath of that command were entirely annulled. Does Tertullian refer to the total Sabbath in every aspect of the fourth commandment, in such sense that the Lord's day could not come into the place of the seventh day? Turn to the next page of the same volume: "But the Jews are sure to say, that ever since this precept was given through Moses, the observance has been binding. Manifest accordingly it is, that the precept was not eternal nor spiritual, but temporal, would one day cease. In short, so true is it that it is not in the exemption from work on the Sabbath—that is of the seventh day—that the celebration of this solemnity is to consist, etc."[3] It was according to Tertullian, merely

[1] Sabbath Essays, p. 229.
[2] Ant. Nic. Lib., Vol. xviii. p. 211.
[3] Ant. Nic. Lib., Vol. xviii. p. 212.

the "seventh day," the ordinal time-element, of which he spoke. It was that which the Jews said was still "binding," and which Tertullian said was only temporary and not binding; and his whole argument in this connection is to show that there consistently could be the cessation of obligation to keep that day. That there was no special sacredness in the seventh-day time itself to forbid a termination of duty to keep it sacred, he argues from Joshua's march of seven successive days—including the seventh—around Jericho. Other Jewish history he brings to the same point. 2. Tertullian does not say that the fourth commandment is abolished, he does not intimate that we are released from obligation to do our secular work on six days; but, on the contrary, says elsewhere, that we should defer from the Lord's day "even our businessess, lest we give any place to the devil."[1] That statement is recognizing our obligation still to work six days and rest a seventh, which he claims is the first. 3. Tertullian says that Christians "ought to observe a Sabbath from all 'servile work' always, and not only every seventh day,"[2] by which he calls attention to the spiritual significance of all Sabbaths, but does not thereby stulify himself by meaning that Christians should not sacredly observe one day in the week. He had said the contrary. 4. His especial care in speaking of the Sabbath, to say that he meant the "seventh day," as we have seen, seems nearly or quite to indicate the thought which was in his mind, that the Lord's day was very much like the original

[1] Ibid., xi. p. 199. Sunday p. 44.
[2] Ibid., Vol. xviii. p. 211.

seventh-day Sabbath. 5. Tertullian did make a clear distinction between God's sabbaths and men's sabbaths, and hence he could consistently teach that certain sabbaths were set aside without implying that the Sabbath of the fourth commandment was annulled. In his argument against Marcion, the heretic, he comments on God's language in Isaiah (i. 13. 14) thus: "Reckoning them as men's Sabbaths, not his own, because they were celebrated without the fear of God by a people full of iniquities."[1] And on the next page he speaks of the "Creator's Sabbaths," thus distinguishing them from the false. Others of the fathers had the same distinction in view. 6. Tertullian betrays an aversion to the use of the word "annul" respecting the true Sabbath. He says: "Good reason . . . had the Lord . . . in the annulling of the Sabbath (since that is the word which men will use)."[2] He refers to Joshua's continuing his March around Jericho on the Sabbath, and to Christ and his deciples plucking ears of corn on the Sabbath, and to other acts which to some "seemed to annul the Sabbath," but which Tertullian claimed did not annul it. It would therefore seem that the true Sabbath of God, as embraced in the fourth commandment, he was never accustomed to consider "annulled," but merely "men's Sabbaths," and the "seventh day." His chief concern on this subject was to show that Christians were authorized to keep the Lord's day, and not bound to keep the seventh day.

Dr. Hessey quotes Irenaeus, and finds evidence,

[1] Ant, Nic. Lib., Vol. vii. p. 219.
[2] Ibid., p. 217.

he thinks, of the "abolition of the Sabbath;"[1] meaning, we suppose, the total abolition of the sabbatic institution of the fouth commandment. *Reply:* 1. We do not find, and Dr. Hessey does not show, that Irenaeus said that the Sabbath of the fourth commandment is abolished. 2. Irenaeus says expressly that the "words of the decalogue . . . remain pemanently with us,"[2] which means that the decalogue is not abolished. Would he not have made exception of the fourth commandment, or of the purely sabbatic part of it, if he considered it in all respects annulled?

Dr. Hessey regards Irenaeus as teaching that the Sabbath was "temporary,"[3] and quotes as evidence this: "Abraham himself, without circumcision and without observance of Sabbaths, believed God, and it was imputed unto him for righteousness."[4] *Reply:* 1. We are in a better condition than Irenaeus was to judge whether Abraham was without Sabbaths. 2. Irenaeus has in mind the seventh-day Sabbath, which he argues is not now to be observed, but he does not come to the point of saying that all that was meant by the Sabbath in the fourth commandment is utterly abolished. He certainly held to the "Lord's day," the weekly celebration of Christ's resurrection; and concerning that in the testimony of the fathers, as Dr. Hessey says, "no diversity exists."[5] 3. Irenaeus makes a clear distinction between the "decalogue" and the "laws

---

[1] Sunday, p. 44. [2] Ant. Nic. Lib., Vol. v. p. 424.
[3] Sunday, p. 44.
[4] Ant. Nic. Lib., Vol. v. pp. 422, 423.
[5] Sunday, p. 45.

of bondage,"[1] and in the laws of bondage he places the Sabbath; and yet says that the decalogue is permanent, and that the laws of bondage—the ritual law—were "cancelled by the new covenant of liberty." Apparently, then, the Sabbath which he has in mind is not the pure one of the fourth commandment, but the ceremonial one of the Jews, which they insisted the Christians ought to keep. It had, indeed, its root in the commandment, but was sadly misshapen and perverted in its growth. Irenaeus and all the fathers could say that that was no longer binding; but not one of them, we think, says that either the fourth commandment or the total sabbatic part of it is abrogated. 4. Irenaeus takes the language of Paul in Col. ii. 16, and ascribing it to all the apostles, says: "The apostles ordained that we should not judge any one in respect to meat or drink, or in regard to a feast day, or the new moons, or the Sabbaths."[2] It is certain that by "Sabbaths" he means the seventh day, the day that the Jews contended all ought to keep. Tertullian also quotes Col. ii. 16, with the same interpretation,[3] and teaches that the law "has been abolished"; but informs us that he refers to the "figurative types" of Christ, the ceremonial law. Yet he denies to Marcion his claim that there is any "breach of peace between the gospel and the law."[4] He also in one instance, we have seen, explains that by the word "Sabbath" he means "seventh day." These two, Irenaeus and Tertullian, are among the

---

[1] Ant. Nic. Lib., Vol. v. p. 425.
[2] Ant. Nic. Lib., Vol. ix. p. 177.
[3] Ibid., vii. p. 473.
[4] Ibid., p. 35.

most noted and reliable of the Fathers. Their interpretation of the passage in Colossians agrees with that we have heretofore given; and since they are so united and positive, that must have been the current view in the primitive era, and it utterly disallows seventh-day sabbbatarianism. On the other hand, since by "Sabbath" they mean the seventh day merely, which the Jews kept in distinction from the Christian keeping of the first day, their view gives no sanction to the theory that the setting aside of the seventh day cancels the whole fourth commandment, or the whole sabbatic part of it. They by no means would give so much credit to the Jewish seventh day as to confess that dropping it was dropping one tenth part of the decalogue.

The writer in "Sabbath Essays" Prof. Smyth, appeals to the fathers "as witnesses that the early church betrays no consciousness of a legal institution of the Lord's day by the apostles."[1] *Reply*: 1. The apostles and early Christians did not regard their new law of love, or any part of it, as cold legalism. They had too much pleasure in keeping their "first of all the days"[2] to look at it with the eye of mere legality. 2. Yet, we claim to have shown that they regarded it as one of their most serious obligations, as well as privileges, to observe "Sunday," or the "Lord's day."[3] They traced that day to the apostles for its authority,[4] just as truly as Israel of old traced the seventh day observance to Sinai. Its establishment had with them the force of law.

[1] Page 230.
[2] Justin Martyr; Ant. Nic. Lib., Vol. ii. p. 189.
[3] Bib. Sac., Vol. xxxvii. pp. 672-677.
[4] Epiphanius; also Irenaeus, Ibid., p. 667.

The same author in "Sabbath Essays" says again: "I cannot but think it impossible that they [the apostles] should have appointed the Lord's day as a continuation of, or literal substitute for, the sabbath of the commandment, and the early churches have remained in ignorance of the fact, and the early fathers have written as they did."[1] *Reply:* 1. None claim that the Lord's day is "a continuation of, or literal substitute for the sabbath of the commandment." It is another day, and has another commemoration, and some other services. It has none of the peculiarly Jewish ceremonial services, which are not named in the command, but were added after it was given. 2. We think we have shown in a previous Chapter, that under apostolic direction a change of observance was made from the seventh to the first day of the week, the latter taking its place in the weekly cycle as the former did, and having other elements of the fourth commandment. We think also, that thus far we find no testimony in the writings of the early fathers which presupposes or teaches that the fourth commandment is abolished, or even the whole *sabbatic* part of it. Hence, since the fourth commandment in a sense, or to some extent, still stands, while one sacred day in the week has been abrogated and another instituted, it is proper to suppose and say that the latter day has in substance, though not in full form, taken the place of the former, and it is both proper and obligatory to appeal to the fourth commandment as still binding, the modification of it being only in the ordinal time element. We are cut off from permission to dismiss the fourth com-

[1] Page 230.

mandment by various facts; among others by the one that the Lord's day pertains to the very week, so constantly recurring, which the original fourth commandment so strictly designated and adjusted. If the Lord's day did not at all touch the week so solemnly appointed and constituted by the decalogue, then we might say that it is wholly a new institution, and not a part of the old one. The moment we step on the threshold of the first day of the week, we tread on the ground which had the legislation of Sinai's fiat. And it is singularly felicitous that the *language* of the fourth commandment needs no change to suit it to the new circumstances. We have simply to understand the word "seventh" in the proportional and not in both the proportional and ordinal sense. And the abrogation of the sacredness of the seventh day while another day in the week is made sacred, is a very different thing from the abrogation of the whole command, or of all in it that pertains to sacred time.

Victorinus, opposing the doctrine that the Jewish seventh day should be kept, said it was abolished; but he did not have in mind all septenary sacred time, for he advocated keeping the Lord's day,[1] in which he embraced like moral elements with those of the Sabbath. The non-Sabbath advocates, to sustain their views, have to assume that the Jewish seventh day under the new dispensation, is the same as the Sabbath of the fourth commandment under the old dispensation. We do not find that they have proved this assumption. When they do prove it they will have also in substance shown that the Jewish Sab-

[1] Ant. Nic. Lib., Vol. xviii. p. 390.

baths which in Isaiah's time the Lord could not endure, were like that Sabbath which he commanded at Sinai. The fact that the Fathers called the Jewish seventh day of their time the "Sabbath," does not settle the question. Did they embrace by that title then the Sabbath institution of at least fifteen hundred previous years? If they did, it seems strange they did not say it. We shall see they said something to the contrary. Even if they thought the outlawed Jewish Sabbath of their own time, were the Sinaitic Sabbath, did Jehovah know they were right?

Dr. Hopkins cites the Apostolical Constitutions—a work of uncertain date and author, though probably of not later date than the close of the fourth century —to sustain his view that Christians are emancipated from the fourth commandment as a law, and he quotes thus;[1] "He who formerly commanded to keep the Sabbath by resting thereon for the sake of meditating on his laws, has now commanded us to consider the work of creation and providence every day, and to return thanks to God."[2] *Reply:* 1. The foregoing language does not say that the fourth commandment is abolished. The author of it is speaking of modifications or enlargements of divine laws under the Christian dispensation. 'He who forbade murder now forbids causeless anger. He who forbade adultery now forbids unlawful lust. He who forbade revenge now commands long-suffering. So he who appointed religious reflections on one day now requires them on all days.' Thus the influence of even the seventh-day Sabbath is brought down to us. Yet

[1] Pittsburgh Address.
[2] Ant. Nic. Lib., Vol. xvii. p. 168.

this writer, like some others in the Eastern church enjoined some observance of the seventh day, as well as of the first;[1] of the seventh particularly as a fast day once a year, on the anniversary of Christ's lying in the grave.[2] He has in mind the command merely in its seventh-day aspect. 2. This patristical author, treating of the law, says: "The law is the decalogue, which the Lord proclaimed to them with an audible voice. . . . And the law is righteous, and therefore it is called law, because judgments are thence made according to the law of nature."[3] "And he that was the Lawgiver became himself the fulfilling of the law; not taking away the law of nature, but abrogating those additional laws that were afterwards introduced, although not all of them neither."[4] The next paragraph takes up various laws of the decalogue, apparently assuming that they were laws of nature, and in that paragraph is the passage quoted by Dr. Hopkins. Also in it the writer says, that the Lawgiver "abrogated circumcision, when he had himself fulfilled it." He does not say that he "abrogated" the fourth commandment, or any other of the decalogue. His thought evidently is, that the seventh day—which was the form of Sabbath known in the command—had received an amplification of its teaching to men, and an "abrogating of those additional laws that were afterwards introduced." 3. It cannot be that this patristical author held that the fourth commandment, or even the sabbatic part of it, is

[1] Ibid., p. 143.
[2] Ibid., pp. 134, 186.
[3] Ibid., p. 163.
[4] Ibid., 167, 168.

really abrogated; because, as we have stated, he enjoined religious services and a fast on that day. He implied the continued existence of the Sabbath to an extent, and therefore did not hold that it was abolished. Yet he did not allow that day to come into competition with the Lord's day. In the same short section on feast-days and fast-days, he speaks of the Lord's day seven different times by that name, and repeatedly elsewhere. On that day he enjoins holding "solemn assemblies" and giving thanks and offering praise and being joyful without fasting,[1] and, while enjoining the celebration of Christ's resurrection on the Lord's day, he cautions against doing it "on any other day than a Sunday."[2] 4. This author of the Apostolical Constitutions speaks four times, at least, of the "law" or "laws of nature"; twice affirming that they are not taken away, and twice implying it.[3] In a fifth instance, referring to the same, he says: "He [the Lord] did not therefore take away the law from us, but the bonds."[4] That sentence is a key to the writer's thought. The pure "law" was not taken away; the "bonds" were. In the bonds he included "those additional laws that were afterwards introduced," and the seventh-day Sabbath doubtless more or less; yet not wholly, for he would still have it to some extent observed. He therefore could not have meant that the fourth commandment was wholly swept away. He must have regarded it in some sense as still a "law of nature," and hence permanent.

[1] Ant. Nic. Lib., Vol. xvii. pp. 143, 186, 189.
[2] Ibid., pp. 138, 186.
[3] Ibid., pp. 163, 167, 168, 170.
[4] Ibid., p. 169.

By "law of nature" he doubtless meant moral law. The laws of nature include all moral laws, but moral laws do not include all laws of nature; for example, none of the material laws. He must have been ready to assent to this,—that the fourth commandment has some moral laws, or laws of nature. Those the Lord did "not take away." Nearly all writers on this subject, in all ages, have claimed or confessed that there are moral elements in the fourth commandment. Dr. Richard Hooker, nearly three centuries ago, gave language relative to natural or moral laws, which has guided the thinking of many, and obtained the consent of all: "Even nature has taught the heathens . . . first, that festival solemnities are a part of the exercise of religion; secondly, that praise, liberality and rest are as natural elements whereof solemnities consist."[1] The fourth commandment having those elements, and being apparently so recognized by the author of "Apostolical Constitutions," and he having said that such laws or elements are not taken away, it will not be right for us to say that he held that the fourth command is abrogated, unless we trace such a sentiment to his pen. This we cannot do. Therefore we must conclude that that one of the Fathers, whoever he may have been, said nothing to justify the theory that Christians "are emancipated from the fourth commandment as a law." Christians should accept the command with such changes as they find have been divinely made.

Prof. Smyth has said this: "The enforcement of a positive commandment like the fourth would have been an impossibility in the early propagation of

---

[1] Works, v. 70. 5; also Dr. Hessey on Sunday, p. 100.

such a religion. It would have been necessary to interpret the statutes in such subordination to the higher law of mercy as practically to have suspended its operation.'"[1] *Reply:* 1. Whatever religious service the early Christians rendered, they gave from love, not compulsion. No doubt they faithfully observed the seventh day until the revelation came that its obligation was revoked. Even after that many of them attended its services. They had nothing of the modern spirit which begs off from as many religious services as possible. Neglecting to assemble together was left to the perverts, and other false professors. The complete transition from the seventh day to the first could not have been suddenly made. 2. But, when it came to be understood that the Lord's day was sacred, which must have been early, and as soon as it received that name, the reasons indicate that it was conscientiously observed. It is certain, as we have seen in a previous Chapter, that the apostles by precept and example taught its sacred character. The name of their "Lord" given to it was a guarantee for that. It being a sacred, religious day, the customs of the times required that it as a whole be to some extent at least sacredly observed. It certainly soon became the most sacred of all their days. The Christians would, then, so far as they could, keep it as sacredly as they had thought their most sacred days should be kept. They would therefore soon naturally refrain not only from all servile work, as on Jewish feast-days, but from all work, as on the Sabbath and day of atonement. Yet the Pharisaic superstitions respecting the Sabbath they would

[1] Sabbath Essays, p. 231.

reject. Stillingfleet, about two centuries ago, said: "As an evidence of the solemnity of the times for worship, the Romans as well as other nations had their several *feriae*, their days set apart for the honor of their gods . . . If any work were done upon those days of rest, the day was polluted . . . By which we see as from the light of nature, that what days and times, whether weekly, monthly, or anniversary, were designed and appointed as *dies festi*, for the service of God, were to be set apart wholly in order to that end, and not to give some part to God and to take others to themselves."[1] We see no reason for believing that the early Christians only half kept the "Lord's day." Where Tertullian speaks of deferring business on the Lord's day,[2] we do not understand it as the inculcation of a new rule, but a prompting to vigilance in keeping an old one. The citation from Jerome by Dr. Hessey, which we have heretofore considered, respecting the making of garments on Sunday in his time and locality, is sufficiently replied to by saying, that there is no evidence that it was common, or that it was done except in stress of circumstances for the poor, the sick, and the enslaved. The fact that Tertullian, nearly two centuries earlier, laid down the principle that Christians should be careful to defer all of their secular "businesses,"—which probably implied strictness much more to defer all secular *labor* from Sunday, according to Jewish customs,—forbids inferring even a partial secularization of the Lord's

---

[1] Stillingfleet's Irenicum, Book i. chap. v. sect. 4 (London ed.), pp. 216, 217.

[2] Ant. Nic. Lib., Vol. xi. p. 199.

day in Jerome's time, unless there had been a falling away.

The same writer says again: "Moreover—and the fact I am about to state is very significant—the apostolic epistles and the early Christian literature bring to light many a question of practical duty about which the Christian mind of those days was more or less perplexed; but there is no trace of such discussions as must inevitably have arisen had the law of abstinence from labor on the Lord's day for master and slave, and ox and ass, been regarded as obligatory upon Christians in the same way that it had been upon the Jews."[1] *Reply:* 1. Mark, that the Jewish sabbatic laws which were superadded to the fourth commandment the Christians did by no means undertake to apply to the Lord's day. 2. Various elements of worship, rest, convocation, inhering in that command, they did embrace in their observance of the Lord's day. 3. The fact that Constantine and other emperors who ruled in favor of the Christians, did make laws emancipating them from secular sabbath employments, shows that the Christian mind of that age really demanded release from secularities on that day long before the laws were made. The emperors followed Christian sentiment, and did not create it. Constantine enacted that all suits and courts of justice should be suspended on Sunday, except to emancipate slaves. He also forbade all military exercises on that day, and gave the privilege of attending church to all Christian soldiers;[2] and these things before his real conver-

---

[1] Sabbath Essays, p. 231.
[2] Neander's Church History (American ed. 1852), Vol. ii. pp. 26, 300.

sion, if he was converted at all, which fact indicates that he acted from public Christian opinion, and not from personal choice. The joint edict of Constantine and Licinius in behalf of religious freedom—which freedom is thought to be the product of modern civilization alone,—made A. D. 313, ran thus: "That each one, and the Christians among the rest, have the liberty to observe the religion of his choice, and his peculiar mode of worship."[1] This implies previous religious oppression toward the Christians; and consequently, that they often could not do as they would. The same restraint is doubtless alluded to in the twenty-ninth canon of the Council of Laodicea, in which it was declared that on the Lord's day "all Christians should abstain from their worldly business *if they were able.*"[2] This implies that abstinence from worldly business on Sunday was the desire, and the usual custom, of Christians in that age, if left to their choice. So it was, it would seem in Tertullian's time, which was half way back to the apostle John's day. 4. Now, where did this custom of sacredly keeping the Lord's day begin, if not in the beginning; during, at least, the apostolic era? We find the Lord's day most sacredly cherished through all the centuries back to the apostles; none of the fathers speaking more tenderly and reverently of it than did Ignatius, contemporary of the apostle John, and second bishop of the church at Antioch after the apostle Peter.[3] At some time subsequent

---

[1] Eusebius, Bohn's Eccl. Lib., p. 406; Neander's Church History (ed. 1853), Vol. ii. p. 13.

[2] Bib. Sac., Vol. xxxvii. p. 676; Neander's Church History (ed. 1852), Vol. ii. p. 300.

[3] Eusebius, Bohn's Eccl. Lib., p. 93.

to him we know that the early Christians customarily refrained from business and labor on the Lord's day, and who can show that that sacred observance did not begin as soon as the day became sacred. We trace its sacredness in Christian esteem to the apostles. Who can show that its observance did not begin with them, and uninterruptedly continue, except as necessity made some breach upon the custom. We do not find many traces of "discussions" about keeping the seventh day; but such "discussions would naturally not exist in respect to the Lord's day among those who kept or observed it; as so early fathers as Ignatius and Barnabas testify that the Christians of their time did. None but Christians were interested in the question of keeping that day. Universal agreement would prevent controversy among them. Universal custom required the sincere observance of all sacred days so far as practicable. Hence, few or no "discussions" on the question of keeping the Lord's day.

We have now examined all of the patristical passages adduced by three noted and able writers to show the abrogation of the fourth commandment, or its abrogation except some of its "principles." We do not recall, indeed, any publication besides theirs which discusses this specific subject beyond a mere notice of it. What do we find?

1. These three authors fail to bring forward a single passage from the fathers which declares or indicates the belief of even one of them that the fourth commandment is abolished. No passage which they have cited refers at all to that part of the command which enjoins labor during six days of the week. We

must infer that there is no patristical evidence in existence which shows or claims that the fourth commandment is wholly revoked.

2. Some of the passages which they cite do claim or indicate a partial abrogation of the fourth command, and men are now left to decide how large a part.

3. There are only two possible interpretations as to the part abolished; one being the whole sabbatic part, and the other the ordinal seventh day part.

4. We are bound to suppose that it is the least part, if that satisfies or exhausts the language respecting it.

5. The least part does exhaust the meaning of the language, for several reasons. (1) It was that part which was almost the whole theme of discussion between the Christians and the Jews respecting the Sabbath question. (2) It was almost the sole object of the Christians on this point, to have the Lord's day kept, and the seventh day not kept in any sense as its rival. (3) In the nature of the case the Christian mind of that age would be satisfied to have the first day observed, and a release given from obligation to observe the seventh day. (4) After satisfying the Christian demand then, certain moral elements of the original Sabbath would remain. (5) Much of the patristic language concerning the Sabbath refers simply to the false Sabbaths observed by the Jews, and not to the "Creator's Sabbaths." (6) The patristic language which refers to the sabbatic part of the fourth commandment does not declare, assume, or imply that that part is totally annulled, not seeming to be directed to that precise point; just as it does not teach that the command itself is annulled. But (7) that language is devoted to two thoughts: first, that the seventh day, which was the Sabbath pointed out

in that command, still subserves valuable ends, as the typifying of rest and of holiness, and hence is not utterly abolished; and, secondly, that the seventh day no longer held its regal place among all days, since the Lord's day had been given to Christians for them to observe as the chief of days. (8) The fathers do not expressly teach that the Lord's day took the place of the seventh day in the fourth commandment; but that is a latent idea with them. having subsequent development, and they teach nothing contrary to it. Their analysis and philosophy on the subject were not completed, and the circumstances did not then particularly call for the completion; for, the chief point was, to show that the divine recall of obligation to observe the seventh day was consistently possible in the new dispensation, and that such recall had been made, and that Christians by good right had another day to keep. Without sayiug all that might have been said on the subject, they were wonderfully preserved from saying what would have been inconsistent with the full truth of this point.

Murphy, Lange, Bush, the Septuagint, and the original Hebrew itself, make the injunction of "labor" in the fourth commandment positive to the extent of doing "all thy work" that thou hast to do. Since a part of the command remains, shall it stand there defaced, mutilated, dishonored? Or, has it always been whole, honored, by receiving the Lord's day when the seventh day was recalled?

But the foregoing we regard as only the negative part of the argument,—a reply to three modern authors on this subject, whose writings and veiws we have quoted, and whose citations from the fathers we have considered. There is a positive side.

CHAPTER X.

THE CHRISTIAN SABBATH IN THE NEW DISPENSATION.

There are sabbatic elements in the Lord's day. They constitute its substance. Hence there is the Christian Sabbath in the new dispensation.

1. The Lord's day has in substance the same nature and design as the original Sabbath. (1) Both are days for bodily and mental, secular and spiritual, rest. The word "Sabbath" means *rest*, and for rest Christians have ever used the Lord's day. Even Dr. Hessey, though utterly severing the two days from each other, says, "The Lord's day should be considered a day of rest."[1] Professor Hopkins says, "The proper end of the Christian Sunday is rest with cheerful worship, beneficent activity, self-help, and self-culture."[2] Two days so much alike would seem to be related to each other. (2) Both days have a high religious purpose. The Sabbath was sanctified, and was to be kept holy. The New Testament observance of the Lord's day was certainly religious, and in no sense secular, so far as appears. Dr Hessey says of it, "It is a divinely sanctioned, religious day . . . *the* religious day of Christians."[3] The wonder is that the Sabbath is completely "abrogated." as he claims, if Sunday is for the same end. (3) The

[1] Sunday, p. 229,
[2] Sabbath or Sunday—Pittsburgh Address.
[3] Sunday, p. 229.

acknowledged religious services of the early Christians on the Lord's day were fully equal to or more than those of the Jewish Sabbath. The fullest description extant is that given by Justin Martyr. The two chapters preceding are on these important topics: "The Administrations of the Sacraments," and "The Eucharist." Then, on the "Weekly Worship of the Christians," he says: "And we afterwards continually remind each other of these things. And the wealthy among us help the needy; and we always keep together; and for all things wherewith we are supplied we bless the Maker of all through his Son, Jesus Christ, and through the Holy Ghost. And on the day called Sunday," etc.[1] According to Justin's description there were in the primitive Lord's-day services prolonged reading of Scripture, instructions, exhortations, prayers, thanksgiving, the Lord's supper, collection of alms, distribution of food and other articles to the absent sick, widows, and orphans. All in country and city assembled; and this was the chief meeting of the day. Sometimes there were other meetings on that day,—as that of early morning, spoken of by Pliny. The Jewish and Christian public religious services were nearly identical, with the addition among the Christians of observing the Lord's supper, exercising spiritual gifts, and considering new truths.[2] (4) The early Christians held more lengthy services on the Lord's day than on other days; it was especially appropriated to their religious assemblies. (5) Their Lord's day services necessitated

---

[1] See remainder of paragraph in previous chap.
[2] Smith and Barnum, Comp. Dict., p. 1074; Jahn's Archaeology, pp. 501, 502.

rest from secular labor. Those coming from the country had but little time in the morning before coming, and little at evening after returning: No evidence appears among the *earliest* fathers or their contemporaries that they considered the Lord's day open to secular purposes. Lapses afterwards do not concern us now. We have seen that Tertullian taught the duty of abstinence from secularities on Sunday.[1] Though Dr. Hessey quotes Jerome as sanctioning the making of garments and visiting the sepulchres of apostles and martyrs on Sunday, he yet acknowledges that the testimony of that father is positive in respect to the religious observance of that day.[2] Moreover, Tertullian's era was two centuries nearer the apostles than that of Jerome, and was also one of more Christian devotion. Besides, the garment-making may have been exceptional — for the poor and enslaved. Dr. Pusey, after examining many passages of the early fathers, comes to the conclusion that "abstinence from business on the Lord's day, as a religious duty, was an early universal tradition."[3] Professor Hopkins says, "Agricultural labor, marketing, and all other necessary buying and selling went on upon the Sunday as upon any other day; that amount of time only being reserved which was necessary for attendance upon worship. From the church Christians went forth to their ordinary occupations."[4] *Reply:* Dr. Hopkins gives no proof of the truth of these statements; we do not think he can find any. He seems to

---

[1] 218 p.
[2] Sunday. p. 14.
[3] Morris's Lib. of the Fathers: Ephrem's Homilies, p. 391. note:
[4] Pittsburgh Address.

confound Jewish feast days with the Sabbath and day of atonement. On the former all servile labor was forbidden, but not business and on the latter all manner of labor and business were forbidden. The Lord's day was not a mere feast day or less than that. Doubtless Christian servants, bound to Jewish or heathen masters, were sometimes obliged to labor on the Lord's day. But it is wholly improbable that Christians spent the "first" and "chief" of all their days in a secular manner unnecessarily. They regarded it as superior to what the Sabbath was under the old covenant. It was the *day* that they observed, and not merely the Lord's supper on that day. The fact that they placed their usual observance of that sacrament on that day shows that they especially regarded the *day*. The supper and *agapae* were so important that their most sacred time would naturally be set apart for them. *Objection:* Reports of law cases in the English courts affirm that in the early Christian ages judicial courts were held on Sunday, and that not until the sixth or seventh century did Christians deem it wrong to try law cases on that day; hence they could not have regarded the Lord's day as holy. *Reply:* We notice this objection, though it comes late to hand. It is based on "Reports of Cases argued and adjudged in the Court of King's Bench," by Sir James Burrow.[1] We hold that Burrow, first, does not quote the earliest authorities on the subject, and, secondly, that the courts to which he refers were ecclesiastical, or had a religious purpose. We have already adduced language from the fathers which shows that they did regard the Lord's day as holy.

[1] Am. Ed. 1808, Vol. iii. pp. 1597-1662.

Dionysius, about A. D. 170, termed it "holy."[1] Tertullian, about A. D. 200, taught that Christians ought to defer their "business" from the "Lord's day."[2] Eusebius, about A. D. 315, said of the Lord's day, "On this day . . . we assemble, , . . and celebrate holy and spiritual Sabbaths."[3] The Council of Laodicea, A. D. 363, voted that Christians should rest from labor on the Lord's day, if they were able.[4] As soon as Christianity obtained civil power in Constantine, he abolished courts on Sunday, except for the manumission of slaves. Such is the testimony of Eusebius, given about A..D. 330.[5] Sozomen, about A. D. 420, said that Constantine "commanded that no judicial or other business should be transacted on these [the Lord's] days."[6] Neander, drawing from the original authorities, says, "The emperor, Constantine, in a law enacted previous to the year 321, commanded the suspension of all suits and courts of justice on Sunday. . . . By a law of the year 386 those older changes effected by the emperor, Constantine, were more rigorously enforced, and, in general, civil transactions of every kind on Sunday were strictly forbidden."[7] It was Theodosius I. who gave the law of the year 386, to which Neander refers.[8] But previous to that, A. D

---

[1] Euseb. Eccl. Hist., book iv. chap. 23.
[2] Ant. Nic. Lib., Vol. xi. p. 199.
[3] Patrologiae Graece, Tom. xxiii. pp. 1170, 1171; Stuart's Citation and Translation in Guerney on the Sabbath, Appendix B.
[4] Neander's Church History (Am. ed. 1852), Vol. ii. p. 300.
[5] Life Const., book iv. chaps. 18, 19.
[6] Eccl. Hist. (Bohn's ed.), p. 22.
[7] History of the Church (Am. ed. 1852), Vol. ii. p. 300.
[8] Hessey, Sunday, pp. 83, 84.

368, under Valentinian and Valens, a law was made which forbade the collection of taxes and other dues on Sunday.[1] And in 469 Leo and Anthemius granted the Christians relief from civil proceedings and annoyances on the Lord's day.[2]

It follows from the foregoing evidence that the objection based on Burrow's Reports, namely, "That not until the sixth or seventh century did Christians deem it wrong to try law cases on that day [Sunday]," is utterly wrong. For those rulers would never have enacted so many laws against the holding of courts on Sunday, if Christian sentiment had not desired it. That the edicts of emperors always prevailed with all the people cannot be claimed. The early laws of Christian emperors against paganism were often transgressed. Their edicts forbidding theatres and other spectacles on Sunday were even opposed by some nominal Christians. Yet such laws and edicts showed the trend of the better Christian sentiment, which finally effectually forbade the sitting of courts on Sunday. Burrow quotes Sir Henry Spelman, an English lawyer and student of judicial antiquities, of about three centuries since. Spelman quotes a church canon against holding courts on Sunday, of A. D. 517, and speaks of that as "fortified by an imperial constitution" made by Theodosius while yet Britain was under the Roman government which constitution must have dated a century and a half earlier than the canon. This is a confession of the more influential Christian views that moved

---

[1] Schaff's Church History, Vol. ii. p. 381; Hessey, Sunday, pp 83, 84.

[2] Hessey, Sunday, pp. 83, 84.

Theodosius. Spelman seems not to have known of Constantine's edict against Sunday courts a half century previous to that of Theodosius, nor of the many others given by other rulers of the fourth and earlier part of the fifth centuries. But he refers to Epiphanius, of the latter part of the fourth century, —without giving page or book of his work—as implying that on the Lord's day "In his time (as also many hundred years after) bishops and clergymen did hear and determine causes, lest Christians, against the rule of the apostle, should go to law under heathens and infidels."[1] But these were only ecclesiastical courts to settle difficulties among brethren, or such as they had with unbelievers, or "they had a religious purpose." Whether these courts in the circumstances were advisable or not, Christianity finally ruled them out, and they do not show or imply that the early Christians at any time held or justified purely secular courts on Sunday. Spelman also refers to Philo Judæus as saying in his life of Moses that the cause of one charged with gathering sticks on the Sabbath was heard on that day, and he cites the Talmudists as saying that their Sanhedrim did the same.[2] But these, too, were religious courts, even if they were the only ones the Jews had. Yet such courts on the Sabbath are without evidence of the divine approval.

Spelman gives a fine array of evidence showing that the ancient Gentile nations refused to hold secular courts during religious occasions. He says:

[1] Spelman's Works, Original of the Terms (London ed. 1727), p. 76.
[2] Spelmans' Works, etc., p. 75.

"The Romans likewise (whether by instinct of nature or precedent) meddled not with lawcauses during the time appointed to the worship of their gods, as appeareth by the primitive law of the twelve tables . . . It was so common a thing in those days of old to exempt the times of exercise of religion from all wordly business that the barbarous nations, even our Angli, whilst they were yet in Germany, the Suevians themselves, and others in those northern parts, would in no wise violate or interrupt it. Tacitus says [etc.]."[1] It is not possible that the early Christians cared less for the day that they named after their Lord than the barbarous nations cared for their religious occasions. (6) Since the early Christians *worshipped* their Lord, the day called by his name must have had their sacred regard. That name, "Lord's day," we find repeated by teaching of the twelve apostles Ignatius, Dionysius, Melito, Irenæus, Clement, Tertullian, Origen, Anatolius, Victorinus, Peter, Eusebius, Athanasius—all within about two hundred and fifty years after the apostle John's death. (7) Some essential *principles* involved in the Lord's day would of themselves soon make it more sacred to the early Christians than the seventh day. Regarding the Lord Jesus as divine, they would esteem his day as divinely sanctioned. Redemption by him would soon be more precious in their sensibilities than the original creation. In their regard the new creation in Christ Jesus would soon supersede the old in material nature. The freshness of Christ's personal presence on the earth would join with their sense of forgiven sin to make the day

[1] Ibid., p. 74.

which commemorated the completion of his mediatorial work more dear to them than the Sabbath of the old dispensation. Accordingly, history presents the fact which these first principles prophesy. The Lord's day gathers to itself in the Christian heart the special sacredness of days, and the chief assemblies and festivals naturally transfer themselves to it, aside from the previously shown fact that the first day was made sacred by the apostolic and divine authority.

Have we not here in the Lord's day the substance of the original Sabbath, when not cumbered with pharisaic rules and rites? The Jewish and other Christians had been accustomed to suspend labor on their most sacred days. Would they not ordinarily abstain from it on that day, more precious to them than all others had been? Theodore Parker, discussing the Sabbath question, here and often correct, says; "The Romans, like all other ancient nations, had certain festal days in which it was not thought proper to labor, unless work was pressing. It was disreputable to continue common labor on such days without an urgent reason; they were pretty numerous in the Roman calendar. Courts did not sit on those days; no public business was transacted."[1] And did the Christians unnecessarily labor to transact business on *their* most precious day—more precious far than any Roman day to Romans? Unreasonable to suppose it?! Mr. Parker says "*All other ancient nations*" thought it not proper to labor on their festal days, unless work was pressing.

[1] Christian use of Sunday, p. 22.

He includes the Jewish nation; and the Christian nations after they became Christian.

We have, then, on the Lord's day sacred time, rest, spirituality, holy convocations, Scripture reading and instruction, the Lord's supper, almsgiving, prayer, praise, and thanksgiving. What more was ever had on the seventh day, save sacrifices and ceremonies now passed away? What more can be named for the Lord's day to make up the substance of the Sabbath?

2. The Lord's day and the scriptural Sabbath of the old dispensation were similar in respect to the actual restrictions imposed upon men, and the religious liberties granted them. The Lord's day was religiously observed. The real Sabbath was always free from useless and burdensome exactions. Pharisaic restrictions should not be confounded with the true scriptural law of the Sabbath. Work for worldly gain was forbidden, but works of mercy were allowed. Healing the sick (Matt. xii. 13) and taking medicine were right. Rescuing an animal from the mire or a pit was proper and obligatory (Luke xiv. 5). Feeding and watering animals was a duty (Luke xiii. 15). Plucking ears of corn to appease present hunger was permitted, opportunity for provision the day previous not having been given (Matt. xii. 1-8); but gathering manna on the seventh day was forbidden, because it would interfere with religious services, and it could be gathered sufficiently on the sixth (Ex. xvi. 29). Proper eating without vain feasting was right (Luke xiv. 1). A "Sabbath day's journey" was proper by pharisaic rule, though the distance varied with the size of cities, and probably was with-

out rule by the real Scriptures.[1] The use of arms for defence or other necessity was not interdicted, though the Rabbins had taught otherwise.[2] The slaughter and sacrifice of animals in worship was allowed, enjoined, and even doubled on the Sabbath (Num. xxviii. 9, 10); and the shew=bread, twelve loaves with frankincense, was to be renewed on that day (Lev. xxiv. 5-9). The building of fires for ordinary, or at least culinary, purposes was forbidden (Ex. xxxv. 3); for, the climate was warm, their food could be sufficiently prepared without it, and allowing it would encourage gathering wood on the Sabbath. After sunset of the seventh day they could build fires, and probably often then they had their chief meal of the day. Some restrictions were ceremonial and national, and hence not always binding. God blessed the seventh day, and it was therefore propitious of good, cheerful, joyful, though not to be given to finding secular pleasure (Isa. lviii. 13). Religious songs and instruments of music were, with the divine sanction, used in Sabbath services. The appointment of the day symbolized a covenant made with God, enjoining upon his creatures to give him praise and thanksgiving for their creation and keeping.

In all this, where are the burdens from which we should wish to be delivered? Where any marked requisition in the original Sabbath, not ceremonial or national, which the early Christians did not cheerfully give in their observance of the Lord's day?

---

[1] The Rabbins doubtless perverted Scripture (Ex. xvi. 29), and without authority made a Sabbath-day's journey to be anywhere within a city, and two thousand cubits outside of it.

[2] Smith's Dict. of the Bible, p. 2762.

Have we not in the first day the true sabbatic elements?

3. The Old Testament gives significance and emphasis to the first day of the week, and thus prepares for its sacred, religious distinction in the new dispensation. (1) The dawn of creation, when God said, "Let there be light, and there was light," was the first of all the first days.[1] With this beginning of light associate the fact that Christ is "the light of the world." (2) The next significant first day was that on which the wave-sheaf of the first-fruits of the harvest was offered before the Lord on behalf of all the people (Lev. xxiii. 11). That sheaf was the symbol of life. With that associate the fact that Christ was "the life . . . of men." (3) Another significant first day was that on which the two wave-loaves were offered to the Lord (Lev. xxiii. 15-17). That offering was emblematic of double life. Associate with that the fact that Christ is doubly the 'resurrection"—to the body and to the soul; to the mortal and to the immortal part. First days in the Old Testament are symbolical of Christ's attributes and relations to mankind, and seem to pre-figure the first day of the new dispensation, which he by his resurrection has made immortal and glorious.

4. The apostles gave a sabbatic character to the Lord's day. They embalmed it in sacred regard. They dedicated it to the holiest religious services, and such dedication was the chief feature of the Sabbath. One of them gave to the Lord's day its most excellent name, or else copied it from the lips of his Master. *Objection:* Robertson says there is no com-

---
[1] Prof. Murphy.

mandment for changing Sabbath observance from the seventh to the first day.[1] Professor G. P. Fisher says the change was not by any explicit ordinance.[2] Therefore Sunday is an entirely new day, without connection with the old. *Reply:* The moral elements, which are the *chief* of the two days, being alike make the days alike, and in chief part identical. The fact that there is no positive command to keep the first day, with the fact that the early Christians *kept* it, indicates a somewhat natural transition from one to the other.[3] If the Lord's day were wholly new there would probably have been given specific and recorded directions respecting its observance. The fact that the fathers argued against observing the seventh day, and in favor of observing the first instead, indicates a similarity between the days, and in part a transition of observance. The fact that the Christians strictly kept the seventh day until they changed to the first tends to the same conclusion; also the fact that they kept the Lord's day weekly, and not annually, and that they observed, not merely the supper on the Lord's day, but the whole day itself. Again: There was no "explicit ordinance" for a change from *any* Jewish to Christian institutions. The new commenced at a specific time; the old *gradually* disappeared. Circumcision lingered after baptism began; passover ceremonies after the Easter Lord's supper commenced its yearly recurrence;[4] purifying of the flesh after the pentecostal

---

[1] Sermons (First Series), p. 118, Shad. and Sub. of Sabbath.
[2] Beginnings of Christianity, p. 562.
[3] Prof. Egbert C. Smyth, Am. Theol. Review, Vol. iv. p. 306.
[4] Smith's Bible Dict., Art. "Easter," p. 637.

purifying of the Spirit came so wondrously to the early church; Sabbath observance after that of the Lord's day began its control of all Christian hearts and lives. Peter, even after the effusion of the Spirit at Pentecost, did not immediately learn the fullest Christian fellowship (Acts x. 28, 34, 35) Paul, notwithstanding all his knowledge and Christian liberality, did not in his early ministry omit all ceremonies of circumsion, vows, and feasts (Acts xviii, 18, 21). Baxter likens Paul's temporary observance of the seventh day after that of the Lord's day commenced to his observance of circumcision, purification, and Pentecost after the new dispensation began.[1] It is evident from the writings of Origen,[2] Eusebius,[3] and other fathers, also from Neander's investigations,[4] that some ceremonies of Jewish feasts were for a long time mingled with the Christian festivals. Christian institutions commenced promptly: the Jewish only gradually disappeared. There having been no "explicit ordinance" for a change from Jewish ceremonies and institutions to the Christian ones, none need be expected for a change from the Jewish Sabbath to the Lord's day. Much was left to the evolution of Christian thought and experience.

5. The early fathers so sacredly regarded the Lord's day, and devoted it to so holy purposes, as to warrant the inference that it contains all the moral and unchangeable sabbatic elements. They derived

[1] Lord's Day, chap. vii. Arg. iv. Vol. xiii. p. 423.
[2] Against Celsus, book viii. chap. 22.
[3] Church History, book v. chap. 23.
[4] Church History, Vol. i. p. 294-302.

their views from the apostles—the earlier fathers directly, the later from the earlier. In answer to the seventh-day Sabbatarians we have seen that the early fathers without exception taught, *first*, the observance of the first day of the week, and, *secondly*, that the observance of the seventh day was not binding. In reply to the Lord's day non-Sabbath advocates we have seen that the fathers in rejecting the seventh-day Sabbath did not discard the moral elements of the original Sabbath. These three facts point to a fourth—that the Lord's day contains sabbatic elements. We now adduce further evidence of the same.

(1) The fathers frequently contrast the Lord's day with the Sabbath; contrast implies similarity; that similarity indicates sabbatic elements in the Lord's day. Many seem to have assumed that contrast implies so much dissimilarity as to indicate an utter difference. On the contrary, Alford says, "*Contrast* partakes of two ideas; that of *opposition* and that of *comparison*."[1] Crabbe says, "Likeness in the quality and difference in the degree are requisite for a *comparison;* likeness in the degree and opposition in the quality are requisite for a *contrast.*"[2] The Lord's day and the seventh day stand opposed to each other in respect to the day of the week, but are alike in respect to their sacred character. Being opposed to each other in time-element or "quality," and having "likeness" to each other in "degree" or sacredness of character, according to both Alford and Crabbe the two days may be both

---

[1] The Queen's English p. 234,
[2] Synonyms, "Contrast."

contrasted and compared, and yet in the former case not be utterly dissimilar. The contrast or the comparison will depend on the specific view at any time taken. Ignatius speaks of Christians as "No longer observing the Sabbath, but living in the observance of the Lord's day,"[1] which is a contrast of the two days with each other. Barnabas speaks of Christians as keeping the eighth day,[2] and of the Lord as abolishing Sabbaths,[3] so that they should be no longer kept, and of the two days as differing from each other,[4] all of which combined show a contrast of the two days, and yet imply a similarity. Justin Martyr gives Trypho the reasons why Christians do not observe Sabbaths,[5] and elsewhere relates how they observed Sunday,[6]—in substance a contrast. Bardesanes speaks of both the Jewish Sabbath and the Lord's day, in one passage, as different institutions, observed by two classes, yet in each instance for the same religious end.[7] Tertullian speaks of the Sabbaths as once beloved of God,[8] and of the sacred rites of the Lord's day,[9] implying a religious purpose in each day, though in different eras. Origen expressly contrasts the two days with each other, giving the superiority to the Lord's day.[10] The elements of

[1] Ant. Nic. Lib., Vol. i. p. 180.
[2] Ibid., p. 128.
[3] Ibid., p. 103.
[4] Ibid., pp. 127, 128.
[5] Ibid., Vol. ii. p. 109.
[6] Ibid., pp. 65, 66.
[7] Spicilegium Syriacum, p. 32.
[8] Ant. Nic. Lib., Vol. xi. p. 162.
[9] Ibid., Vol. xv. p. 428.
[10] Comm. Ex. Patrologiae, Tom. xii. p. 345.

opposition in the contrast made by these and other patristic writers must have been difference of days in the week, difference in the objects commemorated, and to some extent in services,—all of positive appointment. The elements of similarity must have been rest, holy convocation, study of the inspired word, worship of God,—all moral and enduring.

(2) Some of the fathers in effect even *compare* the two days, without contrasting them, so great is the similarity of the two in their conception. They all would have done it, doubtless, had not the discussions of that period been on the *differences* between the two institutions. Irenaeus speaks of the religious design of the Sabbaths,[1] and of that of the Lord's day.[2] Clement of Alexandria indicates that the seventh day in its time was sacred, and that the Lord's day is also.[3] Victorinus speaks of the original Sabbath as blessed and sanctified, and, in the same passage, of the Lord's day as the one now devoted to religious service. In his conception the design of the former in its time was similar to that of the latter in this time.[4] Athanasius, in his treatise on the Sabbath, and circumcision, clearly teaches that the Sabbath commemorating the end of the old creation has passed by, and *in its place* has come the Lord's day commemorating the beginning of the new creation.[5] Elsewhere he says he compares the Lord's day with the Sabbath.[6] Augustine speaks of Christians as ob-

[1] Ant. Nic. Lib., Vol. v. p. 422.
[2] Ibid., Vol. ix. pp. 162, 163.
[3] Ibid., Vol. ii. p. 284.
[4] Ibid., Vol. xviii. p. 390.
[5] Opera, Tom. ii. fol. pp. 55-59.
[6] Hom. vii. in Exod. v.

serving the Lord's day, and then says: "In the same way the fathers observed the rest of the Sabbath . . . because it was incumbent at that time."[1] He thought the two days were similar, both having religious purposes. Similar citations from other fathers might be made. When any of them speak of the Sabbath as devoted to rigid fasting, while the Lord's day is given to religious joy and praise, it is not of the original Sabbath, but of the seventh day after the Lord's day has taken its place. They sometimes consented to fasting on the seventh as a compromise with Judaizing Christians, but intended not to observe it in the manner the Jews did. Victorinus even says, "Lest we should appear to observe any Sabbath with the Jews."[2] It is a restricted view that notes only the *differences* between the two days. Dr. Hessey says Clement recognized the Lord's day as a "Christian ordinance quite distinct from the Sabbath."[3] On such basis he and others regard the fourth commandment as obsolete. But the contrasts and comparisons made by the fathers between the two days indicate elements common to both and identical with the moral elements of the Sinaitic Sabbath. Commenting on Justin's reasons for calling the Lord's day first or chief, Dr. Hessey says he speaks of a "Christian ordinance on its own independent grounds."[4] Independent as to its positive elements, not as to its moral. Every day has something common with every other. The Sinaitic Sabbath and

[1] Works (Clark's ed.), Vol. v. p. 324.
[2] Ant. Nic. Lib., Vol. xviii. p. 390.
[3] Sunday, p. 46.
[4] Ibid., p. 44.

the Lord's day have common elements of *rest* and *worship*, though distinct from each other in time, and chiefly distinct in events commemorated, and partly in services. The Lord's day, in a sense, commemorates God's rest from his work of creation, as well as Christ's resurrection, because of its septenary element. The fathers kept this in mind and linked the day to the weekly division of time by making it a reminder of the beginning of creation. Anatolius probably had this in mind when he said, "On the Lord's day was it that light was shown to us in the beginning."[1] Gregory of Nyssa speaks of that day as commemorating both Christ's resurrection and the beginning of creation.[2] Gaudentius of Brescia speaks of it similarly.[3] Socrates, the historian, distinctly notes the weekly occurrence of the Lord's day.[4]

(3) The fathers employed ideas and phraseology descriptive of the Lord's day which they borrowed from thoughts and language descriptive of the Sabbath. Dionysius says,
"To-day we kept the Lord's *holy* (ἁγίαν) day."[5] His descriptive word has the same root that the Septuagint employs in the fourth commandment: "To keep it holy;" the same that it employs in Isaiah (lviii. 13): "my holy day." Dionysius gives the same idea of sacredness to the Lord's day that he found given in the Old Testament to the Sabbath; and Eusebius, copying his expression, does not dissent from it.

---
[1] Ant. Nic. Lib., Vol. xiv. p. 420.
[2] In Christ. Res.; Opera, fol. Colon. Agrip., p. 454.
[3] Biblioth. Veterum Patrum, p. 945, De Paschae, Tract 1.
[4] Greek Eccl. Hist., Vol. iii. p. 436, book vi. chap. viii.
[5] Patrologiae, Euseb. Eccl. Hist., book iv. chap. 23.

Athanasius speaks of the command to keep the Sabbath, and then says, "So (ὅυτως) we *honor* the Lord's day."[2] He borrows the idea of veneration for the first day from that given the seventh on Sinai. The Council of Laodicea says, "Christians ought not to Judaize, and be at-ease on the Sabbath, but to work on that day, and, giving the chief honor to the Lord's day," etc.[3] The implication is that the honor formerly given the Sabbath should now be given the Lord's day. Theodoret speaks of Christians as consecrating, sanctifying (χαθιεροουσί), the Lord's day;[4] and though condemning the Ebionites for doing it in connection with their observance of the Sabbath at that time, it is evidently the same kind of consecration as that formerly given to the Sinaitic Sabbath. Augustine speaks of the Sabbath as a "figure" of the spiritual rest,"[5] and elsewhere of the Lord's day as "prefiguring the eternal repose."[6] Conceiving of both days as figures of the same glorious state, he must have derived that of the Lord's day from that of the Sabbath. Eusebius entitles the ninety-first (ninety-second of our version) psalm "A psalm of singing for the Sabbath day"; then shows that there is a like provision under the new dispensation, and that spending the Lord's day spiritually is like observing the Sabbath of old spiritually.[7] In his view the spiritual character of the Lord's day is ac-

[1] Patrologiae, Athan. Tom. iv. 6, p. 138, de Sab. and Cir. 4.
[2] Council Laod., Canon 29 ; Morris's Lib. of the Fathers ; St. Ephrem, p. 391, note.
[3] Patrologiae, Theodoret, Tom. iv, Haeret. Fabulor. Lib., ii. 1.
[4] Letter, lv. c. 12. 22.
[5] Works, City of God, book xxii. 30.
[6] Patrologiae, Euseb. Com. on Ps. xci.

cordant with, and copied from, that of the original Sabbath. *Objection:* Eusebius does not identify the Lord's day with the Sabbath.[1] *Reply:* It is not necessary for the present argument that he should. We look for *moral* elements common to the two days. They could not be identical, because their positive elements are of necessity different. *Objection Second:* Eusebius does not "build the observance of the Lord's day on the fourth commandment."[2] *Reply:* Enough that he claims the Lord's day as religious and the chief of days, and does not, with Dr. Hessey and some other modern authors, suppose or pronounce the fourth commandment obsolete. When it is considered that the early Christians from the first made the Lord's day religious, and that it was septenary, like the weekly religious day in the old dispensation, it would naturally be expected that sabbatic thought and language would become associated with the first day of the week. That tendency we find developed more and more as the centuries increase. It proves that some essential elements of the two days are alike.

(4) The early fathers, though not designing any such analysis and distinction, rejected from the Lord's day the positive elements, and retained for it the moral elements, of the Jewish Sabbath. They did a like thing relative to the original Sabbath as separate from peculiarly Jewish rules and provisions. They aimed to discard all that was merely Jewish, not as always evil, but now superseded. They refused longer to accept the seventh day as first and chief. They rejected the animal sacrifices appointed for the Jewish

---

[1] Hessey, Sunday, p. 301.
[2] Ibid, p. 300.

Sabbath. The Jewish sabbatic penalties they would not transfer to the Lord's day. They early dropped the Jewish method of reckoning the civil day from evening to evening, and adopted the Roman, from midnight to midnight. They discarded also all the Pharisaic and Rabbinical prohibitions respecting the Jewish Sabbath. But, on the other hand, they preserved the weekly division of time. One day in seven they turned aside from their usual worldly occupations, rested from them, and held religious services. They put their most valued religious services on the first day, as the Jews did theirs on the seventh. Many Christians, dependent for employment on Jews and heathen, could not observe the Lord's day to their own satisfaction, but the Christian desire and purpose found expression in the writings of bishops, the decrees of councils, and the edicts of emperors, at last. There is unity in all moral elements, and those of the Jews' sacred day entered into that of the Christians, and there received addition in the commemoration of the Saviour's resurrection.

But objectors cite the language of the fathers where they liken the Judaizing observance of the seventh day in their time to the vain observance of the Sabbath by formal and heartless Jews in the prophet's time. This they deem proof that the Sabbath is no more. *Reply:* The fathers rejected merely the Jewish Sabbath, and observed the moral elements of the real Sabbath in the Lord's day. The Jews of their time, alike with the formalist Jews of the prophet's time, were busy with the mutable positive, while the acceptable worshippers of each age absorbed the moral elements. The Jewish positive was no more: the moral of both the original and the Jewish continued. That God would not accept the Sabbaths of the Pharisaic Jews in the prophet's time is no proof that the fourth commandment is abrogated; and that the fathers would not sanction and copy the Judaistic observance of the seventh day after the Lord's day was made sacred to Christians is no evidence that the original Sabbath is wholly abolished, or that the fathers thought it wholly abolished.

(5) The fathers recognized the distinction between the moral and the ceremonial law, and regarded the former as inabrogable, and therefore we may well expect to find the moral elements of the fourth commandment in some form in the Lord's day. Barnabas says, "Thou shalt not forsake the commandments of the Lord."[1] Justin Martyr speaks of law as "abrogated," but it was the ceremonial, because succeeded by "the new covenant."[2] He also speaks of the moral law under the term "two commandments" in which Christ "summed up all righteousness,"[3] and of that "righteousness" as "eternal,"[4] which implies that the moral law is eternal and inabrogable. Irenaeus says, "The Lord did not abrogate the natural [precepts] of the law."[5] "Preparing man for this life, the Lord himself did speak in his own person to all alike the words of the decalogue; and, therefore, in like manner do they remain permanently with us, receiving, by means of his advent

[1] Ant. Nic. Lib., Vol, i. p. 131.
[2] Ant. Nic. Lib., Vol. ii. p. 100.
[3] Ibid., p. 217.   [4] Ibid., p. 147.
[5] Ibid., Vol. v. p. 412.

in the flesh, extension and increase, but not abrogation . . . He has increased and widened those laws which are natural, and noble, and common to all."[1] Clement of Alexandria teaches that the Mosaic law was the source of all moral truths[2]—the imperishable law; yet one law " was only temporary," —the ceremonial, the "shadow of Christ."[3] Tertullian speaks of the "primordial law of God . . . given to Adam and Eve in paradise," and "to all nations the selfsame law";[4] also of "a law temporal and a law eternal, formally declared";[5] and of the suppression or abolition of law which was the sacrificial and ceremonial;[6] and of the law which prefigured Christ, and was replaced by the gospel.[7] Cyprian: The prophets foretold the abolition of the old and the giving of a new law,—the typical, pertaining to Christ and the new covenant;[8] Theophilus: The "great and wonderful law, which tends to all righteousness,"[9]—eternal and permanent; The Clementine Homilies: The original law, perpetual to all, and cannot be abrogated;[10] The Apostolical Constitutions: The " law, complete in ten commands, . . . is never to fail "; the " additional precepts " —ceremonial—Christ " abolished," but he confirmed

[1] Ibid., pp. 424, 425.
[2] Ibid., Vol. xii. p. 47.
[3] Ibid., Vol. iv. pp. 153. 154.
[4] Ibid., Vol. xviii. pp. 203, 204.
[5] Ibid., p. 215.
[6] Ibid., p. 216.
[7] Ibid., Vol. vii. pp. 436, 437.
[8] Ibid., Vol. xiii. pp. 86, 87.
[9] Ibid., Vol. iii. p. 115.
[10] Ibid., Vol. xvii, p. 141.

the "decalogue";[1] Archelaus: The law of Moses is established, and is consonant with the law of Christ;[2] Augustine: A law which Christ came not to destroy, but to fulfil; parts of a law were in Christ fulfilled and removed.[3] The foregoing testimony shows that the early fathers do not justify modern fathers or sons in saying that the fourth commandment is obsolete. They imply, on the contrary, that the decalogue in general and the whole moral law remain. Though rejecting the Jewish Sabbath in their time, they do not assume to reject the fourth commandment proclaimed at Sinai. They evidently are not clear in their apprehension of the whole subject, but they cannot find a heart to discard even one of God's commandments. *Objection:* Epiphanius, bishop of Constantia, A. D. 367, and Cyril, bishop of Alexandria, A. D. 412, say that the Sabbath was abolished.[4] *Reply:* Neither says that the fourth commandment was abolished. *Reply Second:* Both have in mind the positive Jewish Sabbath as contrasted with the Lord's day. That Sabbath *was* abolished; but that was not the whole of the Sabbath of the fourth commandment; it was only a small part of it. Epiphanius argued that the Lord's day was established by the apostles; that there was no sacredness in the Sinaitic seventh day which forbade transacting secularities upon it, if religiously called for, as he says, the march around Jericho and the sacrifices in the temple on the Sabbath fully testify.[5] His aim

---

[1] Ant. Nic. Lib., Vol. xvii. pp. 163, 166.
[2] Ibid., Vol. xx. p. 368.
[3] Works, Manich. Heresy, pp. 321, 323.
[4] Hessey on Sunday, pp. 71, 79.
[5] Epiphanius, Adv. Haer., xxx, Opera, Tom. i. pp. 158, 159.

was to justify observing the Lord's day and not observing the seventh day. Cyril had the same object.[1] Even Dr. Hessey admits that it was the Sabbath as an "observance" which Cyril pronounced abolished. His debate was with the Judaizing Christians. He attempted to show that their demands that believers should observe the seventh day were unjustifiable. Neither of them pronounced a tenth part of the decalogue obsolete. Dr. Hessey does not claim that they did. *Reply Third:* Whatever these fathers may have said, they lived, one of them nearly two hundred and the other nearly two hundred and fifty years subsequent to Irenaeus, bishop of Lyons, A. D. 178, who, removed only three fourths of a century from the apostle John, declared that the "words of the decalogue" by the advent of Christ received "extension and increase, but not abrogation."

Objection Second: Theodoret. bishop of Cyrus, A. D. 420 or 423, says, "The Sabbath was not an institution of nature but a matter of positive precept."[2] *Reply:* He, too, is speaking of the positive Jewish Sabbath,[3] the observance of which some men of his time would impose upon all Christians. We do not find that he denied that there were moral elements in the Sabbath of the decalogue. We do not hear him say that Christ abolished such moral elements. If we did hear it, we hear the wise Irenaeus saying two hundred and fifty years earlier than Theodoret, that Jesus Christ "has increased and widened those laws which are natural, and noble, and common to all,"

---

[1] Cyril, in Esaiam, Tom. ii. Lib. v. p. 790.
[2] Hessey on Sunday, p. 80.
[3] Theod. in Ezeck. chap. xx.

that the "words of the decalogue . . . remain permanently." Victorinus speaks of a Sabbath which Christ in "his body abolished."[1] But examination shows that he has in mind only the Jewish seventh day in the time of the new dispensation.

(6) The fathers recognized a perpetuity in the original holy Sabbath, and in the Lord's day a sacredness which by its nature must also be perpetual; and we may, therefore, so far as they are authority, identify elements of the former day in those of the latter. Justin Martyr speaks of the "perpetual Sabbath."[2] There were, then, sabbatic elements which would not be abolished. The spirit of holiness taught by one holy day in the week should be made to pervade all days. But Justin did not mean that there is now no special weekly religious day, for he has taught us more of it and its services than any other patristic writer. The elements of the "perpetual Sabbath" were especially embodied in the "Sunday" which he describes. Tertullian tells us of a Sabbath "temporal" and of one "eternal." The former is "of the seventh day,"[3] of the letter, the outward, which the Jews were so careful to observe. Underlying it is the spirit of the Sabbath, and that is "eternal." When Tertullian enjoins deferring our business on the Lord's day,[4] he involves in it somewhat of the eternal Sabbath. His conception of the eternal would not allow him to say that the whole soul of the fourth commandment was abolished. Perpetuity is embraced

[1] Ant. Nic. Lib., Vol. xviii. p. 390.
[2] Ibid., Vol. ii. p. 101.
[3] Ant. Nic. Lib., Vol. xviii. p. 212.
[4] Ibid., Vol. xi. p. 199.

in his idea of the "Creator's Sabbaths,"[1] and also the idea of man's proper observance of them, Irenaeus wrote of the Sabbaths as teaching the continual service of God.[2] Though the Jewish seventh days have passed by, the real Sabbath is in some sense teaching and therefore existing still. Its special outward manifestation now is in the Lord's day. There is a Sabbath as inabrogable as the moral law. A mere formal observance of the Lord's day does not teach it, but a spiritual observance does. The Lord's day is a teacher of the true rest still. As Augustine says' it prefigures the eternal repose.[3] The seventh day Sabbath was based, in the fourth commandment, on the "eternal" Sabbath. The Lord's day, having divine appointment and a like design and observance, has the same basis. But when the fathers speak of a localized sabbatic institution, having "Sabbath" for its usual name, it is the seventh-day Sabbath, which they regarded as "temporal" and not "etermal."

(7) The doctrine was set forth among the early fathers and their contemporaries that the fourth commandment, or real Sabbath, was not abolished, whatever the changes, and though the first day was observed, and the seventh was not. It is reputed that the presbyter Diodorus writes to Bishop Archelaus A. D. 277, that one Manes in his vicinage is teaching heresy. He reports him as, among other things, citing the punishment under Moses' law for gathering sticks on the Sabbath as inconsistent with Christ's healing a cripple and allowing his disciples to pluck

[1] Ibid., Vol. vii. p. 220.
[2] Ibid., Vol. v. p. 422.
[3] Works, City of God. book xxii. 30.

ears of corn on the Sabbath. Archelaus in replying to Manes describes his error as an "effort directed to prove that the law of Moses is not consistent with the law of Christ," and says: "As to the assertion that the Sabbath has been abolished, we deny that he has abolished it plainly (*plane*), for he was himself also Lord of the Sabbath. And this (the law's relation to the Sabbath) was like the servant who has charge of the bridegroom's couch, who prepares the same with all carefulness, and does not suffer it to be disturbed or touched by any stranger, but keeps it intact against the time of the bridegroom's arrival, so that when he is come the bed may be used as it pleases himself, or as it is granted to those to use it whom he has bidden enter along with him."[1] This passage occurs in the "Acts of a Disputation" said to have been held by Archelaus with Manes. Its authenticity is not positively traceable to Archelaus. But if not his, and not dating in the third century Beausobre is probably correct in ascribing these "Acts" to some Greek writer of the fourth century.[2] And Neander no doubt correctly remarks that there is in them "much in the representation of the doctrine which wears the appearance of truth."[3] This passage on the Sabbath of the fourth commandment written in the third or fourth century, certainly indicates a view held thus early, and we deduce from it the following: (1) Christ could abolish or change the Sabbath; (2) The law kept the Sabbath for him till he came, and then he did with it what he would; (3)

---

[1] Ant. Nic. Lib., Vol. xx. p. 373.

[2] Smith's Dict., Christ. Biography, Archelaus.

[3] Church History (ed. 1852), Vol. 1. p. 485.

One thing he did not do,—he did not abolish it; (4) The Sabbath therefore in some sense remains, though Christians keep the first and not the seventh day.

In respect to this, as with some other subjects, there are distinctions not readily seen, which are yet so important that error will result unless they are perceived. Luther failed to see clearly the distinction between works as a means of self-righteousness and works as a necessary fruit of justifying faith, and hence he questioned the genuineness of the Epistle of James. Some modern writers do not distinguish clearly between a system of law—moral, typical, and ceremonial—as the way and means of acceptance with God, and law—moral merely—as the expression of the divine pleasure under a system of grace, and hence do not perceive that law in the latter sense is never repealed. And some, failing to bear in mind the difference between the merely positive Judaic Sabbath and the moral-positive Sinaitic or Adamic institution, and seeing evidence in Scripture and the patristic writings of the abrogation of the former, erroneously conclude that both are abrogated, and that therefore the fourth commandment is entirely obsolete. This last error has done much to break down the divine order of sacred time.

Augustine distinctly teaches that the fourth commandment is not abolished. He says, "'Observe the Sabbath day' is enjoined on us more than on them, because it is commanded to be spiritually observed. For the Jews observe the Sabbath in a servile manner, using it for luxuriousness and drunkenness. How much better would their women be employed in spinning wool than in dancing on that day in the balconies? God forbid, brethren, that we should call that an observance of the Sabbath. The Christian observes the Sabbath spiritually, abstaining from servile work. For what is it to abstain from servile work? From sin. And how prove we it? Ask the Lord: 'Whosoever committeth sin is the servant of sin.' Therefore is the spiritual observance of the Sabbath enjoined upon us. Now all those commandments are more enjoined on us, and are to be observed: 'Thou shalt not kill. Thou shalt not commit adultery,'" etc.[1] It was merely the outward observance of the seventh day that Augustine considered annulled, not its spiritual teaching or moral elements. We need not be circumscribed or limited by his philosophy as to the observance of the fourth commandment. Our one point now is, he did not deem it abolished, but still in force, with the single exception of outwardly keeping the seventh day. He makes no allusion to any contrary opinion among the early fathers or Christians. The language of the other fathers is entirely consistent with his view. It follows, therefore, that Drs. Hessey, Hopkins, F. W. Robertson, and many others, who have inferred the abrogation of the fourth commandment from the patristic writings, have made a wrong deduction in respect to that vital question.

Calvin held the same view that Augustine did, and perhaps derived it from him. He says, "Besides, the Sabbath, although its external observation is not now in use, still remains eternal in its reality, like

[1] "Lectures or Tractates on the Gospel according to St. John," Vol. i. p. 39; Tractate, iii. sec. 19 (Edinburgh ed. 1873).

circumcision. . . . They (the Jews) calumniate us falsely, as if we disregarded the Sabbath; because there is nothing which more completely confirms its reality and substance than the abolition of its external use."[1] It is plain from this that Calvin would by no means countenance the idea that the fourth commandment is abolished. Let it not be claimed that Calvin held what Dr. Hessey says the fathers taught, that the Lord's day is a "Christian ordinance, quite distinct from the Sabbath."[2] For Calvin teaches that the Sabbath was instituted at the creation, and thus has some obligation for all men; that it has a moral nature, since it belongs to the decalogue, which he denominates the "moral law"; that the fourth commandment binds men in "every age" to religious services on stated days, and to rest from labor; that the early Christians properly "substituted what we call the Lord's day for the Sabbath," and that we should follow that order.[3] He also held that the specific seventh-day Sabbath had a typical or ceremonial character, which shadowed forth spiritual rest, and that in that respect it was abolished with the other types. Yet in that abrogation the fourth commandment as a whole was not abolished. His co-laborers in the Reformation generally agreed with him. Luther says, "I believe that the apostles transferred the Sabbath to Sunday, otherwise no man would have been so audacious as to dare to do it."[1]

[1] On Fourth Commandment Ex. xxxi. 18; Harmony of Penteteuch (Edinburgh ed. 1853), Vol. ii. p. 444.
[2] Sunday, p. 46.
[3] Institutes, book ii. chap. viii.
[1] Tischreden, Luther's Works (Erlangen ed. 60), p. 388; Pres. Valentine, D. D. "Is the Lord's day only a human ordinance?" p. 27.

(8) It was taught among the fathers that the Lord's day under the new covenant actually took the place, in substance, of the seventh-day Sabbath under the old covenant. When Tertullian teaches that the observance of the seventh day was to be temporary, and that business and labor ought to be suspended on the Lord's day; when Athanasius says we ought to honor the Lord's day even as it was commanded to keep the Sabbath; when Augustine speaks of both the Sabbath and the Lord's day as figures of the heavenly rest, they all plainly regard the Lord's day as legitimately occupying the place of the Sinaitic Sabbath. But Eusebius, of eminent learning, who must have known the testimony and practice of the two preceding centuries, is fullest on this point. In his commentary on the ninety-second psalm, entitled "A Psalm or Song for the Sabbath Day," he says. "Wherefore as they [the Jews] rejected it [the sabbatic command], the Word [Christ] by the new covenant translated and transferred the feast of the Sabbath to the morning light, and gave us the symbol of true rest, viz. the saving Lord's day, the first [day] of the light, in which the Saviour of the world, after all his labors among men, obtained the victory over death, and passed the portals of heaven, having achieved a work superior to the six days' creation . . . On this day, which is the first day of light and of the true sun, we assemble after an interval of six days, and celebrate holy and spiritual Sabbaths, even all nations redeemed by him throughout the world, and do those things according to the spiritual law which were decreed for the priests to do on the Sabbath; for we make spiritual

offerings and sacrifices, which are called sacrifices of praise and rejoicing; we make incense of a good odor to ascend, as it is written, 'Let my prayer come up before thee as incense,' . . . and all things, whatsoever that it was duty to do on the Sabbath, these we have transferred to the Lord's day as more appropriately belonging to it, because it has a precedence, and is first in rank and more honorable than the Jewish Sabbath; wherefore it is delivered to us that we should meet together on this day, and it is ordered that we should do those things announced in this psalm." [1] Eusebius here teaches, (1) That Christ or his apostles translated and transferred the feast of the Sabbath to the Lord's day; (2) That the early Christians on the Lord's days celebrated holy and spiritual Sabbaths, such as were enjoyed under the old dispensation; (3) That they on that day presented unto God spiritual offerings and sacrifices in place of the ceremonial ones required of priests and people under the Jewish law; (4) That they transferred to the Lord's day all the duties, in substance, which formerly belonged to the seventh-day Sabbath; (5) That they were divinely directed to make this change of duties and services from the seventh to the first day of the week. He must have held that the Lord's day contained the chief sabbatic elements. *Objection:* Dr. Hessey says on this commentary, " Such is the passage in Eusebius of which so much has been recently made, as if it identified the Sabbath and the Lord's day. It really does nothing of the kind, but is only a strong instance of that resort

---

[1] Patrologiae Graecae, Tom. xxiii. pp. 1170, 1171; Stuart's Translation in Gurney on the Sabbath. Appendix B.

to the analogy of the Jewish law."² *Reply:* We do not claim that it "identifies" the two days, but in substance identifies the moral elements of the two days; *that it teaches that the Lord's day under the new covenant takes in substance the place of the seventh day under the old covenant, it is the Christian Sabbath, and in respect to moral elements has the authority of the fourth commandment.*

(9) It seems that the idea and even the name "Sabbath" was applied by one of the fathers to the Lord's day, near the close of the second century, about one hundred years after the last of the apostles. Clement of Alexandria, widely known and highly influential in his time, commenting on the fourth commandment says, "The seventh day, therefore, is proclaimed a rest,— abstraction from ills,— preparing for the primal day, our true rest; which, in truth, is the first creation of light, in which all things are viewed and possessed . . . The discourse has turned on the seventh and the eighth. For the eighth may possibly turn out to be properly the seventh, and the seventh manifestly the sixth, and the latter [the eighth] properly the Sabbath, and the seventh a day of work."¹ Among Clement's thoughts are these: (1) There is a near relation and clear similarity between the seventh day and the first, or "eighth"; (2) The first day of the week is analogous to the first of creation; (3) In the new dispensation the seventh day in a sense becomes the sixth, "a day of work," and the eighth becomes the seventh, a day of "rest"; (4) The first or "eighth" day has sabbatic endowments, might "properly" be

²Sunday, notes, p. 301.

termed the "Sabbath," and "possibly" will yet be so named. Such thoughts, being in Clement's mind, and writings, were certainly entertained in that early age by others. The primitive Christians, having certainly perceived the likeness between the seventh and Lord's day, must have also seen that the name of the former—Sabbath—would in many respects be suitable as a name of the latter, except that it already had a better one, in their conception. *Objection*: "It is not certain that Clement refers directly to the eighth *day*. The word for day does not appear in the original." *Reply:* The word "day,"—"seventh day,"—had been previously used in the same section; the passage is distinctly on the fourth commandment, and therefore "day" may well be supposed to be understood, especially as Clement speaks of the "seventh" as a "working,"— day for work. *Objection Second:* "The meaning may be that under the gospel dispensation the Christian has a true rest, or Sabbath." *Reply:* Clement is speaking of particular numbers,— seventh and eighth,— and not expressly of dispensations or of Christian privileges. Those numbers have no significance here unless they refer to days, nor the days any significance unless the writer has the conception that the "eighth" or first day of the week is in substance a "Sabbath," and might yet be called, or even proved to be, such. *Objection Third:* "The use of the passage to support an authoritative transfer of the ancient Sabbath to the Lord's day is hazardous." *Reply:* It is not proposed to use it for an "authoritative transfer," but to show that the early fathers recognized sabbatic elements in the Lord's day, and were very far from saying that the fourth commandment was void because the seventh-day observance was no longer binding. We have aimed to show that the fathers' testimony does not forbid finding a basis for the Lord's day in the fourth commandment. We claim to have shown that Scripture does not forbid it. Therefore the fourth commandment asserts its own demand, subject only to such modification as the New Testament gives. There we find an absolute release from the observance of the seventh day (Col. ii. 16), and in its place the privilege and obligation to observe the Lord's day. The appeal to patristical lore is to interpret and confirm the New Testament instruction. In the writings of the fathers we find ample proof that the Lord's day in that age was kept "holy," though not according to all Judaic sabbatic rules. The commandment itself has not varied its demand for holiness. *Clement's reflections above given show that in his mind was doubtless the same thought that naturally has come to many other minds in the centuries past, and comes to many still,— the Lord's day does in substance take the place of the seventh day in the fourth of the Sinaitic commandments*

But why is there so great importance in finding a basis for Sabbath observance in the fourth commandment, and in holding tenaciously to that basis? Because, (1) If such is God's revealed will it is transgression and peril to disregard it. (2) It gives the most consistent and beautiful array of divine truth. On any other theory the fourth commandment stands mutilated in the most wonderful body of laws that ever existed among men. That commandment made whole accords with the fact that a day of rest was set apart and hallowed from the close of creation, and with the evidence that such a day was given for the observance of mankind previous to the existence of the Jewish nation. The divine common law, or law of precedent, in which the ante-Mosaic Sabbath was based, might be expected to receive expression in some divine statute like that of the decalogue, and that statute might be expected to continue. By divine common law, in distinction from divine statute, the Lord,s day, or Christian Sabbath, has its authority in the new dispensation. This doctrine of the continuity of sacred time from the beginning, based in both the divine law of precedent and the decalogue, accords best with the importance of the Sabbath and the welfare of men. (3) We may know *a priori* that human nature needs to anchor to the firm foundation of God's commandments. (4) History tells us that wherever the doctrine of the abrogation of the fourth commandment has found sway, there Sabbath desecration has been the sure result. The Jews ever disregarded and despised the Sabbath unless confronted with the divine sabbatic requirements. Many who condemned the principles of the Puritan Sabbath acknowledged its conservative and healthful influence. Many noted men who have advocated the theories of the European continental Sabbath have mourned over their evil fruits, and have in the comparison admired and desired the purer American Sabbath when free from foreign embarrassments and corruptions. Man left to his own free will, without the divine will, is sure to go astray. Therefore we should enthrone forever the whole moral law. the moral elements of the fourth commandment with all the rest. We must choose whether to regard them as void or binding. Who, with fair and full consideration, can accept the former alternative?

NOTES.

1. It should be noticed that the modern general view of the Sabbath is well supported by that eminent theologian and reasoner Jonathan Edwards, of more than a century and a half ago. He held that the Sabbath was instituted at the close of creation as a personal blessing to man, and is therefore binding upon him now as it has been in all ages past whereever known. He held also that the Sabbath is one day in seven and that under the gospel dispensation this day is the first day of the week and that the Christian Sabbath in the sense of the fourth command is as much the seventh as the Jewish Sabbath, because it is kept after six days of labor as well as that. Its observance honors God as the keeping of His command, and should be kept free from worldly concerns that it may be devoted to religious exercises.

2. The discussion of this subject shows that the Christian Sabbath, or the sacred observance of one day in seven, is not a merely Jewish Institution. It was not only ante=Sinaitic, but ante=Mosaic, dating at the close of creation: it has a moral principle, therefore that principle is a law founded on the nature and needs of man and irrepealable. Its repetition at Sinai was simply its engrossment; a few outward observances were merely adaptations to Jewish ceremonial and civil laws subsequently repealed; a

change of time was a later adaptation to the Christian dispensation which must stand while the Christian dispensation remains.

3. When Christ told his hearers that the Sabbath was made for man and not man for the Sabbath, his chief motive was to rebuke Judaic superstitions. But the truth he cited concerning the Sabbath was no less a truth because brought forward incidentally and not as the primary object. The Sabbath is of such a nature as to be applicable to all men and not to Jews merely. The distinction between the secular and the spiritual is adapted to all classes of men and lasts while life lasts. Therefore it should be observed by all men: neither Christ nor his apostles said any thing contrary to this.

4. Let it never be forgotten that apostolic unity in doctrine and in practice constitute divine instruction and authority. Let it be also remembered that the earliest Christians were taught by Christ and his apostles and that the Early Fathers, some of them contemporory with the apostles, are agreed in holding the first day of the week as sacred. In actual history there is no division of testimony.

5. Let those who speak lightly of the Puritan Sabbath remember that imperfect though it may have been, it was a magnificent protest against great worldliness in the church at that time and served a grand purpose. Much of its spirit might well be retained.

CHAPTER XI.

THE ADVANTAGES OF THE SABBATH FOR MAN'S PHYSICAL BEING.

When the Savior said, "The Sabbath was made for man " (Mark ii: 27), he announced a fundamental and most valuable divine law for human welfare. The human body of necessity occupies a large place in man's attention and wants. The efficiency of that body is very wide and serviceable when it is possessed and governed by a right mind. There must be then, a great importance in due attention to the real wants of the physical nature in this life. How many sick beds and how many faint and drooping forms demonstrate, that there has been a lack of appliance for the health of the body; and also, that there should be strict vigilance with all the healthy and robust, to preserve the physical force and strength which they already possess. One law of demand for the human system is that of rest. Laws for rest are stationed all along the physical nature. The lungs rest after each breath we take; the blood-vessels rest between the heart-beatings; the nerves and brain will have rest and will revenge themselves upon us if we cut short the supply.

The ordaining of day and night to follow each other in quick succession through all ages of the world, was a merciful appointment of God. —Without it the human species would probably have become extinct at a very early period of time. The night is needful to refresh and invigorate our weak bodies, that can endure but a few hours of toil without sleep. If rest be not willingly given, the body will take it against will. The person long wearied by *sorrow*, in spite of himself will fall asleep, if he persists in denying the demand for rest. So was it apparently with the three disciples whom Christ asked to watch with him in the garden of his agony. So is it often with criminals the very night preceding their execution. They have been known to sleep soundly for nine successive hours the last night of their earthly existence. Bonaparte once passed three entire days and nights without sleep; but he could no longer contend against this law of rest, and sank to sleep on his horse. As surely as there is a God, one of his laws in our physical being is that which calls for *rest*.

But, experience and observation have shown, that the rest of night, and all forms of daily and nightly rest put together, are insufficient for the highest good of man's physical being. There must be days as well as nights of rest. The steady routine of day and night, without breaks and openings in its course, is inimical to man's highest state of health and physical efficiency. Dr. Carpenter, the distinguished English physician, physiologist, and author, says it has been found by those who employ horses in coaching, that in traveling a certain distance, it is better to work a horse four days, and give him a fifth day for rest, than to divide the same distance into five parts for five days, and give him no one day of rest. Mr. Bionconi, to whom Ireland is much indebted for "establishing and maintaining its system of public cars," at a meeting of the British Association for the advancement of science, in Dublin, in 1857, said, "I found that I could work a horse with more advantage eight miles a day for six days, than six miles a day for seven days; and therefore I discovered that by *not* working on Sunday I made a saving of twelve per cent."[1] Intervals, changes, that shall give variations to the course, are demanded by the physical nature.

But some regularity in the intervals is important. A term of twenty days for work, and then of four days for rest, will not suffice like the four for work and one for rest in regular order. It is found that the physical nature looses its vigor by a long succession of working days without intervening rest days; that the tone of vigor grows less and less as by a regular falling scale. Numerous experiments have demonstrated this.

Whether the physical being shows that the day of interval and rest should be every *seventh* may not be so clear. But the law of God, copied from his law of creation, has revealed to us that the seventh day for interval and for rest is for the best, and destruction would doubtless come if any other ordinal than the seventh were taken. The distinguished Jonathan Edwards held that there was probably some Divine law in human being, which demands the *seventh* rather than any other ordinal day for rest, though the reason of it is as yet unknown to us. The once infidel France tried the *tenth* day in place of the

[1] Rev. Joseph Cook, Sabbath Essays, p. 40.

seventh, and that was doubtless one of the evil elements that plunged the nation into anarchy and blood. The long centuries have given numerous opportunities for experiment in this matter. The conclusion of all candid and well-informed minds put to this question has been, that a seventh day for rest is needful for man's physical being. The communities where this law is observed are healthier, stronger, more temperate, of greater longevity. The better soldiers in physical capacity during the late American war, did not come from the Sabbath-breaking communities, but from those in general where God's law of weekly rest had been observed. When the great "New West" was almost unknown, and emigrants from the East went in caravans from the Mississippi across the Rocky mountains to California, it was repeatedly demonstrated by experiment, that the companies of travelers that stopped their teams on prairies or hill-sides, and gave to them, and took for themselves, the Lord's day rest, reached their journey's end the soonest and safest. Years ago, when the Crystal Palace exhibition was at its height, six hundred and forty one physicians of London subscribed a petition to the British Parliament against opening that Palace for profit on Sundays, and in the petition they said, "Your petitioners, from their acquaintance with the laboring classes and with the laws which regulate the human economy, are convinced that a seventh day of rest, instituted by God, and coeval with the existence of man is essential to the bodily health and mental vigor of men in every station of life." The British House of Commons many years since made an investigation of the effects of laboring seven days in the week compared with laboring six and resting one. Among the many witnesses they summoned, was Dr. Farre of London, who had been in the early part of his life the physician of a public medical institution and had been engaged in the study and practice of medicine forty years. He gave a lengthy and important testimony, showing that one day in seven is greatly needed as a day of rest to restore to the body and mind, that energy and vigor and strength which they lose by six days of laborious application. He gave it as his opinion that the night was not a sufficient restorative power to secure the attainment of long life. He considered the Sabbath not only a positive institution which should be observed because the Divine Will demands it, but that it should also be kept as a *natural* duty to preserve life; that he who habitually violates it by labor is virtually guilty of *suicide.* He regarded the Sabbath as a great "sustaining, repairing and healing power." A committee in the Pennsylvania Legislature, in their report in regard to the employment of laborers on their state canals on the Sabbath, asserted it as the result of their own experience, that man and beast will perform more labor by resting one day in seven than by working the whole seven. Years ago the Minister of Marine in France ordered that no workmen be employed in the government dock-yards on the Sabbath, on the ground that more labor will be performed by resting on the Sabbath than by working seven days in the week.

During some years past there has been a somewhat popular call for more holidays. Without now judging whether there should be more or not, one thing is certain, there ought to be more *holy days* and even a well-kept and universally kept Sabbath. The more holidays some people have, the worse they are off. A laboring man of New York city who had freely patronized Sabbath excursions under the plea for more recreation, recently abandoned them, saying, that he found himself by them made more weary and unfit for his week's work then to come, than he was on Saturday night. Jorgensen says, "The moroseness occasioned by the want of a Sabbath in France has an effect on the cleanliness of young men engaged in manual labor; they pursue their daily drudgery in their dirty working dresses, and habit renders them at length averse to a change of linen and clothes." Cleanliness is one protection against disease. It is found that suicides occur more in Sabbath breaking than in Sabbath keeping countries, and far more among Sabbath breakers than among Sabbath keepers." Coleridge says, I feel as if God had, by giving the Sabbath, given fifty two Springs in the year." All laboring men who are dependent on others for employment, have a direct and important interest in maintaining the Sabbath. No Sabbath means for many of them eventually more labor with no more pay. John Stuart Mill said, "Operatives are perfectly right in thinking that if all worked on Sunday, seven days' work would be given for six days' wages."[1] It is seen that there must be a well-observed law of rest for all, or there will be no liberty of rest for those who wish it. Sir David Wilkie, a celebrated painter, said, "Those artists who wrought on Sunday were

[1] Sabbath Essays p. 42.

soon disqualified from working at all." Professor Ernest Curtius, a distinguished philologist and antiquary of Germany, says, "The alternation of working and resting days appeared, even to the ancients, as something so primeval in its origin, so indispensible, and so closely connected with religion, that they perceived in it, not an innovation of human cleverness, but a divine ordinance; as Plato says, 'Out of pity for the wretched life of mortals, the Deity had arranged days of festal recreation and refreshment.'"[1] William Von Humboldt says, "I am satisfied that the six days are really the true, fit, and adequate measure of time for work, whether as respects the physical strength of man, or his perseverance in a uniform occupation. There is also something human in the arrangement by which those animals which assist man in his work enjoy rest along with him. To lengthen beyond the proper measure the periods of returning repose, would be as inhuman as it would be foolish. An example of this occurred within my own experience. When I was in Paris during the time of the Revolution, it happened, that, without regard to the divine institution, this appointment was made to give way to the dry, wretched decimal system. Every tenth day was directed to be observed as a Sunday, and all ordinary business went on for nine days in succession. When it became distinctly evident that this was far too much, many kept holiday on the Sunday also, as far as the police laws allowed; and so arose on the other hand, too much leisure. In this way one always oscillates between

---

[1] Sabbath Essays, p. 26, note, quoted by Rev. W.W. Atterbury, Sec. N. Y. Sab. Com.

the two extremes, so soon as one leaves the regular and ordained middle path."[1]

Lord Macauley, in discoursing on the physical benefits of the Sabbath says: "While industry is suspended—while the plow lies in the furrow—while the exchange is silent—while no smoke ascends from the factory, a process is going on quite as important to the wealth of the nation as any process which is performed on more busy days. Man, the machine of machines, is repairing and winding up, so that he returns to his labors on Monday with clearer intellect —with livelier spirits—with renewed corporal vigor."

Rev. Dr. C. A. Huntley gives the following: "Ordinarily, men are no losers by giving up one day in seven, to God, even in temporal things, but gainers rather. Indeed, man was not made for unceasing labour, whether bodily or mental. For a little while he may, perhaps, do more work in seven days than in six; but not for a continuance. God's physical laws forbid the attempt as plainly and intelligibly as his moral laws. In the end he will be found to have done the most who has at due intervals suspended his labor, that he may return to it again with recruited strength and renewed vigor, and with that calmness and self-possession which he has gained by communion with God in those intervals."[2]

We could add to the foregoing matter on this subject a great multitude of other facts and testimonies. Enough have been given to show that there is a deep-seated law in the physical nature of man, which absolutely requires a weekly day of rest. It is a

[1] Letters, etc. Vol. i. p. 207; Sabbath Essays, p. 29.
[2] Form of Sound Words, p. 269.

law of God, nearly or quite as well established as any law in nature can be. And since Jehovah has revealed that one seventh part of time should be given to rest, the allotted weekly day of rest should be one day in seven.

CHAPTER XII.

THE ADVANTAGES OF THE SABBATH FOR MENTAL REST, CAPACITY, AND CULTURE.

A sane mind works best in a sound body. Being shown that the weekly rest is needful for the physical man, it is in that already shown that the rest is needful for the intellectual man. The dependence of the mind upon the body in this mortal state, is so great and constant as to be beyond human calculation. We know that none of us now have any command of our intellect without the body. And we know that a diseased body gives a beclouded mind; and sometimes even goes so far, that though the mind remain in the body it becomes useless, helpless. We know also, that *rest* of mind means rest of body too, and often we can not tell whether it is body *only* that is tired, or body and mind both. Rest for the body is rest for the mind. Weekly rest for the body is weekly rest for the mind. A Sabbath for the body is a Sabbath for the soul. As the day of weekly rest is economy for the physical being, so it is for the intellectual powers; as it enhances the physical capacities, and increases the amount of their executive power, so it does the same for the endowments and executiveness of the understanding. Numerous demonstrations have shown, that men of great intellectual labor must take the weekly rest, or risk the failure or ruin of their mental powers. Close observation has shown, that under secular labor and mental application, the intellect loses more vigor each day than it regains each night, until at the end of the week the rest-day can make full reparation ; or if it be not allowed to do that that then premature failure of mental capacities is quite sure to be the result. Many men of long life and great intellectual labors have attributed their long-continued success to the fact, that on each weekly rest-day they have unstrung the bow, and given it relaxation. A man of twenty-five year's observation in New York City, has said that those merchants of his acquaintance who have kept their counting rooms open on Sunday, have failed without exception. William Wilberforce, the celebrated philanthropist, one of the most laborious men that ever entered the British Parliament, said he could never have accomplished so much public business as he did, except for the rest of the Sabbath. Many public men who began life with him, found an early grave. Some became maniacs, and put an end to their own existence.

The cause of their premature and untimely end, Wilberforce attributed to their violation of the law of nature in disregarding the Sabbath, and allowing themselves no mental rest on that day. A distinguished financier, charged with an immense amount of business during the memorable years of 1836 and 1837, said: "I should have been a dead man, had it not been for the Sabbath." Isaac Taylor says: "I am prepared to affirm, that to the studious especially, and whether younger or older, a Sabbath well spent, —spent in happy exercises of the heart—devotional and domestic—a Sunday given to the soul is the best of all means of refreshment to the mere intellect."

It is a law in general, that they who give best observance to the Sabbath, give also the best and most successful attention to pursuits and studies, and studies that most promote culture, civilization and social happiness. Lord Macauley says: "If the Sunday had not been observed as a day of rest, but the axe, the spade, the anvil, and the loom, had been at work every day during the last three centuries (in Great Britain), I have not the smallest doubt that we should have been at this moment a poorer people and a less civilized people than we are." The blessing to *domestic* life, of keeping the Sabbath, is incalculable. The Sabbath kept holy, will bring a peaceful and contented spirit, will diffuse solid comfort and enduring prosperity. There is a conservative power in "not doing thine own ways, nor finding thine own pleasure, nor speaking thine own words" one day in the week, according to the ancient Divine instruction respecting the keeping of the Sabbath. Jonathan Edwards says: "A peculiar blessing may be expected upon those families where there is due care taken that the Sabbath be strictly and devoutly observed."

Even Pierre Proudhon, the Atheist, yet penetrating philosopher, in discussing the Mosaic Sabbath, relative to its hygienic, social, political and moral bearings, aims to show, and does show, that it is really fitted to the nature and wants of man.[1] As quoted by Dr. Paul Niemeyer, Proudhon says concerning the septenary element of the Sabbath,

[1] Sabbath Essays, p. 28.

"Shorten the week by a single day, and the labor bears too small a proportion to the rest; lengthen the week to the same extent, and labor becomes excessive. Establish every three days a half=day of rest, and you increase by a fraction the loss of time, while in severing the natural unity of the day you break the numerical harmony of things. Accord, on the other hand, forty=eight hours of rest after twelve consecutive days of toil, you kill the man with inertia after having exhausted him with fatigue." Niemeyer, himself professor of hygiene in the Leipsic universities, has entered into similar investigations and comes to the same conclusions. A summary of what he says he expresses thus: "If religion calls the seventh day 'the day of the Lord.' the hygienists for the reasons I have exhibited, will call Sunday the day of man."[1] Other hygienists and social philosophers, as Ochsenbein,[2] and Dr. Haegler[3] of Bale, have come to like opinions on purely scientific grounds in our own day. The evidence accumulates, and may be called sufficient for the positive deduction, that *nature* accords with Scripture in demanding a septenary Sabbath.

The Sabbath expands and cultivates the intellect through the study of the holy Scriptures which it secures. The chief part of the study of the Bible is done on the Sabbath. There would be but little Biblical study in the week=time were it not for the influence and sacred occupation, of the Sabbath. An open Bible is a true symbol of knowledge opened to

[1] Ibid, p. 33,
[2] Ibid, p. 30.
[3] Ibid, p. 33.

the people. Ignorance is the mark set upon the people wherever the Bible is withheld from them. The Bible bestows a view of the only living and true God, and of his infinite attributes. There is an elevating, strengthening, and expanding power in looking daily towards the eternal Jehovah. We can not think of the great " I am," who is without beginning and without end, Almighty, Omnipotent, heart-searching, holy, and merciful, without intellectual expansion and culture. It produces due sobriety, reflection, and thought on high themes, as well as on the minutiae of life, that each person may do all to the glory of God. The Bible is also superior to all other books in making man acquainted with himself, and that enlarges and improves the understanding. Self-knowledge is a way to success. Self-acquaintance may guide the doom of our destiny. It enables one to supply the defects of his character. It shows him his need, and where to go for help. And yet, all the books of the world are not equal for self-knowledge to many a single page of the Bible. That book also gives one a glance into the future state and eternity, which promotes carefulness and depth of thought, and that promotes intellectual discrimination and strength. It also to a wonderful degree reveals the distinction between sin and holiness, and that gives sharpness, watchfulness and strength to the mind. The raised and exalted character of Biblical literature is also in a high degree fitted to expand and cultivate the mental powers. And all of this and yet other gains are secured by remembering the Sabbath-day to keep it holy.

But it is not designed that this mental culture shall

be sought as a chief end on the Sabbath. It is rather an incidental benefit. It comes in connection with the convocation services which God has appointed for the Sabbath, and with our enjoyments as intellectual beings, who *must* have something for the mind to feed upon during its waking hours. Mental *rest*, we should remember, is one of the Sabbath's advantages. A member of the English Parliament, Hon. Hugh Mason, gave November 30, 1880, at Free Trade Hall, Manchester, the following: "There is nothing to which I look forward with greater pleasure, hope, and thankfulness, than the periodical return of the Day of Rest. It is not only that I may have the pleasure and the profit of assembling in the House of Prayer with other men and women likeminded; there is something in addition to that, something which every busy brain and busy mind relishes—the day of rest from worldly work, the throwing away of every mean and secular occupation, and feeling that the mind is completely at rest from all the distractions and all the anxieties which beset busy people in the course of their daily life,"[1]

Bishop John Hooper, a Reformed clergyman of the sixteenth century, who died a martyr under Queen Mary, left valuable writings on the subject of the Sabbath, in which is the following: "That man might breathe and have repose, this Sabbath was instituted, not only that the body should be restored unto strength and made able to sustain the travails of the week to come, but also that the soul and spirit of man whiles the body is at rest, might upon the Sabbath learn and know so the blessed will

[1] Time's Feast Heaven's Foretaste, pp. 112, 113.

of his Maker that it leave not the labor and adversity of sin only, but also by God's grace receive such strength and force in the contemplation of God's most merciful promise, that it may be able to sustain all the troubles of temptation in the week that followeth. . . . God by this commandment provideth for the temporal and civil life of man, and likewise for all things which be necessary and expedient for man in this life. If man, and beast that is man's servant, should without repose and rest always labor, they might never endure 'the travail of the earth.'"

CHAPTER XIII.

THE ADVANTAGES OF THE SABBATH FOR SOCIETY AND SOCIAL REGENERATION.

The family is one of the first and best of the institutions ever given by God for the human race. And the Sabbath is one of the best and most potent friends which the family ever had. On the Sabbath, and especially in the house of God, the claims of our social nature, and the kinds of needed social regeneration, receive their most pungent and thorough consideration. Reforms in society receive more their origin and impetus on the Lord's day, than on all other days of the week. The nature of a happy family, and the duties it involves, are especially thought of and fashioned on the Christian Sabbath. The old Jewish family was superior to all heathen families around it. The Christian family excels all others of its time, other opportunities being equally distributed. And it is the Christian Sabbath that gives a great part of its character and value to the Christian family. In the Christian family the desire is to know what God wants, and generally in the unchristian, to get what self wants. In the Christian family, when some new intimation comes of what is pleasing to the Lord, there is an endeavor to conform the rules and regulations of the family to the new light. So that that family becomes constituted and ordered somewhat according to the Divine pattern, much as Moses' artificers conformed the tabernacle and the furnishing of it to the pattern which Moses saw in the mount. And in all this process lie the principles of social regeneration. By these principles society can be purified and built up in righteousness. In this way in heathen lands Christianity entering the souls of individuals, leavens families, and they leaven society and moral renovation ensues, and the Sabbath is a potent agency for it all.

The servants of God in general live longer and do more for the benefit of society than others do; and they in great part get their Christian character and abilities through means and agencies given by the Sabbath. It is found that the average length of human life in Christian lands is increasing. The increase is greatly owing to religion; and the religious people on an average live longer than others. And they live longer because of right and useful business, and because of Divine solace in their burdens and cares. This is a part of the blessings conferred by the Lord upon those that serve him. And that service of the Lord is always a means of regeneration in society.

A servant of the Lord must and will bear his testimony against evil. The witness of many combined becomes a powerful lever for social improvement. But without the Sabbath these grave questions of purity and reform and happiness would get but little faithful and impressive consideration. The heathen moral philosophers of old, could write well some moral maxims and principles, but they had no sacred *Sabbath* in which to get the listening ear of the people, even if they would. Widely extended reformations could not follow.

Canon Farrar says this:

"For families in which, like sheltered flowers, spring up all that is purest and sweetest in human lives; for marriage exalted to an almost sacramental dignity; for all that circle of heavenly blessings which result from a common self-sacrifice; for that beautiful unison of noble manhood, stainless womanhood, joyous infancy, and uncontaminated youth; in one word, for all that there is of divinity and sweetness in the one word *Home!* for this—to an extent which we can hardly realize—we are indebted to Christianity alone."[1] But how could we have Christianity without the Sabbath? Count Montalembert says: "There is no religion without worship, and there is no worship without the Sabbath." From the testimony of these two distinguished writers we may deduce the lesson, that good society depends in great measure upon the Sabbath.

The mere fact of the frequent *change* from the secular to the religious given by the Sabbath, and then back again to the secular for provision for our earthly needs in itself makes the Sabbath an especial blessing to society. A French writer has the following: "God knows that we have need of change, and he provides generously for this necessity of our nature. He does not, indeed, grant to most of us the costly pleasure of travel, but he gives something else—the Lord's day—the Christian Sabbath, which interrupts the rude labour of the week, which brings with it family joys and rest of conscience, which gives us communion with our father and our brethren, and which procures to us here below a fore-

---
[1] Witness of history to Christ, p. 183.

taste of the life to come. Ah! if only, in our feverish, harassed age, each toiler would but accept the blessings of the Sabbath! *Without the Sabbath life is but one long sigh.* Woe to the poor toiler, above all, who on that day gives himself to work as a beast of burden, incapable of discerning the needs of his body, or as if he had no soul to guide him!" "*Le Besoin de Changement*," *Bulletin Dominical*, *May, 1880*.[1]

The Earl of Shaftesbury says: "Sunday is a day so sacred, so important, so indispensable to man, that it ought to be hedged round by every form of reverence. Its adaptability to the wants and necessities of society, the wisdom of its institution, proves it to be Divine; and, my lords, the working people of this country—the great bulk of the working people—regard it in that light. They differ, no doubt, many of them. Some take a religious view of the matter; others take a more political view of it; but all are of this mind, that the sanctity of Sunday is to them a grand protection."[2]

Says Emerson: "Two inestimable advantages Christianity has given us—first, the institution of preaching, the speech of man to man; and, secondly, the Sabbath, the jubilee of the whole world, whose light dawns welcome alike into the closet of the philosopher, into the garret of toil; and into prison cells, and everywhere suggests, even to the vile, the dignity of spiritual being. Let it stand for evermore a temple, which new light, new love, and new hope shall restore to more than its first splendour to mankind."

---
[1] Dr. Gritton's Times' Feast Heaven's Foretaste, p. 114.
[2] Dr. Gritton's Time's Feast, etc., p. 117.

It cannot be that the best state of society is ever secured without the Sabbath. We may judge so from first principles involved in the case, and we may know it also from the history of society in many lands. The purest state of society has always existed where the Sabbath has been best kept. The family there has been less disintegrated by sin, divorce has there been less frequent. Morality has there most prevailed. Improvement in Sabbath observance in any community means social improvement. A profanation of the Sabbath means a lower state of morals, and society more impure. The Sabbath converted from a holy day to a holiday means other looseness of morals, and general social degradation. A thorough social regeneration were impossible without the aid of a holy Sabbath.

CHAPTER XIV.

THE ADVANTAGES OF THE SABBATH FOR THE WELFARE AND PRESERVATION OF THE STATE.

What can save nations and give them enduring life? This has been one of the questions of the ages. Many sad and disastrous experiments have been made. The rise and fall of nations fill many pages of history. Mankind are clambering for wealth. Can wealth really exalt and perpetuate a nation? It gives a basis on which men erect their pride and ostentation. It often gives convenience and comfort, though not as much as general prosperity gives with neither extreme poverty nor great riches. Wealth often secures praise and glory, and even sycophancy and worship from some. Will any tell us that a nation rich in resources and treasures is a splendid object? Its splendor is no insurance for permanence. Will any point to memorable examples of antiquity, and read to us the full roll of opulent nations of the past? Their splendor passed away as the mist of the morning. They are fallen and destroyed. Not even the name of some is any honor to them in history. With many or all of them their riches were their destroying worm.

Can physical power, force of arms, mighty armies, fleets and navies, cause a nation to endure? Where now is ancient Rome, that sat upon her seven hills of glory and power, that sent her fleets and governors and armies abroad among the nations on schemes of conquest, and left scarcely a dominion of the world beyond her wide embrace? Rome is now only one of the feeblest of states instead of a kingdom, and it were almost forgotten among men, except for the dazzling views of her former splendor. What could have saved Rome so that no historian should have ever written the sad story of her decline and fall?

Alexander the Great was so endowed with power that he conquered the world, as we say, and then sat down and wept that there was no more for him to conquer. And yet, with all his might, he was so weak that he was seduced and ruined by the vices of the very people whom he had vanquished. He has no honorable name like even that of Socrates, and yet Socrates never had ten soldiers at his command.

Can literature and the arts truly perpetuate a nation? The wisdom and learning of all Greece, which stretching downwards in the stream of time become a fascination and a wonder for the present world, were unable to save. Neither her learning nor eloquence could uproot the slavery of her masses, or cast out the demon of her corruption. Her transgressions of even nature's holy laws finally swept her away with all the rubbish of nations long since destroyed and lost.

Can commerce give the elements of endurance to nations? What power has commerce which wealth has not? Since the latter fails the former must. Does our system of almost universal education, now so noted and so absorbent of attention and admiration, our common schools strewn abroad in almost every district where universal freedom has long prevailed, and our seminaries of learning, dotting and enlightening and gilding our nation, do all these really give a guarantee in themselves of endurance to this nation? Education, learning, separate from gospel conversion and culture of the soul, after all the glorying it has received, is of very doubtful influence and character. Mere knowledge may be used for sin and corruption, and often has been. Many statistics among civilized nations go to show that the morals of men have often grown worse while their intellectual advantages have grown better.

Not even morality has the power to preserve if destitute of the element of *righteousness*. The outward moral life, without the inner heart of piety, will leave the heart of sin to break forth in ulcers of corruption. Morality is not righteousness itself. If a man goes into a field where grow both wheat and corn, and coming to a plant which of course has leaves and stems, begins to contend that it is wheat because it has leaves and stems, when it is plain to every beholder that the plant is only a tare, he would not be more unwise than one who claims that *morality* is *righteousness* because the two have some features in common. One inherent property of gold is malleability, the capacity of being drawn under the hammer or rolling press. But what folly for one to bring us a piece of *iron*, and, demonstrating that it also is malleable, should set up a stout argument that the iron is gold and that we ought to receive it as such in payment of debt. Greater folly is it to contend that morality is righteousness, or equally valuable for a nation.

But what can preserve nations? The Divine word says that "Righteousness exalteth a nation." In that exaltation continued there is permanence. Righteousness is so right, so pure, so fair and so full of love to God and men, that it will not itself perish, nor suffer that which it permeates to perish. The very elements of righteousness are purifying and exalting. It will drive out evil, it will contend against all corrupting and degrading forces. Righteousness can not work at all, either with individuals or nations, except it makes pure, or keeps pure, or prospers and builds. A nation that receives and cherishes righteousness may be sure that it has a preserving and elevating force within itself. Righteousness put into the heart and life of a nation, will cleanse and ennoble, will give a national and normal power, will make the laws and functions of being do the part which the all-wise God has assigned them.

The *sine qua non* of national prosperity and preservation is righteousness, and a *sine qua non* of national righteousness is a holily kept Sabbath. But even an outwardly observed Sabbath is of great national value. Since the physical, intellectual and social man requires the Sabbath for his good, then the *state* demands it on the same grounds. The highest interests of the state are made up of the highest interests of the individuals comprising the state. Says Blackstone, the noted law commentator, "The keeping of one day in seven holy, or a time of relaxation and refreshment, as well as for public worship, is of admirable service to a state, considered merely as a civil institution." Adam Smith, a Scottish philosopher and political economist, says: "The Sabbath as a political institution, is of inestimable value independently of its claims to Divine authority." History and reason, the analysis and synthesis of the whole subject, overwhelmingly confirm all this testimony of so able men.

Nations may rise or fall by the observance or non-observance of the Sabbath. Sabbath desecration will eat out industry, integrity and honor, in the long trial. No nation can afford to do without a well-observed Sabbath. Criticize the Puritans as much as we will, admit though we may that some of them were over-rigid in their Sabbath observance, it still remains true, that their sacredly observed Sabbath was a great means of their grand exaltation and honor among men, and of their being the salt of preservation and purity to both England and America. The days of a lax Sabbath in England, have been eras of deterioration and corruption. A forerunner of ruin in the French nation was the attempt to annihilate the Sabbath. When private and public virtue begins to rise in any land the Sabbath begins to be better observed. Even a poorly observed Sabbath is better than none for national integrity.

The Sabbath is one of the bulwarks of the state. Strange that so many are blind, to its value. Laws to protect the Sabbath, are wise and just if within the bounds of discretion, and not an interference with rightful liberty. Sir Charles Reed, chairman of the London School Board says: "The defence of the Sabbath is a patriotic duty. Those who would remove the ancient landmarks are not the workingman's true friend. Their success means a loss, and not a gain, to the laboring man."

And laws for the defence of the Sabbath as a civil institution, are not laws for the establishment of religion, nor for the union of church and state. Some regard for morals, and for the means of good morals, must be had for the true welfare of the state. The Sabbath being filled with blessings for the physical, intellectual, and social man, it can be protected without any just charge of ecclesiastical legislation or oppression. "Laws which suspend labour on Sundays are not laws to enforce the religious observance of the day. They give men the opportunity of religiously observing the day; but they do not, they can not enforce the keeping of the day holy to God. They protect men in the enjoyment of a great physical and moral blessing. They secure the labourer from the grip of his employer by declaring ordinary labour to be illegal on Sundays."[1]

Pere Hyacinthe, at Geneva Conference, gave this testimony: "The Lord's day is not the day of God only; it is the day of humanity. This is the true democratic festival—this day of God and man. And yet this is the day which certain friends of the people wish to deprive them of. False friends that cheat them with the name of liberty, thinking only of their bodily needs, and not wisely even of those."[2] Thus do men of different nationalities, and of different schools of the Christian faith, agree in their testimony respecting the Sabbath.

[1] Sunday Laws, by Charles Hill, p. 10.
[2] Dr. Gritton's Time's Feast, etc., pp. 115, 116.

Another French writer, Monsieur Loyson, pleading for a well-observed Sabbath in France, points to two nations which in some measure exemplify what he desires: "Let us examine two industrial powers which are fully our equals, if they do not surpass us —England and the United States. In London, in the great city, where floods of busy men fill the streets, in the midst of the repeated incessant sound of all the echoes of labour, there occurs every week a day which recalls to me those of my childhood. The gigantic machine which, on the eve of that day, put all in movement, stops: everywhere repose and silence; the bells alone—Protestant bells, I know, but —they send their sweet melodies heavenwards. It seems as if the very fogs of the Thames and of the ocean had grown lighter. Let me not be told that the Sunday rest in England is a remnant of feudality and aristocracy, soon to be swept away by the breath of Liberty. Behold in America that strong and young Anglo-Saxon race, which certainly is not of the Middle Ages, and which has in its constitution the most complete liberty. It also observes Sunday . . . and sends us across the ocean the same answer as England—the silence of God at the blasphemies of men. No; we do not ask that the Sunday should be imposed upon the people by laws of which the application would offer more inconvenience than advantage. We ask the liberty of the Sunday, and Sunday by liberty."[1]

While the wise and good of European lands look with longing desire to the Christian Sabbath of the

[1] "Daily News," Sept. 27, 1867. Dr. Gritton's Times Feast, etc., p. 132.

United States, shall we of this union be so false to our own weal and honor as to adopt the European Continental Sabbath, which changes the weekly holyday into a worldly holiday, and which is so great a sorrow to all the godly that have to endure it?

CHAPTER XV.

THE ADVANTAGES OF THE SABBATH IN ITS REWARD FOR OBSERVANCE.

Encouragement and hope for doing right are primal qualities. These the Sabbath gives. One exemplifying passage is this; "Then shalt thou delight thyself in the Lord, and I will cause thee to ride upon the high places of the earth, and feed thee with the heritage of Jacob thy father; for the mouth of the Lord hath spoken it" (Isa. lviii:14). In the scriptures the keeping of the Sabbath is supposed to be accompanied with the keeping of the other commandments. It is so important and cardinal a duty that often around it seem to circle, as the planets around their central orb, all the other duties of the Christian religion. Great is the reward for striving to keep all of Christ's words. He says: "Blessed are the poor in spirit." "Blessed are the meek." "Blessed are the pure in heart." He says, also: "Blessed is the man . . . that keepeth the Sabbath from polluting it. . . . Also the sons of the stranger, . . . every one that keepeth the Sabbath from polluting it, or taketh hold of my covenant" (Isa. lvi:26). Sabbath-keeping is placed by the side of keeping covenant with God. Has God any rewards for his servants? Has he blessings for his people? They are vouchsafed to him who keeps the Sabbath holy.

And punishment awaits those who profane the Sabbath. "Her priests have violated my law . . . and have hid their eyes from my Sabbaths, and I am profaned among them. Therefore have I poured out mine indignation upon them" (Ezek. xxii:26, 31). The same Divine principles pertaining to reward and punishment pervade the new dispensation that belonged to the old. We have the sacred day and the sacred convocations of the day to observe now as much as ever. The weight of obligation is increased as we come into the new dispensation, for the light and the advantages are the more. They who do not regard the Sabbath may know that they have not the guarantee for the Divine blessing. They may receive mercies still, but not because of the promise. The young have peculiar advantages for prosperity in observing the Sabbath. If they will early begin to do it, and then persevere, they will in some way ride upon the high places of the earth; they will be safely borne through the stormiest trials; they will have Divine provision for their wants; they will be fed with the heritage of Jacob. Pres. Wayland, in speaking of the observance of the Sabbath, says: "Every attentive observer has remarked, that the violation of this command by the young, is one of the most decided marks of incipient degeneracy. Religious restraint is fast losing its hold upon that young man, who, having been brought up in the fear of God, begins to spend the Sabbath in idleness, or in amusement."

When it is found that the law of the Sabbath is trampled upon by individuals or communities, there is no surer evidence that there has become an insane love of the world; reason is subjected to appetite and passion; a heaven-daring spirit has begun its rule; recklessness is engendered; carnal pleasure—not duty and the highest happiness—has become the law of the soul, and the judgments of God are upon the track, and without repentance and reformation the doom of final condemnation is sealed.

On the other hand, if the law of the Sabbath is observed, if the day is esteemed a delight, if it is pleasure to the soul, or to the community, to honor the day as that which God has honored, then the blessing will be that which God gave to the day in the beginning. He "blessed the seventh day and sanctified it"; he will assuredly bless those who also sanctify it. No sabbath-keeping person was ever without the special and peculiar blessing of God; no sabbath-keeping nation has ever perished; no sabbath-keeping soul has ever been lost.

In the keeping of his commandments there is great reward (Psalm xix:11). This is true respecting the statute of the Sabbath or of any other command. Very many are the evidences of providential prosperity and preservation to those who keep the Sabbath. Working seven days in the week instead of six, on the score of economy has many times been proven a failure, both for man and beast; for man both physically and mentally. Those who would make haste in journeying by traveling on the Sabbath, have often been defeated in their object, besides abusing their own souls by their disregard of God's requirements, and doing harm to others by their evil example. Those who sacredly rest on the Sabbath, clearly obtain physical, intellectual, and religious reward. Besides that, they seem on the whole to have a peculiar favoring of *Providence*, which gives them blessings in addition to those of the natural laws ordained of God. Sabbath-breaking causes recklessness, and that causes more accidents, and more deaths by accidents on that day than on any other in proportion to the amount of exposure. And in addition, providential judgments often especially seem to follow those who trample on the Sabbath.

In the Boston Sabbath convention, year 1879, M. Field Fowler, Esq., gave the following testimony concerning the running of the Metropolitan horse-cars in that city: " Soon I saw some of the evils growing out of this business. In the first place, we had much trouble with our conductors in keeping them honest. It is impossible to get honest men, and keep them so, and make them work on Sundays You employ them to violate the Fourth commandment, and expect them to respect the Eighth; you find human nature is such that both conductors and drivers suffer. Drivers become reckless, are not careful, their faculties become blunted, and more accidents result. The managers employed detectives. I remember a young man came to one of the directors, and wanted to know why he was discharged. " Because we think more money goes into your pockets than comes out." He confessed it; and the reason he gave was, that his driver said if he would not divide with him, he would put him over the road so that he couldn't get half as many passengers. In every way it was demoralizing.

Furthermore, as to the horses, what is the result? You work horses every day, year in and year out. Talk about cruelty to animals, why, it is like putting a horse on a treadmill, and keeping him going until he almost drops. The result is, you use up horses in a very short time. Of course some work them harder than others, but I believe two or three years is considered about the average length of usefulness of a horse on New York roads, and three or four here, perhaps. The harder you work them the more you have to feed them. The president of one of the horse railroads of New York told me he made an experiment, and decided the thing to his satisfaction. He found that, on every thousand horses, it cost them a thousand dollars a day more to feed them than if they had Sunday to rest in . . . I am convinced by investigation that the running of horse-cars on Sunday involves the employment of certainly twenty-five per cent. if not more of horses, than if you rest them on that day. Take the omnibuses; they don't run Sundays. Mr. Hathorne tried it one year, and he said if kept up it would ruin him. New York omnibuses do not run on Sundays; there is no profit in it."[1]

The Hartford Steam Boiler Inspection & Insurance Company, discern the same principle of reward for keeping the Sabbath, and express themselves thus: "The custom of making repairs and improvements on the Sabbath is, in our opinion, a loss in the end. . . . If men are required to work on the Sabbath, the influence will be demoralizing. They will not have the same respect for any law as they otherwise would, nor will they, in our opinion, have the same respect for their employers' interest. The whole practice is wrong, and contrary to the instinct of those even who have religious convictions. . . .

[1] Sabbath Essays, pp. 422, 423.

Work of necessity is different and there would be no difference of opinion on that point. But be careful not to imagine a mercenary feeling into a necessity!"

The unprofitableness of violating the fourth commandment is being more and more acknowledged and considered by the truly observing. Rev. W. W. Atterbury, Secretary of the New York Sabbath Committee, in the Boston Convention said: " In Germany many of the prominent pastors have felt the vital need of a more religious observance of the day, and are actively engaged in promoting it; and the Supreme Church Council of Prussia, and several of the provincial synods, have earnestly taken up the matter. The Reformed Church assemblies of Bohemia and Hungary have recently called attention to the same subject. In the Roman Catholic Church, in France and to some extent in Belgium and elsewhere, there exists a similar movement; and a religious association formed for this purpose a few years ago received the special benediction of Pope Pius IX. . . . Societies have been formed in nearly every country of Europe for promoting the secular and civil as well as the religious observance of Sunday. The Social Democrats of Germany, at their Conference in 1877, affirmed as one of their principles, the suspension of work on Sunday to be assumed by the State."[1]

If we contrast the Sabbath observed with the Sabbath desecrated, we shall everywhere see that there is *reward* for sacredly regarding the fourth commandment. The Church=going throngs are far more attractive to the candid eye than the Sabbath=breaking excursions. The quiet Sabbath=keeping family

[1] Sab. Essays, pp. 406, 407.

is far more beautiful at home, than the pleasure-seekers abroad. The young man who goes to the Sanctuary and the Sabbath-school, and then to his father's roof for Sabbath-reading and conversation, gives far better promise than the young man who sleeps away the church-going hours, and then strolls off through fields and woods, or dashes through the streets on a Sunday afternoon ride. The Sabbath-keeping, church-going young lady is far more lovely and promising than the worldly, vain, church-hating young woman—hardly a lady—who invites company to her parlors, or seeks it by walks with young men on the Lord's day. Children trained to Sabbath observance, have far superior manners, and graces of spirit, as compared with those that are trained in an utterly Sabbathless home.

An English Sabbath is thus described by one born and loved in it: " Which of the Sabbath-desecrating nations of Europe does not envy us? They may throw out the taunt against our English Sunday of *tristeness*, and melancholy, and gloom: but hardly can they look upon the glad multitudes as they throng to the house of God—the closed shop and warehouse announcing that the inmates are enjoying their privileged and protected rest—the well-dressed artisan and his family meditating in the fields at eventide—and the great city, with its silence unbroken by the sound of axe or hammer,—hardly can their eyes rest on such a scene as this, without the thought forcing itself upon them, Happy are the people that are in such a case: yea blessed are the people who have the Lord for their God."[1]

[1] Our Sundays, by Dr. Moore, p. 29; Dr. Gritton's Time's Feast, etc. p. 119.

Yet another English writer, Dr. James Hamilton, says: "Oh! blessed Sabbath, needed for a world of innocence! Without thee, what would be a world of sin! Like its Lord, it rises upon us as the light of seven days with healing in its wings. It has been the coronation=day of martyrs—the feast=day of saints. It has been from the first until now, the sublime custom of the Churches of God. Still the outgoings of its morning and evening rejoice. It is a day of heaven and earth, life's sweetest calm, poverty's best birthright, labour's only rest. Nothing has such hoary antiquity upon it—nothing contains in it such a history—nothing draws along with it such a glory. Nurse of virtue! Seal of truth! The household's richest patrimony, the nation's noblest safeguard! The pledge of peace, the fountain of intelligence, the strength of law! The oracle of instruction! The ark of mercy! The patent of our manhood's spiritual greatness—the harbinger of our soul's sanctified perfection—the glory of religion—the watch=tower of immortality—the ladder set up on earth whose top reacheth to heaven, with angels of God ascending and descending upon it."

CHAPTER XVI.

THE ADVANTAGES AND NECESSITY OF THE SABBATH IN RESPECT TO MORALS AND RELIGION.

The highest commendation of the Christian Sabbath or Lord's day, is its inestimable moral and religious benefits. The religious nature of man is the crown of his being. Our Creator designed that it should preside as ruler over all our other endowment. How it would impoverish us all to be deprived of our religious capacities. Benefit our moral nature and you send a refreshing, fructifying stream through all the other human faculties and interests. It is a fact many times proven, that the allowed desecration of the Christian Sabbath is followed by a depraving of morals. On the contrary, it is equally proven, that the sacred observance of the Sabbath results in well-kept laws, and purified morality. Who are the criminals that die on the gallows? With few exceptions they are Sabbath-breakers. Who fill up our jails, prisons and penitentiaries? Desecrators of the Sabbath. Who become maniacs through vices of any kind, and afterwards crowd our lunatic asylums, or go so often into the suicide's grave? The great proportion are Sabbath-breakers. Go through all the by-ways, highways, and avenues of society, from the lowest and most degraded of mankind, to those the most opulent and proud, and ask, Who are the vicious? who are contaminators of private and public morals; who are swearers, thieves, gamblers. robbers, defaulters, murderers; who are sowing the seeds of death, and scattering the fire-brands of hell? One of the most comprehensive replies to these questions will be, Sabbath-breakers. Sir William Blackstone says again, "The profanation of the Sabbath is an offense against God and religion." And again he says: "A corruption of morals usually follows a profanation of the Sabbath."

"A committee in the British House of Commons in 1832, on the observance of the Sabbath, was composed of the following eminent men: Sir Andrew Agnew, Mr. Burton, Sir Robert Peel, Lord Morpeth, Sir Thomas Fowler Baring. One gentleman testified before them, that he had been employed as chaplain of prisons twenty-eight years, that during that time not less than seven thousand prisoners had annually passed under his care, and that during the twenty-eight years he had had, in a measure, the religious instruction of one hundred thousand criminals. He said he made it a point to see in private those who were charged with capital offences, and that he did not recollect a single case among them all, where the party had not been a Sabbath-breaker, and in many cases they had assured him, that Sabbath-breaking was the first step in their course of crime. He adds, "I may say in reference to prisoners of all classes that nineteen out of twenty of them have neglected the Sabbath." An investigation on this point was once made in the State prison of Connecticut, and at that time ninety out of one hundred of its inmates had been habitual Sabbath-breakers. A similar examination with a similar result was had in Massachusetts prisons. Of the one thousand, six hundred and fifty-three criminals who had been committed to the New York State Auburn Prison previous to the year 1840, only twenty-nine had kept the Sabbath. Such has been the result of all investigations ever made on the subject, so far as they have been made known.

The enemies of religion understand this subject. They know that to make the name of Jesus Christ forgotten, they must blot out the Sabbath as a religious day. Bold and rank infidelity has no respect for the Sabbath. The infidels of France fitted their means to their ends as well as they could, when they changed the week of seven days to that of ten, thus hoping to rid themselves and the French nation of the remembrance of the Lord's day. But the result of the experiment proved two things; that man needed the *rest* of the Sabbath; that also he needed its *religious influence*. For, the nine days of labor, with the tenth for a holiday," *increased* the exhaustion of man and *diminished* the aggregate amount of labor." What else? The total abrogation of the Sabbath by Revolutionary France was followed by a general corruption of morals; the sense of moral obligation between man and man was greatly extinguished; the marriage relation was widely broken up and men and women lived together almost as brutes. Twenty thousand divorces were registered in the short space of eighteen months. Then the Frenchmen fell to the work of chopping off human heads. The faction to-day in power filled the gutters of the streets of Paris with the blood of their enemies, and to-morrow their own headless bodies were carted out of the city by thousands. Human sympathy and affection were well-nigh gone. Men became tigers, the dupes and servants of hell. All these fruits were in fact the manifest indignation and desertion of God, because of the impious attempts to blot out the Sabbath from the memory of man.

The observance of the Lord's day is a necessity for the due and full worship of God by the human race. Without it the spirit to glorify God and to praise him will not have adequate development and growth. Nor will man cultivate properly his religious nature without that day. Without it worldliness will overwhelm him, and leave his soul barren, and hard, and unfruitful of good. Cruel unbelief will come in, the heart of man will become beaten down into fallow-ground desolation, or will run into the thickets of vice and corruption.

It may unqualifiedly be said. that spiritual religion never prospers without the Sabbath. Every revival of religion results in the more faithful observance of the Lord's day, or creates that observance where it had not been before. Dr. Chalmers said, "We never, in the whole course of our recollections, met with a Christian friend, who bore upon his character every other evidence of the Spirit's operations, who did not remember the Sabbath day to keep it holy." And the pious and ardent McCheyne said, "Can you name one godly minister of any denomination in all Scotland, who does not hold the duty of the entire sanctification of the Lord's day? Did you ever meet with a lively believer in any country under heaven—one who loved Christ, and lived a holy life—who did not delight in keeping holy to God the entire Lord's day?" Even if there be exceptions to McCheyne's rule, what he has in mind shows the united trend of true piety and the sacred observance of the Sabbath. Lord Kames said, "Sunday is a day of account, and a candid account every seventh day is the best preparation for the great day of account:" Lord Bacon said, "The first creature of God in the works of days was the light of sense, and the last was the light of reason, and his Sabbath work ever since is the illumination of the Spirit." Indeed, who are emphatically illumined by the Spirit save they who regard the Sabbath. They who keep the Sabbath holy are under the training ef the Holy Spirit; at least during its sacred hours. Blessed Teacher! able to make wise unto Salvation, and for eternity.

The Lord's day thus becomes one of the best evidences of the truth of Christianity, and even an evidence of the existence of God. It is the *Lord's day*, that now, in the new dispensation, becomes the highest evidence. It commemorates Christ's resurrection. Therefore it is the *Lord's* day. It is a remembrance of Christ's completed work. It points ever to the capstone of the perfected evidences of Christ's sonship with God. "If Christ be not risen, then is our preaching vain, and your faith is also vain" (1 Cor. xv. 14). The Lord's day is also a remembrancer of the Divine assurance that all men will be raised from the dead. "If there be no resurrection of the dead, then is Christ not risen." "And if Christ be not raised, your faith, is vain; ye are yet in your sins." (1 Cor. xv. 13, 17. Christianity has an immense superiority over Judaism; the new covenant is better than the old. (Heb. viii:6-8). We can not dispense with the Lord's day. We can not go back to the ancient types and symbols. The benefits of Christianity can not be without Christ. Christ can not be to us the *Life* without his resurrection. We in part deny his resurrection if we deny the Lord's day. If we deny or discard even a *part* of the day, we deny or discard, or profane a part of the power of the religion of Christ. Sir Walter Scott said, "Give to the world one-half of Sunday, and you will find that religion has no strong hold of the other."

It is one of the laws perceived in nature, and demonstrated in history, that the highest success of religion requires frequent entire days sacredly devoted to her service, and not merely parts of days. The holiness of the day passes out if worldliness comes in. Pure spring water will not retain its clearness, if a coloring liquid be intermingled with it. God has appointed sacred services for secular days; but he has never made half of the same day sacred and the other half secular, and men will never successfully do it. They will not desire to do it when they are illumined and led by the Holy Spirit. In lands where the half religious, and the half secular system for the Lord's day has been adopted, the intelligent and devoted Christians look with longing to the countries where the Christian Sabbath is sacredly kept through all its hours. These various truths confirm the doctrine that the holy observance of the Lord's day is of perpetual obligation for the well-being of man in his entire nature, physical, intellectual, moral and religious.

We come in this discussion to a trilemma, a choice **between three alternatives.** One choice is, that the world have no weekly Sabbath. Both reason and scripture cry out against such a horrid preference. Another choice is, that only the seventh day be observed as the Sabbath. Such a decision would put mankind back into Judaism, the old dispensation; whereas we know that the new covenant is better, and by Divine purpose takes the place of the old, The remaining choice is, to follow the teaching of Scripture and providence, and accept the Lord's day as the Christian Sabbath, of *perpetual obligation* and of so *great and peculiar advantages*, that they conspire with Scripture evidence to pronounce it the day of Heaven. This view comports with reason as well as with the word of God. Christianity is better than Judaism, though not contrary to it, since it grew out of it. The Christian Sabbath has in the Old Testament its basis and in the New Testament its capstone. No candid and thorough examination of Scripture can set aside all Sabbaths, even though the old dispensation has closed; nor can it adhere only to the Mosaic Sabbath. We do despite to the revelation from God in the new dispensation, if we discard all testimony in favor of the Lord's day as the sacred weekly rest day in the Divine economy. Since we must choose for our Sabbath between the seventh day and the first, the great mass of the Christian world would do violence to their most intelligent and devout convictions, if they were to reject the Lord's day and choose the seventh. Such a gross anomaly mankind will never witness. And if Christians universally were to contemplate abandoning the Lord's day and observing no Sabbath, even the Godless, in their sober reflections, would protest against such a profanation of both reason and Scripture. They who love the Christian Sabbath have unbounded reasons for rejoicing, and thanksgiving to God, because their holy day stands on so firm a basis, and is so replete with blessings to the Church of God, and to mankind.

CHAPTER XVII.

HOW TO KEEP THE SABBATH.

The Scriptures tell us that by steadfastly, and with open face, beholding the glory of the Lord we may be made partakers of his glory. But we all, with open face beholding as in a glass the glory of the Lord, are changed into the same image from glory to glory, even as by the Spirit of the Lord. (2 Cor. iii. 18) So the Sabbath may be a *mission* to us, in which we may behold the *holiness* of the Lord and thus be made partakers of his holiness. The Divine command is, to "Remember the Sabbath-day, to keep it holy." By endeavoring to keep this command men may find great assistance for personal holiness of heart and life. A part of the assistance lies in the aid to a real *conception* of the nature of holiness. The Sabbath demands the putting away of all secular things, beyond the requisites of necessity and mercy, and the taking of the spiritual and religious for our thoughts and our ways during its sacred time. This in its true spirit involves a most salutary training for holiness, without which no man shall see the Lord.

One passage of Scripture preeminently sets forth the Divine *method* for keeping the Sabbath-day holy. It is this: "If thou turn away thy foot from the Sabbath, from doing thy pleasure on my holy day; and call the Sabbath a delight and the holy of the Lord, honorable; and shalt honor it, not doing thine own ways, nor finding thine own pleasure, nor speaking thine own words: Then shalt thou delight thyself in the Lord; and I will make thee to ride upon the high places of the earth, and I will feed thee with the heritage of Jacob, thy father: for the mouth of the Lord hath spoken it. (Isa. lviii. 13, 14)

The foregoing passage is kindred to the Fourth Commandment. The latter tells us to keep the Sabbath "holy." The former says it is a "holy day," and therefore, it is to be holily kept. The very holiness is to be regarded as a "delight," and not as a dread. It is to be esteemed "the holy of the Lord, honorable." God in his *holiness* is to be honored upon it, Secular "ways," and "pleasure," and "words," are not to be indulged. With such holy observance one will "delight" himself "in the Lord," and will be transformed into likeness to Christ the Lord.

More minutely: In the foregoing passage from Isaiah, the Lord sets forth the keeping of the Sabbath both negatively and positively. On the negative side we are to keep the Sabbath by refraining from certain things, and on the positive side by engaging in certain things. The things to be refrained from are these: "Doing thine own ways," "Finding thine own pleasure," and "speaking thine own words." The things to be engaged in are these: "Turn away thy foot from the Sabbath," "Call the Sabbath a delight," and the holy of the Lord, honorable," "Honor him," "Delight thyself in the Lord."

On the negative side:

1. "Not doing thine own ways." It implies, of course, not doing any *sinful* "ways," for those are wrong on all days The reference is distinctly to *secular* "ways," which are *right* on other days of the week, but unnecessary on the Sabbath, and unfriendly to the holy keeping of that day. God has given us, in a sense, six days as our *own*. In them we are to do all *our* work, and engage in all proper and useful ways. But the Sabbath is the Lord's day, and on it we are not to attend to *our* business, our week-day employments, or any of our "own ways." Whatever we do on the Sabbath which is of our "own ways," in that we violate the holy time. Upon that day we are to do wholly according to God's ways.

2. "Nor finding thine own pleasure." To keep the Sabbath one must cease finding not only *sinful* pleasure, but also all wordly pleasures suitable and proper on the six secular days, of the week. "Thine OWN pleasure." That is what the Lord has given us as specifically ours in the week time. It does not embrace God's peculiar pleasure for us on the Sabbath.

3. "Nor speaking thine own words." Words that are wicked on any day should, of course, be excluded on the Lord's day. But, we have a great amount of conversation and public speaking during the six days which should not be admitted to the Sabbath. The inference is necessitated, that if we engage in secular or worldly conversation on the Sabbath, whether about business or about pleasure, except as some necessity or mercy. or some religious end, requires it, we violate the commandment of God. There may be

conversation about the works of God in nature, or about people and society, or even business, which has a religious bearing or design. Such conversation is allowable on the Sabbath. But, the mere gossipy, talk, that has no moral or religious air, or vein about it, is a desecration of the Christian Sabbath. Our conversation on the Sabbath should be appropriate to "the holy of the Lord," which the Sabbath is termed in the text.

We turn now to the *positive* side, to the things which should be engaged in on the Sabbath.

1. "Turn away thy foot from the Sabbath." Turning the foot *to* or upon the Sabbath, would be *trampling upon* it. We are to turn our foot *away* from that. Hence we are to take pains, make calculations, and preparations, to *observe* the Sabbath's sacred hours, hours appointed to a sacred use. We should not pack great worldliness and exhaustion upon ourselves, or upon others on Saturday, so as to load its burden off partly upon the Lord's day, or so as to render ourselves unfit to spend the Sabbath holily, or other than as sleeping animals. While the Sabbath is in part for both physical and mental, as well as spiritual, *rest*, we yet should leave our rational natures for some activity upon it. Without that we can not obtain and enjoy *rest in God*, for which that holy day was in chief part designed. We should have express *plans* to keep the Sabbath holy, plans not to trample on its designs, nature, or claims.

2. "Call the Sabbath a delight." Though we refrain from all *outward* violations of the Sabbath, and though that refraining be useful, yet unless our souls take actual "delight" in the Sabbath, we are found

wanting. Without that the heart which God approves is not in us. It is far better for others, and for ourselves, not to violate outwardly, even if we are destitute of the right heart; but the real and full blessing can come upon us only when we "delight" to observe outwardly and inwardly, and in our hearts really call the Sabbath itself a "delight."

3. "Call the Sabbath and the holy of the Lord honorable." This does not say or mean, "Call the Sabbath the holy *to* the Lord," but "the holy *of* the Lord," "of Jehovah," a day of holiness given of God for men, a day "honorable," of especial honor because it is so sacred a gift from God's great bounties. The early Christians called the first day of the week, "the day of heaven," "the queen of days." To a true saint in the enjoyment of religion, the Christian Sabbath will always be a "delight," and "honorable," the choicest of all the week. Its hours will not drag heavily with him. Communing with God, or being in a state accordant with such communion, his temptations will not be many, or strong, or harassing, to break over the restraints of the day; he will not find his thoughts ever roaming for worldly themes; his heart will not long for the day to be gone. He will rejoice in its coming; for then he may lay aside the secular cares and engagements of the week and yield his soul to the communions and enjoyments more in unison with his spirit; and then his religious thoughts, meditations, and society, may be uninterrupted by the world. Often can he exclaim, with the primitive saints, "Day of heaven!" "Queen of days!"

4. "Honor him." The Sabbath is probably here personified, and the pronoun "him" refers to the Sab-

bath, and not to Jehovah. And the idea is, that men should *honor* the day on which God has bestowed some splendor of his glory by sanctifying it, as recorded in the beginning (Gen. ii. 3). Jehovah honors the day by appointing it to holy purposes. Can we honor it by devoting it to secular purposes? God honored it by making it a day of "holy convocation" (Lev. xxiii. 2). Can we honor it by neglecting the convocation for worship, and by disobeying the command, "Forsake not the assembling of yourselves together," (Heb. x. 25)? How unlike God are those who turn their foot to the Sabbath, and trample upon it. What a difference between those who aim only to refrain from positive transgressions of the Sabbath, and those who rise into a far higher atmosphere, and as by intuition, or the perpetual bubblings of an ever-flowing fountain, pour forth their joy and praise, and Sabbatic honors, unto the Lord!

5. "Delight thyself in the Lord." If we make and treat the Sabbath as a "delight," by that we shall be so trained and built up that God will be a delight to us, and not a being of fear and dread. There is no cause for wonder that those who do not keep the Sabbath holy do not have joy and comfort in the Lord, do not like solid religious reading on the Sabbath, do not love to meet in the sanctuary.

We find that in the text we have, negative and positive together, eight distinct and emphatic principles for our guidance in keeping the Sabbath day holy. From those principles we may deduce many lessons of closer application to ourselves. A few we do well now to name and consider:

1. It is wrong to put seven days' works into six, if

that is going to make us stupid and unfit for God's worship and the sanctuary. For God has provided for only six days' work in the seven, and he has provided for the sanctuary and for our attendance upon it.

2. All intellectual labor on the Sabbath other than what is moral and religious, or what is requisite for spiritual worship, or for necessary mercy, is Sabbath profanation. Children and students who learn their secular lessons of the week on the Lord's day, do wrong, and their parents and teachers do wrong who allow them in it. Keeping secular book-accounts on the Sabbath is also wrong and a kind of partial suicide.

3. Publishing a secular newspaper on the Sabbath day is a violation of the day, and is a very great evil, because it tempts thousands to desecrate the Sabbath by secular, and often corrupting, reading. Purchasing the secular newspaper on the Sabbath is also wrong, as well as advertising in it, and running a train, or being a newsboy to carry it and sell it, is wrong. Editors and publishers are bound to exempt one day in seven from all labor for the secular press. If all laborers in this business, or any other business, can not always keep precisely the same hours free from secularities, and devoted to sacred purposes, still all laborers should keep holy one day in seven.

4. Traveling or journeying on the Sabbath, except from providential necessity or mercy, is violation of the fourth commandment. Pleasure-riding on that day is particularly embraced by one of the condemnatory principles of the text; for it is *finding one's own pleasure* on the Sabbath. Riding to church; in case of need of it, on that day is allowable; for it is find-

ing God's pleasure. Riding to church, as some probably do, for mere fashion and show, is wrong. If any think it hard that they cannot indulge in pleasure-riding on the Sabbath, they should be reminded that their *hearts* are not in unison with the Lord, else the Sabbath properly kept would be their "delight." If any need to ride for health on the Sabbath, that is allowable if they cannot get health enough in that way in the week-time. Yet, they should be careful about it, lest their example encourage secular pleasure-riding. To take all of one's medicine on the Sabbath looks to men a little like sponging from the Lord, and to the Lord no doubt it looks worse still. Walking for mere pleasure on the Sabbath amid sights and curiosities, whether of people or smaller things, is likely to secularize the mind and unfit it for God's holy purposes in this day. Walking for *exercise* on the Sabbath, or getting into the open air for health's sake, where no associations or tendencies are evil, is allowable. Yet, we need to keep strict watch, lest in getting a little good to ourselves by any such indulgence, we do much harm to others in connection with it.

5. Secular visiting on the Sabbath is Sabbath trespassing. A little *religious* visiting in special cases may sometimes be well; yet, ordinarily we should leave people by themselves, and without much company, on the Lord's day, except as they are in church. These restrictive principles will create better personal character, and better society in the end. If any have not a heart for all this, it is sad that they do not love God's ways instead of their own ways; for God's ways are fitted to make the most and the best of them.

(6) Visiting on the Sabbath by means of secular letter-writing, must be accounted a violation of the day. If persons write religiously on the Sabbath, the secular matters should be left until a week-day. Writing on secular matters must be a secular act which belongs to our own six days, and not to the Lord's holy day which he has reserved for our own religious benefit. But, writing *itself* is a mechanical act, and composing is a mere intellectual act, without in itself being religious at all, and it were generally better to defer all of that, doubtless, even the religious letter-writing, from the Sabbath to the week-time, and take on the Lord's day, after our active religious work, and necessary secular duties, such reading and communing as will leave us more in the passive rather than the active state. At least, we should not write of *secular* matters on the Sabbath, unless for an immediate *religious* purpose, or for some real necessity or mercy. If any say that they must write even their secular letters on the Sabbath because they have not time during the week, they should be reminded that there is a way of dishonoring God and doing the less to pay for it, and a way of *honoring* him and doing *more*, and being the greater, in consequence. They who think they can improve upon God's ordering of affairs will be poor at last.

(7) Corporations and joint stock companies violate the Sabbath if they allow their property to be unnecessarily employed in secular business on the Lord's day. Railroad managers should curtail the running of trains on the Sabbath as much as consistent with necessity and mercy. They never should

run them for Sabbath-breaking excursions. Owners of railroad stock should protest against the use of their property in Sabbath desecration and ever protest.

(8) Imposing unecessary labor on employes on the Sabbath is desecration of the day. In the Fourth commandment the prohibition of labor extends to "thy man-servant, nor thy maid-servant" (Ex. xx: 10). As given in Deuteronomy we read, "That thy man-servant and thy maid-servant may rest as well as thou" (v: 14). Employers should provide as much as they can for the keeping of the Sabbath, and the attendance at church, by those they employ. It is one important and legitimate way of doing good.

(9) The Sabbath is violated by undue sleeping and lolling during its hours; and also by undue indulgence of appetite resulting in excessive dullness. Over-eating over-strains internal organs, and sometimes makes the blood settle back too much into the brain, or produces other unhealthy congestion. Many persons can sleep too much at once. With active pursuits during the week, and over-sleep on the Sabbath, there is not sufficient exercise to keep the circulation good on the surface, and so the blood settles in upon internal and sensitive organs, which cannot bear the load without danger to health, and sometimes to life. In this way it is demonstrable that people are better off to get up in proper season, and get out to church, than to lie asleep half the day, and then perhaps go a Sabbath-breaking in the afternoon and evening. Doubtless we have a right to sleep more if we wish on Sundays than on other days, because the Sabbath is in part for physical re-

cuperation and rest; but we have not a right to allow sleep and stupor to trespass on religious service and *spiritual* rest, for which the Sabbath was preeminently designed.

If any object that we cannot found the observance of the Lord's day on the Fourth Commandment we reply: First by disagreeing with that statement; Secondly, there was an ante-Sinaitic Sabbath, a premosaic Sabbath, dating, doubtless, from the close of Creation. That Sabbath was for *man*. Found the Lord's day Sabbath on that.

If any say we are not bound to keep the Lord's day holy, we disagree, for this reason; the early Christians, as we have seen, deemed the Lord's day *holy*, the *chief* of all days and they sacredly observed it. Those early Christians derived their belief and practice directly or closely from the Apostles and the Apostles from Christ or the Holy Spirit. Therefore we should keep holy the Lord's day.

Some object that we are wrongly bound to keep Jewish Sabbatic laws and customs. Not so. We are not bound to keep any merely Jewish laws or customs. Jewish merely civil and ceremonial laws are obsolete. Strong analogy sometimes holds us to a Jewish principle. Circumstances alter cases. The Jews could not build fires on their Sabbath but they could on each Sabbath between sun and sun. Their holy time ending at sunset, they could then have fire and prepare their usually chief meal of the day, it being during the same daylight with their Sabbath. But with the same law in force we could not have that privilege; our Sabbath commencing and closing with midnight. Their gathering sticks on the Sabbath was like our hauling cord wood from the forest to the home door on that day. In both cases it would be a high affront to heaven.

We should take notice that the character of an act depends upon the motive for it, or the end in view. Preparing shew bread for the temple on the Sabbath, and placing it there was a sacred and holy act. But except for its object it would have been secular and sinful. The same difference with the double sacrifice on the Sabbath is to be noticed. So with us; two parties may be riding together by private or public conveyance on the Sabbath, and the act of each will be sinful or holy according to the end in view, which may be seeking amusement or the service of God in divine worship, If the right object is ever made an excuse for pursuing the wrong that also is sinful.

From the Scripture law of the Sabbath the foregoing requisites and prohibitions are deduced. They are drawn from the Sabbatic *moral* law; not from civic and ceremonial provisions or enactments made specifically for the Jewish nation in their particular circumstances, and not made binding upon all men. But these lessons derived from the moral law are preeminently fitted to promote holiness. They require holiness of heart and life during one seventh part of time, The mere outward observance is not satisfactory to Jehovah. Holiness taught one seventh part of the time, is in itself fitted to promote holiness during the secular part of the week, and during the whole life. The Sabbath is God's great training school and university for holiness and for heaven. The holy "convocation" divinely appointed for the Sabbath, is exactly fitted to the design for holiness, and the holiness when sufficiently cultivated, prepares the soul to see the Lord in peace. In the fourth of Hebrews we are taught. that the Sabbatic rest on earth is a symbol of the holy rest which remains for all the servants of God in heaven. This fact assumes that the earthly Sabbath is designed to qualify penitent and obedient minds for the endless condition of heavenly glory. It also suggests that we are not left in the new dispensation without a Sabbath, for, as preparatory for heaven it is as much needful now as ever, and in its added commemoration of Christ's resurrection, its service for the heavenly rest is greatly heightened.

APPENDIX.

I.

Prof. Geo. T. Ladd, D.D., of Yale College in his work, "The Doctrine of Sacred Scripture," in writing concerning the Sabbath speaks of "discrepancies" in the "two editions" respecting that day (Ex. 20:8-11, and Deut. 5:12-15). [Vol. I., pp. 101, 102.] He also speaks of "two variant and somewhat conflicting forms" in the two copies of the sacred Fourth Commandment.

In respect to these statements, "Discrepancy" savors of disagreement or contradiction, we ought not in that sense to admit of discrepancy in the two accounts. One copy may exceed another without contradicting it. The two copies of the command are not, as we think, "somewhat conflicting forms."

He speaks also of a "number of slight variations, noteworthy differences as to the reason for the Sabbath law." In Exodus, the Creation is given as one reason for the Sabbath law; in Deuteronomy two reasons are added, deliverance from bondage in Egypt and the obligation to give rest to laborers. The reasons given in the two cases are not conflicting. The history of the Israelites gave emphasis to the additional reasons for the existence of the Sabbath law.

II.

In the body of this work it is attempted to show that the day of Pentecost occurred upon the Lord's Day. Further discussion of that point may be found in the Bibliotheca Sacra of April, 1880, pp. 368-373.

INDEX

Index of names of persons and subjects not readily found by the Table of Contents.

A

Accadian, 29.
Alexander, 286.
Aldrich, 93.
Alford, 42, 43, 44, 58, 108, 124, 238.
Andrews, 85, 128, 152.
Andrewes, 172.
Apostolic Fathers, 88.
Apostolic Authority, 118, 263.
Appleton, 171.
Artists, 269.
Arnold, 25, 33, 66, 140.
Assos 103.
Assyrian, 27, 29.
Atterbury, 270, 298.
Augustine, 44, 51.

B

Bacon, 33, 51, 66, 103, 140, 305.
Barnes, 128.
Barrows, 47.
Babylon, 27, 103.
Baxter, 139.
Bengel, 41, 58.
Bionconi, 266.
Blackstone, 288, 301, 302.
Bryennios, 165.
Bush, 223.
Bushnell, 59.
Burrow, 227, 229.
Butler, 70, 71, 144.
Buxtorf, 47.

C

Calvin, 138.
Carpenter, 265.
Celestial bodies, 15.
Convocation, 57, 80.
Conybeare, 103.
Collections, 110.
Constantine, 164, 219, 228.
Contrast, comparison, 238.
Coleridge, 269.
Commons, 302.
Continental Sabbath, 292.
Cook, 135, 266.
Chronology, 104, 106, 109.
Changes, 142.
Chalmers, 304.
Corporations, 317.
Crabbe, 238.
Crystal Palace, 267.
Crucifixion, 93, 99.

D

Dale, 10, 25, 33, 36, 66, 79, 140.
De Wette, 53.
Dominicum, 172.
Donaldson, 151.
Dwight, 128.

E

Early Fathers, 263.
Easter, 92, 120, 236.
Ecclesiastical Theory, 180.
Edwards, 128, 138, 139, 171, 262, 266, 275.

Ellicott, 124, 188.
Emerson, 283.
Evenings, 107, 108.

F

Fairbairn, 41.
Family, 280, 282.
Farre, 268.
Farrar, 282.
Feast, 42, 45, 49, 95, 105, 128, 133.
First Day, 235.
Fisher, 236.

G

Gilfillan, 171.
Gladden, 34.
Gurney, 257.

H

Hackett, 90.
Hadley, 22, 38.
Hamilton, 300.
Hessey, 10, 115, 137, 149, 180, 183, 202, 204, 205, 208, 257.
Heylin, 16, 33, 64.
Hodge, 128.
Hooker, 216.
Hooper, 278.
Hopkins, 37, 39, 62, 183, 193, 194, 203, 213.
Horne, 48.
Humboldt, 270.
Hyacinthe, 290.

I

Inscriptions, 27.

J

Jahn, 48.
Jerome, 115, 218, 226.
Jewish Superstitions, 263.
Josephus, 46, 98.
Justification, 62.
Justin on Sunday, 153.

K

Kames, 305.
Kendrick, 38.
Koran, 24.

L

Lange, 58, 108.
La Place, 24.
Law, 70, 73.
Lewis, 15.
Licinius, 220.
Lightfoot, 48, 151, 188.
Littlejohn, 85, 104.
Lord's Day, 120, 161.
Lord's Supper, 120.
Lord Bacon, 305.
Loyson, 291.
Luther, 253.

M

Manna, 17.
Mason, 278.
Memory, 31.
Merrill, 30.
Meyer, 53, 58, 188.
Mill, 269.
Mischna, 49.
Mohammed, 23.
Montalembert, 282.
Moral duties, 36, 70.
Morality, 287.
Morrow, 87.
Murphy, 223.
McKnight, 115
McClintock, 171.
Macauley, 271, 275.
McCheyne, 304, 305.

N

Nations' weekly time, 21.
Neander, 53, 116, 160, 228.
Nisan, 93, 96.
Niemeyer, 275.

O

Olshausen, 92.
Ordinal, 140.

P

Paley, 10, 16, 64.
Parker, 34.
Parliament, 274.
Passover, 95.
Persian, 103.

INDEX.

Peel, 302.
Pentecost, 89.
Pond, 128.
Pusey, 226.
Puritan, 8, 261, 263, 289.
Phelps, 62, 171.
Philo, 46, 47, 49, 230.
Pliny, 152.
Plato, 270.
Philosophers, 281.
Protestants, 178.
Proudhon, 275.

R
Rabbins, 188, 234.
Reed, 289.
Reforms, 280.
Rest, 264, 278, 291.
Resurrection, 83, 101.
Religious freedom, 220.
Righteousness, 287, 288.
Robertson, 35, 50, 139, 192, 254.
Robinson, 98, 108.
Roman Catholic, 9, 178, 298.
Rosetta Stone, 127.

S
Sanderson, 66.
Sayce, 28.
Sabbath perversions, 188.
Septuagint, 54, 223.
Selden, 46.
Seyffarth, 93.
Schaff, 90, 92, 96.
Shabbath, 53, 130.
Supper, 42.
Spellman, 229, 230.

Socrates, 286.
Scott, 306.
Shaftesbury, 283.
Stillingfleet, 218.
Strong, 171.
Smith, 90, 91, 289.
Smyth, 146, 184, 195, 205, 210, 216.
Stanley, 53.
Stuart, 26, 80, 128.

T
Tacitus, 87.
Talbot, 27.
Talmud, 125.
Taylor, 64, 66, 274.
Time differences, 78.
Theodosius, 228.
Trench, 42.
Troas, 102, 109.

U
Upham, 48.

W
Washburn, 30.
Watch, 107.
Wayland, 294.
Westminster, 138.
Wetstein, 48.
Wilberforce, 274.
Wieseler, 92.
Wilkinson, 171.
Whitsuntide, 92.
Winer, 37, 156.
Wilson, 70.
Whately, 58, 66, 67, 72, 144.

SPECIAL SCRIPTURE TEXTS

Lev. 23: 54, 57.
Lev. 16,21: 130.
Nehemiah 8,9: 43, 132.
Isaiah 58,13,14: 310.
Mark 2,27: 36, 38, 263.
Acts 20,7: 50, 87.
Rom. 3,31: 50.
Rom. 6,14: 58.
Rom. 7,6: 51.

Rom. 13,8: 60.
Rom. 14,5: 50.
1 Cor. 16,2: 110.
Gal. 4,10: 50.
Col. 2,16: 50, 55, 141, 127.
Heb. 4,4: 156.
Heb. 10,25: 50.
Rev. 1,10: 120.

www.ingramcontent.com/pod-product-compliance
Lightning Source LLC
Chambersburg PA
CBHW030730230426
43667CB00007B/666